# The ~ Post-Utopian ~ Imagination

**Recent Titles in**
**Contributions to the Study of American Literature**

The Short Fiction of Kurt Vonnegut
*Peter J. Reed*

Enchanted Places: The Use of Setting in F. Scott Fitzgerald's Fiction
*Aiping Zhang*

Solitude and Society in the Works of Herman Melville and Edith Wharton
*Linda Costanzo Cahir*

The Immigrant Experience in North American Literature: Carving Out a Niche
*Katherine B. Payant and Toby Rose, editors*

American Literary Humor During the Great Depression
*Robert A. Gates*

The Marriage of Heaven and Earth: Alchemical Regeneration in the Works of
Taylor, Poe, Hawthorne, and Fuller
*Randall A. Clack*

The Divine and Human Comedy of Andrew M. Greeley
*Allienne R. Becker*

Teaching Faulkner: Approaches and Methods
*Stephen Hahn and Robert W. Hamblin, editors*

Songs of the New South: Writing Contemporary Louisiana
*Suzanne Disheroon Green and Lisa Abney, editors*

American Carnival: Seeing and Reading American Culture
*Philip McGowan*

# *The* Post-Utopian Imagination

## American Culture in the Long 1950s

M. Keith Booker

Contributions to the Study of American Literature, Number 13

Greenwood Press
Westport, Connecticut • London

**Library of Congress Cataloging-in-Publication Data**

Booker, M. Keith.
    The post-utopian imagination : American culture in the long 1950s / M. Keith Booker.
        p.   cm.—(Contributions to the study of American literature, ISSN 1092–6356 ; no. 13)
    Includes bibliographical references and index.
    ISBN 0–313–32165–5 (alk. paper)
    1. American fiction—20th century—History and criticism.  2. Politics and
literature—United States—History—20th century.  3. Literature and society—United
States—History—20th century.  4. Popular culture—United States—History—20th
century.  5. Political fiction, American—History and criticism.  6. Motion pictures—
United States—History.  7. Dystopias in literature.  8. Cold War in literature.  9.
Realism in literature.  I. Title.  II. Series.
PS374.P6 B66 2002
813′.5409358—dc21      2001050100

British Library Cataloguing in Publication Data is available.

Library of Congress Catalog Card Number: 2001050100
ISBN: 0–313–32165–5
ISSN: 1092–6356

First published in 2002

Greenwood Press, 88 Post Road West, Westport, CT 06881
An imprint of Greenwood Publishing Group, Inc.
www.greenwood.com

Printed in the United States of America

The paper used in this book complies with the
Permanent Paper Standard issued by the National
Information Standards Organization (Z39.48–1984).

10 9 8 7 6 5 4 3 2 1

For Debra Rae Cohen and Bob Brinkmeyer

*Colleagues, friends, and rescuers of
the U of A English Department*

# Contents

# Introduction:
## America as Utopia–Or Not

In 1962, the newly formed Students for a Democratic Society (SDS) issued the "Port Huron Statement" (drafted by Tom Hayden), in which they announced their radical agenda and explained why they felt that agenda was necessary at this particular time in American history. Among other things, they argued that radical action was needed because the popular American mind was so thoroughly in the grips of a conformist ideology that it was no longer capable of imagining alternatives to the status quo. Thus,

the message of our society is that there is no viable alternative to the present. Beneath the reassuring tones of the politicians, beneath the common opinion that America will "muddle through," beneath the stagnation of those who have closed their minds to the future, is the pervading feeling that there simply are no alternatives, that our times have witnessed the exhaustion not only of Utopias, but of any new departures as well. (qtd. in James Miller 330)[1]

In this, Hayden and the founders of the SDS oddly echoed the diagnosis of neoconservative social scientist Daniel Bell, who argued in *The End of Ideology* (first published in its original form in 1960 and in a revised form in 1962) that a principal phenomenon of American political thought in the 1950s was the "exhaustion of utopia," and indeed the exhaustion of "ideology" altogether.

In typical Cold War fashion, by "ideology" Bell mostly means "socialism," but the similarity in these diagnoses is not surprising: it arises from the fact that both are simply correct and that the American utopian imagination did, in fact, collapse in the long 1950s (1946–1964)[2]. At first glance, it might seem surprising that this collapse should occur at this time, when American capitalism expanded at an unprecedented rate, producing an ever-expanding domestic prosperity. Meanwhile, emerging from World War II as the most powerful nation on earth, America occupied a position of global prominence it had never had before. This very prominence, especially within the vexed climate of the Cold War, required a rethinking of national identity that triggered a national symbolic crisis. For one thing, America's new place as a global power helped to create a siege mentality in which Americans felt threatened not merely by the communist ghouls of the Soviet bloc but by the savage hordes of the Third World. For another, the new prosperity of the 1950s occurred within the context of a consumerist ethic that derived its energies from the creation of a never-ending and unquenchable desire that, by its very nature, made true satisfaction impossible. However wealthy it might have appeared to be, America at the time was beset with a panoply of anxieties, arising from a set of social, economic, and political problems the increasing complexity of which rendered them more and more intractable. Yet, if the current system was fraught with difficulties, the repressive climate of the Cold War was such that any proposed alternative to the present tended to be equated with communism, while communism tended to be equated with satanic evil.

Little wonder, then, that, idyllic television sitcoms and Disney animated films aside, the cultural products of the 1950s often took an extremely dark turn. *Leave it to Beaver* and *Peter Pan* were offset by film noir and Hitchcock, while the simple worlds of Disney and the domestic sitcom can themselves be taken as compensatory reactions to a world in which problems seemed increasingly threatening and insoluble. And even Disney films, on close examination, contain a dark core of violence, racism, and anxiety over potential challenges to conventional gender roles. Similarly, the comic style of the most critically respected American novel of the long 1950s, Vladimir Nabokov's *Lolita* (published in Paris in 1955, in the U.S. in 1958), belies an extremely dark narrative. Humbert Humbert fills his narration of rape and murder with tremendous linguistic gusto but ends with a note of regret and loss. Having sought an ideal state of happiness through pursuit of a romantic relationship with a prepubescent girl, he now concludes that the state of aesthetic bliss he had sought is not available in life, but only in art. He thus writes his narrative, he claims, in order to immortalize Lolita not as she was but as he, in his hyperaesthetic imagination, envisioned her. "I am thinking of aurochs and angels," he says, "the secret of durable pigments, prophetic sonnets, the refuge of art. And this is the only immortality you and I may share, my Lolita" (311).

In his radical skepticism toward the possibility of achieving an ideal life in the real world, Humbert (foreigner, pervert, and murderer though he is) shows a very mainstream American attitude of the 1950s. His final demise (he dies in jail after losing Lolita and murdering a rival pederast) is also typical.[3] However, other American novels of the years after World War II were more up-front about their own darkness. For example, in one of the first important postwar novels, Norman Mailer's *The Naked and the Dead* (1948), the American forces succeed in their siege of the Japanese-held Pacific island of Anopopei, but the protagonist, Lt. Hearn, is killed in the process. Meanwhile, the Americans win with a savagery that makes it clear that this is no case of good guys defeating bad guys — and that does not bode well for a postwar world dominated by American military power. In the final chapter, the triumphant American forces scour the island, hunting down and killing virtually defenseless Japanese stragglers like troublesome insects. After months of hard battle, we are told, "the mopping up was comparatively pleasant, almost exciting. The killing lost all dimension, bothered the men far less than discovering some ants in their bedding" (718).

Slightly later in the 1950s, Flannery O'Connor's Hazel Motes (the protagonist of 1952's *Wise Blood*) ends by not only giving up his quest to found a Church Without Christ but also murdering a rival; he then blinds and tortures himself until he sickens and dies. By the time of Kurt Vonnegut's *Cat's Cradle* (1963), published near the end of the long 1950s, not only the major characters but every living thing on earth are destroyed. Even if the protagonists of the decade's novels do manage to survive, they tend to do so in a mode of defeat or, at best, paralysis and stagnation. Ralph Ellison's invisible man is still invisible at the end of the text, J. D. Salinger's Holden Caulfield is still an alienated adolescent, and John Updike's Rabbit Angstrom is still trapped in a carceral domesticity, his days as a basketball star behind him, his infant child dead.

This volume is a study of the ways in which a number of products of American culture in the long 1950s demonstrate the decline of the American utopian imagination in the years after World War II. In particular, I associate that decline with the beginnings of postmodernism during that period. In that sense, this study follows directly upon my earlier *Monsters, Mushroom Clouds, and the Cold War* (2000), which discusses the emergence of postmodernism in American science fiction novels and films of the long 1950s. There, as here, I draw heavily upon Fredric Jameson's influential characterization of postmodernism as the "cultural logic" of capitalism in its "late" international phase. After all, the globalization of capital began in a big way during the long 1950s, as the great European colonial empires collapsed, to be replaced by the growing hegemony of transnational corporations and Western popular culture. It should thus come as no surprise that so many important postmodernist writers, from William Gaddis and John Hawkes, to E. L. Doctorow and Thomas Pynchon, began their careers in the long 1950s. Further, if Jameson is right about the status of postmodernism as a cultural dominant, then postmodernist characteristics should be displayed in a wide range of cultural products, not just in *The Recognitions* or *Naked Lunch*. I argue in *Monsters, Mushroom Clouds, and the Cold War* that such characteristics can indeed be found in the science fiction of the long 1950s, even though most of the major works of science fiction from the period do not necessarily appear, on the surface, to be postmodernist in any formal sense.

In this study, I extend that project further, examining a wide variety of American novels of the long 1950s, from highly self-conscious literary artifacts such as *Lolita*, to the realist works of leftist writers struggling to build upon (or, in some cases, repudiate) the proletarian literature of the 1930s, to the pulp crime fiction of Jim Thompson. The novels I examine are often quite different in form, structure, style, and tone. All, however, exhibit postmodernist characteristics of various sorts, the most consistent of which is a failure to project viable utopian alternatives to the present social order. I focus on the novel because that literary genre that has historically been strongest in utopian energies, especially in the eighteenth and early nineteenth centuries, when it participated in a central way in the Enlightenment and in the revolutionary transformation of European society from feudalism to capitalism. Thus, the loss of utopian energy in this genre is particularly striking and significant.

Together, these explorations demonstrate that what I am calling a "post-utopian" vision was quite widespread in American culture in the long 1950s. In fact, I would argue that this attitude became hegemonic during this period and has remained so. Further, I argue that it could hardly have been otherwise, given the rise to complete dominance in America during this period of a consumer culture that, while it offered a limited utopian vision in its association of consumption with happiness, was ultimately anti-utopian, because the desire upon which consumer capitalism is built is, of necessity, a desire that can never be satisfied. Meanwhile, the pursuit of this desire dos not lead to the transformation of society but merely reinforces the status quo. My arguments here thus substantiate much of what Jameson has to say about postmodernism as the cultural logic of late capitalism, or capitalism in its phase of global hegemony.[4] However, my claims are, in most senses, somewhat more modest than Jameson's. For one thing, my study focuses on American culture only. Therefore, I make no claims concerning the global dominance of post-utopian thought, while Jameson envisions the global hegemony of postmodernism, as the cultural logic of an increasingly global late capitalism. I do not dispute Jameson's claim and, in fact, largely agree with it. The information contained in this study simply does not allow me to reach conclusions concerning anything other than American culture. Further, the globalization identified by Jameson was only just beginning in the long 1950s, when what he calls postmodernism and what I call post-utopianism arose first and foremost in the United States, then radiated outward in subsequent decades with the increasing global power of America and American culture.[5]

Still, Jameson's postmodernism and my post-utopianism are related phenomena and, to an extent, can be taken as different names for the *same* phenomenon. I prefer the term post-utopianism, first, because it calls attention to a much more specific aspect of the phenomenon than does the broader designation of postmodernism. Moreover, the greater specificity of the term post-utopianism makes it far easier to demonstrate with actual evidence that the phenomenon actually did occur in the long 1950s. A loss of utopian energy is only one of several characteristics that Jameson has associated with postmodernist culture, though it is part and parcel of several other characteristics, including most obviously a loss in the ability to think in terms of coherent historical narratives. Utopia, in the Marxist sense, is a profoundly historical category, to be envisioned as a goal not just of the imagination but of the historical process. In addition, utopian thought is, to an extent, inherently totalizing, so that a loss of utopian vision can also be associated with the social, psychic, and cultural fragmentation that Jameson and others have associated with postmodernism. In this study, I maintain a secondary focus on this fragmentation but maintain a primary interest in the loss of utopian energy, which I believe to be a more fundamental and telling phenomenon.

Jameson's argument of the hegemony of postmodernism in the late capitalist era has seemed unconvincing to many because so many cultural products of the late capitalist era do not seem postmodernist in the sense of the complex, self-conscious, and playfully parodic works that have typically been associated with postmodernism, especially as manifested in the works of key postmodernist authors such as Pynchon, William H. Gass, and Salman Rushdie. Jameson, of course, has in mind something much more subtle and profound than the mere formal characteristics of specific texts, but the subtlety and profundity of his formulation of postmodernism, combined with its sweeping nature, make it extremely difficult either to prove or disprove. My identification of the post-utopian nature of American culture after World War II is less ambitious than Jameson's characterization of postmodernism, but my post-utopianism grows out of essentially the same historical phenomena as Jameson's postmodernism, while having the virtue of being much easier to demonstrate for specific texts. Thus, my elaboration of the notion of post-utopianism does not contradict Jameson's more ambitious notion of postmodernism but, in fact, tends to support Jameson's analysis by focusing on a clearly definable (and thus demonstrable) subset of the larger phenomenon.

Of course, utopianism itself can be a vague concept that means different things to different people. I use the term in a Marxist sense and, in particular, in the very broad sense that Jameson himself employs throughout his work, that is, in the sense of an ability to imagine a preferable systemic alternative to the status quo, while at the same time imagining a historical process that might lead in the direction of that alternative. This term itself, then, is in danger of getting out of hand. As Jameson has pointed out, by this definition, *all* cultural phenomena, even the most debased and hateful, contain some sort of utopian component.

Indeed, for Jameson, as he makes especially clear in *The Political Uncon-scious*, it is part of the task of any genuine Marxist (or genuine dialectical) critique to tease out this utopian component. In particular, he argues that "a Marxist negative hermeneutic, a Marxist practice of ideological analy-sis proper, must in the practical work of reading and interpreting be ex-ercised *simultaneously* with a Marxist positive hermeneutic, or a deci-pherment of the Utopian impulses of these same still ideological cultural texts" (296).

Jameson's conception of utopia (as with essentially all recent Marxist conceptions of utopia) is strongly influenced by the work of Ernst Bloch, the twentieth century's great thinker (and poet) of utopianism. It is per-haps fitting that Bloch's central work, the massive, encyclopedic, and lyrical *The Principle of Hope*, was initially drafted in the United States (where Bloch, a German Jew, had fled with his family to escape the Na-zis) in the years 1938–1947, that is, in the years just prior to the collapse of an already weak utopianism in American thought in the long 1950s. The title of this vast treatise (reinforced by its initial working title, "Dreams of a Better Life") suggests the flexible and comprehensive na-ture of Bloch's vision of utopianism, as do the amazing scope and breadth of *The Principle of Hope* itself.

This work was published in three volumes in German from 1954 to 1959 and did not appear in a full English translation until 1985, perhaps because there was little market for Bloch's ideas in a United States where utopianism, not to mention Marxism, was decidedly out of fashion. It is thus not surprising that Bloch, along with Theodor Adorno, Bertolt Brecht, and other left-leaning refugee German intellectuals, returned to Germany soon after World War II, fleeing a United States that seemed to him not very different from Nazi Germany. Of course, Bloch, suspected of being a mystic, a subjectivist, and an idealist dreamer, had his own problems with the authorities in East Germany. But Bloch's conception of utopia is largely a practical and scientific one. By definition, Bloch's ver-sion of utopia is never reached, but it can be worked toward; utopian thought is always thought that reaches beyond the real, but for Bloch, genuine utopian thought is shot through with concrete possibility, its goal being the transformation of reality, not an escape from it. Moreover, Bloch's vision, however poetic it may sometimes appear, is resolutely historical. Among other things, his vision of thinking beyond the present is always oriented toward the future, not the past. Utopian thought, for Bloch, must reach toward the "Not-Yet-Conscious ... towards the side of something new that is dawning up, that has never been conscious before, not, for example, something forgotten, something remembrable that has been" (*Principle* 11).

In this sense Bloch's utopianism differs dramatically from consumer capitalism, which also reaches constantly toward the future, spurring constant new consumption, but does so in ways that discourage the imagination of systemic alternatives to capitalism and that thus work against, rather than toward, the transformation of society. The message is clear: capitalism is a wonderful system, and you, too, can be happy, if you only work a little harder in order to be able to consume a little more. Thus, if the rhetoric of consumerism is designed to convince individual subjects that life is fine, despite all evidence to the contrary, Bloch's conception of utopia is a prescription for surviving current hard times by imagining better ones in the future. In particular, Bloch recommends that individuals seek sources of hope to help them cope with the exigencies of life under late capitalism, where he sees fear as the principal emotional experience, a diagnosis that would be hard to dispute in relation to life in America in the long 1950s.

If Bloch is right that utopia is the opposite of fear, then it should come as no surprise that utopian thought should suffer in the era characterized by David Caute as the era of the "Great Fear." The greatest American fear of the long 1950s, of course, was the fear of nuclear annihilation at the hands of the Soviets, along with the associated fear of communism in general. But Americans of the decade, especially white middle-class Americans, were afraid of all sorts of other things as well. They feared a loss of individualism through their absorption into the corporate structure at work or seduction by mass culture at home; on the other hand, they feared that they might be too individual and thus might be found to be "abnormal." They feared incursions into the privilege of white, middle-class life by nonwhites both at home and abroad. They feared the increasingly uppity children of blacks and poor whites, who seemed, in the guise of juvenile delinquents, to be more and more of a threat; and they even feared their own middle-class children, who were getting out of hand, held in thrall by such sinister phenomena as rock and roll music, with its suspiciously African American rhythms and its seemingly satanic impact on the young.

These problems were, of course, obvious to many in the period, however celebratory the official rhetoric of Americanism was at the time. As I note in more detail in *Monsters, Mushroom Clouds, and the Cold War*, the long 1950s is remarkable, among other things, for having produced an impressive number of important works of American social criticism, including such now-classic examples as David Riesman's *The Lonely Crowd* (1950), David Potter's *People of Plenty* (1954), C. Wright Mills's *The Power Elite* (1956), and William Whyte's *The Organization Man* (1956). Summarizing this phenomenon, Richard Pells argues that the works of figures such as Riesman, Whyte, Mills, Hannah Arendt, John Kenneth Galbraith, Paul Goodman, Daniel Bell, Dwight MacDonald, Louis Hartz, Daniel Boorstin, and C. Wright Mills are "superior in quality to any comparable collection of works produced in America during other periods of the twentieth century" (x). Of course, in this decade of explosive consumerism, even social criticism became a commodity, as in the best-selling works of Vance Packard. Moreover, all of these works of social criticism, while pointing out the growing alienation of American individuals and the increasing routinization of American life, are decidedly weak in utopian energy. They fail to imagine any sort of large-scale, systemic alternative to consumer capitalism, largely because such alternatives would, almost by definition, smack of socialism, while the political climate of the Cold War made it essentially impossible to present socialist alternatives in America.

In this environment, the main critique of the capitalist status quo came from capitalism itself, which focused on gratification in the present, but with a dependence on constant innovation and expansion that constantly, insistently, and simultaneously declared the inadequacy of the present. At the same time, any number of cultural forces contrived to create a nostalgic vision of the past, helping to ensure that any critique of the present would offer the past as the only alternative, thus foreclosing radical movement toward the future. This contradictory, but quintessentially late capitalist, combination of nostalgia and a drive for innovation led ultimately to what Jameson calls a "nostalgia for the present" (*Postmodernism* 279). From this point of view, it makes perfect sense that utopian thought should be so thoroughly routed in the long 1950s, the period in which capitalism consolidated the gains of the past three centuries and asserted its full dominance in the Western bloc, a dominance that was only strengthened by the perception of a communist menace lurking in the East. This was especially the case in the United States, where capitalism was particularly strong, but where the postwar capitalist dream contained a strong component of nightmare. It was, after all, the atomic bombs dropped on the Asian populations of Hiroshima and Nagasaki that announced to the world the new global power of the United States, a nation that had been built on bloody racial violence from the beginning.

Tom Engelhardt notes that this violence was both physical and discursive, as European settlers justified their violence against America's native inhabitants with stories of native savagery:

At the beginning, there had been an armed horror that was not yet a story, a bloody hell of torture, dismemberment, and enslavement, of desperate retribution against the less-than-human, and of helplessness and captivity at the hands of peoples referred to as "the devil's instruments" or "barbarians," as "wolves" or "mad dogs," as vermin to be exterminated. (18)

Meanwhile, Engelhardt notes that this same discourse was revived and repeated during World War II to describe and support the American war in the Pacific, thus extending the narrative of violent triumph (usually over a savage racial Other) that had sustained the American national identity for a century and a half. However, according to Engelhardt, this narrative ceased to function with any effectiveness in the postwar years, removing even the problematic and ambivalent utopianism that had long been a part of American culture. In fact, Engelhardt argues that narrative in general becomes difficult to maintain in postwar American culture, a characteristic that would clearly suggest the beginning of postmodernism, with its famously fragmented and inconclusive narratives, in this period.

In a general sense, America in the new postwar world had to present itself as a global defender of peace and freedom, which seriously compromised the value of the national narrative of violent victory over anyone who was different. In addition, for Engelhardt, three specific Asian events contributed to this collapse of the American national narrative. First, the atomic bombing of Hiroshima and Nagasaki made the notion of racial extermination all too real: "Here was a victory in no sense previously imagined, for it was victory as atrocity" (56). Indeed, Engelhardt argues that the unimaginable violence of the final victory over Japan threatened, in the American imagination, to conflate American actions in the war with the atrocities committed by the German Nazi, and thus to undermine the American myth of noble victory in war (57). Moreover, this particular atrocity also threatened to come home to roost, as the subsequent Cold War convinced a generation of Americans that they might very soon be on the other end of the atomic stick. The possibility that Americans might be defeated in the coming nuclear conflict grew all the more real after the next two Asian events cited by Engelhardt, which saw the Chinese communists sweep to victory in their own country in 1949, then help to fight the U.S. to a standstill in Korea a few years later.

In short, those hordes of nonwhites (usually in the form of American Indians) who had for so long been routinely routed by small bands of virtuous whites on American movie screens, were apparently not so easily dispatched after all, a lesson the Vietnam experience would soon drive home all the more. Meanwhile, the 1950s also saw an era of explosive growth in consumer capitalism in some ways even more spectacular than the original rise of consumerism in the first three decades of the twentieth century. However, the consumerism of the 1950s, no longer supported by an effective national victory culture, tended to create at least as much anxiety as pleasure. Affluent Americans had, in a sense, achieved everything they ever dreamed of, only to find the dream empty, leading to a feeling of "entrapment in abundance" (Engelhardt 88).

As I have discussed in more detail in *Monsters, Mushroom Clouds and the Cold War*, even "successful" Americans were caught in a crushing double bind of alienation and routinization. On the one hand, they were terrified of being different, of not living up to the images of normality constantly beamed into the new television sets in their suburban living rooms; on the other hand, they were terrified of losing their individuality altogether, thus joining the series of anonymous and interchangeable cogs that made up the gears of the corporate machine. Meanwhile, there were lurking and potentially ominous reminders that not all Americans were so affluent, not to mention the vast majority of the population of the rest of the world. Thus, white, middle-class Americans came increasingly, in the long 1950s, to think of their lives as an island of prosperity and tranquillity surrounded by a threatening sea of poverty and turmoil, somewhat in the mode of those bands of pioneers who had long circled their wagons to fight off savage Indian attacks on American movie screens.

This ultimate collapse of the American utopian imagination in the long 1950s was, in many ways, the culmination of a long history, the ironic consummation of the dreams of abundance experienced by America's first European invaders. One of the most remarkable stories in the cultural history of Western civilization is the striking rapidity with which the notion of the "New World" captured the popular European imagination after 1492, that seminal year in which Christopher Columbus famously sailed the ocean blue, "discovering" on the other side a magical land where the hopes and dreams of a Europe long impoverished in both material and cultural terms could suddenly come true. Visions of New World gold and silver quickly danced through the heads of European monarchs, and significant deposits of both precious metals were indeed found. However, Caribbean sugar plantations provided the greatest wealth of all, ironically feeding enough wealth into Europe to finance the budding emergence of capitalism, ultimately leading to the demise of those monarchs and their feudal-aristocratic system once and for all. Culturally, the New World spurred a number of imaginative visions. Columbus's own reports made the Americas sound like a biblical paradise, so perhaps it is no surprise that, by 1516, Thomas More had placed his genre-defining Utopia in the Americas. Indeed, by the time Francis Bacon placed his New Atlantis in the Americas in 1627, the notion of America as the locus of utopia was firmly established in the European imagination and in European material practice. In the intervening time, Sir Walter Ralegh had sailed to Guiana in search of El Dorado, reports from the New World had inspired the magical texture of Shakespeare's *The Tempest*, and Spanish conquistadors had tramped about sixteenth-century Mexico, wreaking havoc and seeking paradise.

In the ensuing centuries, America (especially the Caribbean) would provide the setting for so many European (especially English) novels that the well-known eighteenth-century rise of the novel as a cultural phenomenon is absolutely inseparable from the historical phenomenon of colonialism. Identifying the novel as the European colonialist genre par excellence, Edward Said declares that "imperialism and the novel fortified each other to such a degree that it is impossible … to read one without in some way dealing with the other" (71).[6] Meanwhile, calling Defoe's *Robinson Crusoe* (1719) the "prototypical modern realistic novel," Said suggests that it is no accident that the book is "about a European who creates a fiefdom for himself on a distant, non-European island" (xii). It is, in fact, a Caribbean island, while Aphra Behn's even earlier *Oroonoko* (1688), sometimes regarded as the first English novel, takes place largely in Surinam, on the Caribbean coast of South America.

Both *Oroonoko* and *Robinson Crusoe* still contain strong elements of romance, but even when the realist novel emerges in full force, as in Defoe's *Moll Flanders* (1722), America (this time North America) remains a powerful locus of utopian dreams. Continually buffeted by the slings and arrows of English capitalism and forced into a prostitution that makes her (like Crusoe) an allegorical figure of capitalism, the resourceful Moll finds happiness at last on an idyllic Virginia plantation. Indeed, America functions so consistently in European literature from the sixteenth to nineteenth centuries as a utopian alternative to Europe, it is easy to see why the utopian imagination of American literature, as it emerges in this period, is inherently impoverished. American writers, already living in the land of Europe's utopian dreams (but not necessarily finding those dreams to be a reality), have to work all the harder to imagine alternatives.

There was, from the moment Columbus sighted land on October 12, 1492, a real serpent in the imaginary American garden. For one thing, even European accounts of the marvels of the New World were ambivalent from the very beginning. If the Americas were a locus of unprecedented utopian potential, they were also the locus of unprecedented danger, perhaps even of satanic evil. In the New World

> myths of paradise and utopia were complex—and often confused—affairs. On the one hand, in some versions, they represented a rediscovered time of innocent perfection dating from *before* the biblical Fall from Grace; on the other hand, some dreams of such perfection envisioned and were built upon the expectation of a *future* time of anticipated peace and harmony. And bound up with every myth, past, present, or future, was still another contradictory vision of savagery and wildness and the dark. (Stannard 64)

Meanwhile, both the positive and the negative accounts of the strangeness of America were used as discursive justification for the brutal colonization and exploitation of the New World by Europeans. In his study of European travel writing about the Americas (beginning with the diary of Columbus), Stephen Greenblatt notes the consistent tone of magic and wonder that pervades early accounts of the Americas; he also notes that these accounts of American marvels were couched within a confident discourse of European superiority, based, among other things, on a faith that the written culture of Europe marked Europeans as the racial betters (and thus rightful colonizers) of the mostly illiterate populations they encountered in the New World. Meanwhile, David Stannard notes the consistency with which European accounts of New World utopias seemed remarkably unconcerned that the possession of these utopias might require the displacement of a preexisting native population. But it does not require careful analysis of European colonial discourse about the Americas to realize that the European appropriation of American wealth came at great expense to the native populations of America. As many as 100 million Native Americans ultimately died directly or indirectly as a result of the European intrusion into the Americas. Meanwhile, tens of millions of West Africans were also among the victims of American colonization, because the wealth derived from Caribbean sugar was built on the backs of African slaves.

In short, the atomic bombing of Hiroshima and Nagasaki was not an entirely new departure as much as it was a final straw that finally broke the back of the American national narrative, leading it to collapse beneath its own weight. The baleful legacy of slavery and genocide that underlies the American historical experience means that the American national utopian narrative had been precarious long before the sequence of events that led from Hiroshima to Hanoi. The particular nature of the American historical experience complicates the American utopian imagination in other ways as well. American literature as an identifiable cultural phenomenon emerges in the decades following the revolution, which makes American literature not only the first postcolonial literature but the first genuinely postrevolutionary literature as well, even if it would quickly be eclipsed in this area by the literature of postrevolutionary France. American literature, like American society as a whole, emerges within the context of the idealized Enlightenment discourse of the revolution. Thus, while the young United States was hardly alone on the historical stage as a nation born of brutality, exploitation, and murder, it was a nation that found it particularly hard to come to grips with this fact, given that it supposedly represented a fresh start, putting the past behind it via a theoretical devotion to liberty and justice for all. And the long legacy of utopian discourse about America only made this situation more difficult.

The major figures of American literature in the first half of the nineteenth century were very much aware of their postrevolutionary status and drew significant amounts of imaginative capital from the mythos of the revolution. Thus, Sacvan Bercovitch has noted that figures such as Whitman, Thoreau, Melville, Hawthorne, and Emerson all "felt it was incumbent on their generation to give fulfillment to the potentialities freed by the Revolution, to provide a culture commensurate with America's political opportunity" (633). Of course, Bercovitch here is speaking not so much of the attitudes of these writers themselves as of the *interpretation* of their attitudes in the work of F. O. Mathiessen, who made these figures the chief icons of his American Renaissance. Indeed, it is difficult at this point to separate American literature of the nineteenth century from the interpretations of that literature produced in the decades following Mathiessen's groundbreaking work, decades in which scholars working in the emerging field of American studies virtually invented "American literature" and did so within the extremely compromising context of the Cold War.

The seemingly weak utopianism of nineteenth-century American literature may, in fact, be partly due to the fact that this literature now inevitably comes to us refracted through the lens of the invention of American literature in the long 1950s. The central figures in this phenomenon were the New York Intellectuals, whose attempt, during the long 1950s, to build a new American canon drew directly on the work of Mathiessen but also grew out of the attempt of the intellectuals to legitimate their own anticommunist Leftism as true Americanism. Crucial to this project was the apotheosis of modernism as the standard of aesthetic achievement, thus aligning the intellectuals with their presumed ideological foes, the right-wing New Critics, who also glorified modernism. If anything, Lionel Trilling, Alfred Kazin, Richard Chase, Philip Rahv, Edmund Wilson, Irving Howe, Dwight McDonald, and the other critics associated with the New York Intellectuals (and the *Partisan* Review) were even more enthusiastic in their support of modernism than were the New Critics. But the "modernism" of the New York group was a far cry from the Pound/Eliot aestheticism so central to New Critical formulations of the movement. For the New York Intellectuals, modernism was not entirely divorced from politics—at least not from certain kinds of politics. Indeed, their modernists (who included such nineteenth-century figures as Melville and Dickens, as well as the obligatory Proust, Joyce, and Kafka) produced works that, according to the New York Intellectuals, had a powerful subversive potential in their celebration of individual creativity.

If the New Critics saw modernism as an aestheticist refusal of any contaminating negotiation with the debased and dehumanized realities of life under modern industrial capitalism, the New York Intellectuals' preference of modernism over realism involved a vision of modernist experimentalism as an expression of American individualism and refusal to submit to convention, literary or otherwise. But, as Thomas Schaub notes, this turn to literature as a source of political inspiration was part of a larger "liberal narrative" that originated "in the experience of disillusionment and betrayal" revolving around their perception of the failure of the utopian political programs of the 1930s and in their sense of betrayal by the Stalinist Soviet Union, especially in the Moscow show trials of the mid-1930s and the German-Soviet nonaggression pact of 1939. Indeed, one after another, liberal intellectuals of the long 1950s repudiated their former leftist utopian longings as naive and simplistic. This repudiation was specifically anti-utopian. Thus, Rahv notes in "Our

Country and Our Culture," a sort of collective policy statement, that he and others associated with the *Partisan Review* were resolved "to be done with Utopian illusions and heady expectations" (304).

For Schaub, the liberal intellectuals themselves saw this phenomenon as a collective attempt to turn "from innocence to experience, from the myopia of the utopian to the twenty-twenty vision of the realist" (5). In terms of literature, however, these new realists turned away not only from utopia but also from realism, which was inevitably associated with the leftist cultural projects of the 1930s. Indeed, Schaub, among other things, sees this phenomenon as crucial to the beginnings of postmodernism, concluding that "American postmodernism is not separable from the emergence of fiction from the politics of paralysis in the postwar period" (190). It is certainly the case that many of the founding works of American studies during this period tended to glorify the antirealist tendencies of American literature, which is not surprising given that American realism had always been a bit weak anyway and that it became still weaker, especially in terms of its utopian energies, during the long 1950s. Further, this period of unprecedented attention to American literature was also a period of general critical celebration of modernism at the expense of realism. Thus, as the new American Cold War canon took shape, a committed realist such as William Dean Howells had little chance to receive the same appreciation as a protomodernist such as Herman Melville, while the most appreciated American realist, Henry James, was appreciated partly because he drifted toward modernism in the latter part of his career.

But Melville is perhaps the key figure here, a crucial marker of the way in which the 1950s canonization of modernism extended anachronistically into the nineteenth century. *Moby-Dick* was the crucial text here, its encyclopedic intricacies rivaling even those of *Ulysses*. Richard Poirier's later comment is typical of the use of *Moby-Dick* as an illustration of the achievement of American culture: "Americans can take some pride in *Moby Dick* not because it is in a way like *Ulysses* but rather because *Ulysses* is like *Moby Dick*" (149). As Donald Pease points out, the "Cold War consensus" that informed, indeed constituted American literary studies after World War II mobilized *Moby-Dick* to good advantage, making the book "into a figure through which it could read the free world's survival in the future struggle with totalitarianism" (274).[7] Thus Chase described his book-length study of Melville explicitly as a contribution to the new liberalism of the long 1950s and as part of an attempt to move beyond "the ruinous sellouts, failures, and defeats of the thirties" (*Herman Melville* v).

Such readings made *Moby-Dick* a paean to individualism, largely through a celebration of Melville's own eccentric procedure for constructing the book. But such readings also reinterpreted the content of the book, making Ahab (the book's tragic hero per the Melville revival of the

1920s) a figure of totalitarian (maybe even Stalinist) fanaticism, opposed by Starbuck's forthright individualism. Of course, if Ahab can be both hero and villain, *Moby-Dick* can produce other variant readings as well. For example, rather than reading the book as a celebration of individualist resistance to totalitarianism, one might perfectly well do just the opposite, making the book a celebration of the collective efforts of the multiracial, multicultural group of seamen aboard the *Pequod*, who constitute a sort of utopian community disrupted by the arrant individualist designs of Ahab. Read in this way, *Moby-Dick*, which clearly pays more attention to the labor of working-class characters than virtually any other fully canonical American novel, becomes almost a proletarian text, with all those expositions on whaling serving as a demonstration of the substantial knowledge and expertise embedded in the everyday skills of ordinary workers, whose job experience constitutes, according to Ishmael's narration, "their Yale College and their Harvard."

But, of course, the ultimate fate of the *Pequod* casts a considerable shadow on its status as a utopian image. And, in fact, Melville does relatively little to associate his catalogs of information about whaling with the professional expertise of the *Pequod*'s working-class crew. Thus, a critic such as Laura Hapke, looking specifically for representations of working people in American literature, concludes that, in point of fact, Melville "reduces sailors to mindless servitors in the grip of Ahab's obsessional will" (34). In any case, it was not likely that the criticism of the long 1950s, so suspicious of class-based ideals of any kind, would emphasize the potential proletarian aspects of Melville's novel. As Cecelia Tichi suggests, the term "cold war criticism" is appropriate to describe the work of a whole range of American critics after World War II, all of whom sought to argue that "the major American literary texts (those of indigenous 'genius') transcend ideology" (218). Meanwhile, Tichi herself is a key member of the so-called New Americanists, a group of critics who have attempted to elucidate the conditioning of American criticism by the dictates of the Cold War political climate and to suggest potential rereadings of the American literary tradition that might help to surmount that conditioning. This loosely defined group (which also includes such figures as Pease, Bercovitch, Myra Jehlen, Russell Reising, Jane Tompkins, David Reynolds, Paul Rogin, Wai-chee Dimock, Sharon Cameron, and Philip Fisher) has made numerous important contributions, mostly to the study of nineteenth-century American literature. But the New Americanist focus on the cultural politics of American criticism during the Cold War can, by extension, tell us a great deal about American Cold War literature as well.

The critical tendencies of the New York Intellectuals in the 1950s are epitomized in Chase's *The American Novel and Its Tradition* (1957), which comes late in the 1950s and already reflects a decade of modernist-oriented canon building in which realism was gradually de-emphasized.

Thus, Chase largely dismisses the importance of realism in the American literary tradition. In particular, he opposes the realist tendencies of the British novel to the "romance" tendencies of the American novel, though Chase's characterization of "romance" — which emphasizes traits such as symbolism and psychological depth — sounds suspiciously similar to most 1950s characterizations of modernism. Of course, Chase's suggestion that the American novel shies away from realism is meant as a compliment. Among other things, Chase argues that the American tendency toward romance is rooted in the special realities of American historical experience (such as the existence of the frontier), making his argument a version of American exceptionalism. In fact, the American engagement with literary realism *is* exceptional, at least in terms of the powerful utopian potential that critics such as Georg Lukács have located in realism.

Lukács, attempting to provide practical advice to leftist writers hoping to contribute to the global socialist revolution that he felt to be building in the 1930s, identifies the great early nineteenth-century realist novelists, such as Walter Scott and Honoré de Balzac, as appropriate role models, precisely because the works of these writers powerfully reflect the capitalist-bourgeois revolution of the Enlightenment, a revolution that Lukács, following Marx, sees as the immediate and necessary historical predecessor of the socialist revolution. Scott, for example, is a featured figure in *The Historical Novel* because of the way in which his novels portray the inexorable forward sweep of capitalist modernization, especially in Britain, despite Scott's own doubts about the desirability of that historical progression. Similarly, Balzac figures throughout Lukács's work as perhaps the greatest of all realist novelists, partly because of his refusal to back away from a realistic portrayal of the inevitable historical victory of capitalism, despite Balzac's own reactionary horror at capitalist corruption and materialism.

Such writers are great, in short, because their work honestly portrays historical processes at work in the societies in which the writers live. In particular, such writers derive their works from a profound understanding of the revolutionary victory of the emergent European bourgeoisie over the traditions and values of the ancien régime, despite the ongoing power and prestige of the European aristocracy. For Lukács, the work of Balzac is particularly powerful because it captures a historical moment in which the victory of capitalism is not yet total. The ultimate commodification of everything — including humans and human relationships — is not yet complete in Balzac's world and is not yet accepted by his characters as a given fact of modern life. Thus, even in a work such as *Lost Illusions*, that great epic of the commodification of literature itself, "the fact that the spirit has become a commodity to be bought and sold is not yet accepted as a matter of course and the spirit is not yet reduced to the dreary greyness of a machine-made article" (Lukács, *Studies* 59–60). But Lukács further notes that the opportunity offered by Balzac's particular postrevolutionary historical moment would not last long: "Balzac depicted the original accumulation of capital in the ideological sphere, while his successors, even Flaubert, the greatest of them, already accepted as an accomplished fact that all human values were included in the commodity structure of capitalism" (*Studies* 63).

Lukács characterizes *Lost Illusions* as the first great work of "bourgeois disillusionment." However, due to the incomplete victory of capitalist commodification in Balzac's world, even this disillusionment contains a profoundly utopian component. Thus, the corruption encountered by Lucien de Rubempré in the literary circles of Paris is countered by the solid virtue of Daniel D'Arthez (a stand-in for Balzac), so that "the existence of another and a better truth is poetically opposed to the squalid reality" (*Studies* 62). In addition, the very strength of the disillusionment depicted by Balzac and experienced so deeply by his characters arises from a strong sense that things once were otherwise. Meanwhile, the historically dynamic nature of Balzac's world provides at least a glimmer of hope that things might be otherwise again at some unspecified moment in the future. In particular, the historical victory of the European bourgeoisie provides a reminder that revolutionary, class-based, historical change is possible in general. Moreover, the class-oriented nature of the bourgeois revolution lends fuel to the Marxist vision that the bourgeois victory in Europe was an inevitable and necessary condition for the creation of the proletariat that would ultimately sweep the bourgeoisie off the historical stage.

The nineteenth-century American novel, however, is a postrevolutionary genre that arises in a world in which the ancién régime has already been routed and destroyed, leaving the bourgeoisie unchallenged in their domination. It is not for nothing that Marx, despite the backward material development of America during his lifetime, viewed the United States as the most ideologically modern (and most thoroughly bourgeois) nation on earth. Moreover, the American revolutionary victory was imaginatively portrayed in American culture of the nineteenth century as a simple victory of liberty over oppression, not as a class-based conflict. There is, in short, none of the ongoing class conflict from which the novels of writers such as Scott and Balzac drew such important energies.

Without this class conflict, the American Revolution, driven by a rhetoric of restoration of normalcy rather than radical transformation of the norm, was strikingly unrevolutionary. Unlike the French Revolution, in which the bourgeoisie swept to power, displacing the Catholic-aristocratic alliance of the ancién régime, the American Revolution merely shifted power to a postcolonial American bourgeoisie, whose ideology had essentially been hegemonic in England at least since the Glorious Revolution of 1688. In this sense, the United States was a particularly direct predecessor to the postcolonial nations of the second half of the twentieth century, in which independence meant not liberation for the masses but a transfer of power from the European bourgeoisie to their indigenous successors, trained to rule in their image (and often merely to serve as compradors for Western capitalism). Here it is entirely relevant to remember the warnings of Frantz Fanon that the rule of this new postcolonial bourgeoisie, far from leading to a glorious new age of freedom and prosperity, might in many ways make things worse, because they were merely a second-order bourgeoisie, lacking the energy and competence of their European predecessors.

Fanon's insight is informed by his Marxist-influenced realization that the European bourgeoisie had been tempered in the fires of the historical experience of the bourgeois cultural revolution, that centuries-long battle in which they finally solidified their power in Europe through their victory in the class war against the aristocracy. For Fanon, the postcolonial bourgeoisie, especially in Africa, had experienced no such battle and no such victory. As a result, they lacked the historical energy of their European predecessors and came to power in a condition of premature decadence. In his classic essay, "The Pitfalls of National Consciousness," Fanon warns against the potential for disaster in postcolonial African nations if those nations, in independence, simply replace the ruling European colonial bourgeoisie by an indigenous African bourgeoisie, while leaving the basic class structure of the societies still in place. For Fanon, the African bourgeoisie were mere mimic men, imitators of their Western masters, who themselves had already become decadent by the time of their full-scale colonization of Africa in the late nineteenth century. According to Fanon, the African bourgeoisie thus "follows the Western bourgeoisie along its path of negation and decadence without ever having emulated it in its first stages of exploration and invention. ... It is already senile before it has come to know the petulance, the fearlessness, or the will to succeed of youth" (153)

For Fanon, the bourgeoisie, decadent before their time, can never lead Africa in the building of an energetic new society and thus must be displaced from positions of power at all costs. The situation was somewhat different in America, where the postrevolutionary bourgeoisie swept into power at a time when the European bourgeoisie were still on the ascendant and not yet decadent. On the other hand, the American bourgeoisie escaped the class conflict still going on in Europe, erasing the aristocracy from the American scene and leaving the new rulers of America with no clear class enemies to fight. Without this conflict, there is no great historical novelist in early American literature, no Balzac and no Scott, who derive such powerful energies from the conflict of the classes in Europe. Instead, American novelists of the nineteenth century derive their energies from the sense of building a new national identity, forged not so much in historical class conflict as in the adventure of conquering the American frontier. It is no accident that James Fenimore Cooper (who did not at all mind being called the American Scott, however inaccurate the label) tends symbolically to link Native Americans with European feudalism, the victory of white America over Native America thus becoming another version of the victory of the European bourgeoisie over their aristocratic predecessors.

Among other things, this aspect of Cooper's fiction announces, very early on, the tendency of American culture to refigure class conflicts as racial ones, replacing class war with what Richard Slotkin, in an analysis of American culture that in many ways resembles Engelhardt's, calls "savage war," violent destruction of a savage racial enemy.[8] But this refiguration also tends to dehistoricize the conflict, which becomes a confrontation between two timeless racial essences rather than between the modernity of capitalism and the tradition of feudalism, as it had been in Europe. Put differently, from the point of view of literature, the strongest utopian energies in nineteenth-century American literature tended to reside not in realism but in romance, as Chase would ultimately note. For Chase, writing during the Cold War, this turn to romance signaled the unique American ability to solve social problems without resorting to "ideology," that bogeyman of Cold War rhetoric. But this turn also decoupled any vision of an alternative order from material reality. In short, American utopianism tends toward what Terry Eagleton calls "bad" utopianism, or utopianism in the "subjunctive mood." Rather than providing a model for building, or at least imagining, a better future, such visions describe a future that is disengaged from the present, because it can never be reached. This bad utopianism "grabs instantly for a future, projecting itself by an act of will or imagination beyond the compromised political structures of the present. By failing to attend to those forces or fault lines *within* the present that, developed or prised open in particular ways, might induce the condition to surpass itself into a future" ("Nationalism" 25).

This kind of utopianism, for Eagleton, merely makes us miserable by causing us to "desire uselessly rather than feasibly" ("Nationalism" 25). A more useful vision, for Eagleton, would allow us to imagine a leap from the "eternal recurrence of new variants on persistent forms of exploitation" that Marx termed "prehistory," into the realm of history proper, "the kingdom of use value, sensuous particularity, and an endless productivity of difference" (27). Here, Eagleton builds upon a long Marxist tradition that goes back to Friedrich Engels's well-known distinction between "scientific" socialism (a good form of utopanism) and "utopian" socialism (a bad form of utopianism because it is ahistorical and escapist) (Marx and Engels 683–717). The distinction, essentially, is between bad utopian visions that lead to escapism, quietism, and ultimate acceptance of the status quo and good utopian visions that can at least potentially lead to transformation of the existing social order.

The utopianism of American culture has long tended to be of the "bad" sort. The problematic utopianism of American realism was comprehended early on in Kazin's *On Native Grounds* (1942), one of the founding works of the emerging American studies movement. Kazin begins his pioneering study with a discussion of "the opening struggle for realism," the gist of which is that (oddly foreshadowing Fanon), when American realism finally arrived at the end of the nineteenth century, it was belated and prematurely decadent, delayed by the romantic tendencies of the better part of the nineteenth century and overwhelmed by the turn to naturalism and then modernism before it ever really got started. As Kazin puts it, "realism in America, which struggled so arduously to make itself heard and understood, had no true battleground, as it had no intellectual history, few models, virtually no theory, and no unity" (13–14). Thus, he goes on, "there was something dim, groping, unrealized in American realism even when it found its master in Dreiser, and long before Dreiser (himself so perfect a symbol of the crudity and emotional depths of American realism) it foundered on a dozen religious and moral taboos" (16).

The central figure in Kazin's initial chapter is Howells, whose career in a sense encapsulates the belated rise and premature fall of American realism. Howells is still best known for *The Rise of Silas Lapham* (1885), a late entry in the early phase of Howells's career, which bemoans the tawdriness of post–Civil War American capitalism, but from a solidly middle-class perspective that envisions no alternative to capitalist corruption and ruthlessness other than an old-fashioned personal rectitude that Howells himself suspects has no real place in modern America. Lapham's final retreat into the values of the past signals Howell's unwillingness to admit, as had Balzac, that history only moves forward, however unfortunate that movement might be. Howells's novels after *Silas Lapham* then take a darker turn as Howells, partly due to his horror at the summary trials and executions of the Haymarket anarchists in Chicago, becomes ever more critical of American capitalism. In this phase, Howells vaguely flirts with the notion of socialism as a potential alternative but can recover a utopian dimension only by exiting the realism he had so long championed and turning to utopian romance, somewhat in the mode of Edward Bellamy's influential *Looking Backward* (1888), which triggered a flurry of such texts. But even works such as *A Traveler from Altruria* (1894), Howells's most successful utopian novel, have a bitter satirical edge that makes them more complaints about the evils of the present than legitimate attempts to imagine a better future.

All in all, Howells's later realist novels are weak in utopian energy; they might themselves have collectively been titled *Looking Backward*, and they look backward in an even more eulogistic mode than had *Silas Lapham*. As Kazin puts it, the books have the tone of "the funeral of the romantic and facile promise of the American dream" (39). Of course, given the late arrival of American realism on the historical stage, it could hardly have been otherwise. Howells, after all, was a contemporary not of Balzac, who wrote in the midst of capitalism on the rise, but of Zola, who wrote when capitalism had already become decadent and com- modification was fast becoming universal. Zola's basic acceptance of this fact, of course, can be located in his infamous determinism, and his de- piction of the capitalist system does have a tendency to suggest that capi- talism is a natural consequence of a basically predatory human nature. It should come as no surprise, then, that Marxist critics from Zola's con- temporary, Engels, onward have dismissed Zola's work, arguing that, whatever his consciously socialist agenda, Zola is ultimately unable to see beyond his own bourgeois class perspective. Thus, Lukács grants that Zola's novels as a group may be unmatched as an encyclopedic descrip- tion of the French society of their day but argues that they have a ten- dency to weave their astonishing variety of factual material into a sweep- ing organic vision of society that is unable to comprehend the inherent contradictions in the capitalist system (*Studies* 86). With no coherent vi- sion of these contradictions, Zola is also unable, according to Lukács, to construct a viable historical vision. History, after all, proceeds through the playing out of conflicts and contradictions, not by a process of or- ganic growth analogous to that of a plant. Meanwhile, for Lukács, Zola's predicament suggests a larger historical phenomenon in which the nine- teenth-century bourgeois writer was gradually reduced to the status of "a mere spectator and chronicler" as opposed to being a genuine participant in the great historical struggles of his time (*Studies* 89).

Of course, in the United States, all of this was complicated at the be- ginning of the twentieth century by the transformation of capitalism into its consumerist phase, a transformation that occurred throughout the capitalist world but that was at its most powerful and dramatic in the U.S. As William Leach documents in great detail in *Land of Desire*, the decades between the end of the nineteenth century and the end of the 1920s saw a radical transformation in the texture of American life. Dur- ing this period, technological innovations led to fundamental changes in the way Americans lived and worked. Perhaps even more importantly, American capitalism was itself transformed, entering a modern consum- erist phase the ultimate completion of which would occur in the long 1950s. According to Leach, the cardinal features of the new culture that arose in conjunction with this new phase of capitalism were "acquisition and consumption as the means of achieving happiness; the cult of the new; the democratization of desire; and money value as the predominant measure of all value in society" (3).

Among other things, the dramatic changes undergone by American society in the early twentieth century solidified the notion of change itself as the quintessential American paradigm. Of course, the cult of the new was itself already a tradition of sorts by the twentieth century. Colonized by European settlers seeking a New World, then founded by revolution- aries seeking a new political order founded on the new principles of the

Enlightenment, the United States was uniquely prepared for the radical transformations wrought by consumer capitalism in the first decades of the twentieth century. Nevertheless, these transformations, changing virtually every aspect of the texture of everyday life within a generation, were radical enough that they largely wiped out any lingering sense of genuine tradition, in the sense of transgenerational values and practices. Such changes necessarily left a certain emptiness in the American soul, an emptiness that the flood of commodities produced by this new consumer capitalist system was not likely to be able to fill.

After all, as Leach's title indicates, the new consumer capitalism was all about the creation of desire, particularly of the desire to consume more and more commodities and thus feed the capitalist economic system. Moreover, it was necessary, in order for that system to continue to grow and prosper, that these desires could never be fulfilled. Within the logic of this system, acquiring particularly coveted commodities did not make consumers content but merely stimulated them to yearn for even more acquisitions. The system was, in short, fundamentally anti-utopian, and even more so than nineteenth-century industrial capitalism, which drew upon the legacy of the Enlightenment to produce at least the *notion* that a stable happiness could be achieved.

The dynamism of the growth of consumer capitalism in America in the first decades of the twentieth century was such that the phenomenon can genuinely be considered a second bourgeois cultural revolution. This time, however, Americans were at the forefront, rather than on the margins, so it perhaps comes as no surprise that, just as the decades after the French Revolution produced a Scott and a Balzac to document the dramatic changes under way in Europe at the beginning of the nineteenth century, the consumer capitalist revolution in America produced a Faulkner, Fitzgerald, Hemingway, and Dos Passos to document the changes under way in America at the beginning of the twentieth century. Meanwhile, given the profoundly anti-utopian nature of the American consumerist revolution, it should come as no surprise that the works of these American writers were relatively weak in utopian energies. These writers, by and large, rued the effects of consumerism in their work, just as Balzac had railed against the dehumanizing consequences of capitalism in his. But Balzac was writing at a time when capitalism was sweeping away feudalism and thus at a time when, however doleful the present appeared to be, history had a chance to bring something new. By the time of the great American modernist novelists, this utopian possibility no longer seemed so clear. The American consumerist revolution did not replace capitalism (America's ancién régime), but merely moved it in a new and more powerful direction, assuring that the commodification of everything so despised by Balzac would simply shift into a higher gear. Little wonder, then, that modernism, however much informed by a sense of historical crisis, lacked the sense of the forward sweep of history that informed the realism of Balzac and other early nineteenth-century bourgeois writers.

On the other hand, the consumerist revolution of the first three decades of the twentieth century did help to create new and different kinds of culture. In particular, the new consumerist ethos, combined with certain technological advances (such as the development of commercially viable film technologies), helped to trigger an explosive growth in the production and distribution of popular culture. Advertising became perhaps the American cultural genre, par excellence. The film industry was born. Increases in print technology made it feasible to produce large numbers of books to be sold at low prices; rapidly rising literacy rates ensured that the masses, now able to afford books, could also read them. Given the tremendous emphasis on consumption in this phase of American history, the strongest utopian energies in American culture of this period were to be found not in high culture but in popular culture, as writers such as L. Frank Baum assured Americans that it was okay to be prosperous and self-indulgent, while writers such as Edgar Rice Burroughs offered fantasy escapes from the humdrum routine of everyday capitalism, assuring Americans that it was still possible to experience some sense of adventure while living in the workaday world.

Bloch himself, erstwhile devoted reader of Karl May, notes the genuine utopian potential to be found in the adventure story (for which he coins the term "colportage"), which he sees as a modern version of the fairy tale. Bloch grants that such stories, like fairy tales, have an escapist quality; they are "castle in the air par excellence" (369). Yet, for Bloch, such stories nevertheless suggest the possibility of a better golden world, of "happiness which penetrates from the night to the light" (369). Baum's work, of course, is all about happiness, though it is a happiness that is always already commodified. Noting that Baum had a prominent career as a pioneer in the design of store window displays before he became a popular writer, Leach identifies Baum's *The Wonderful Wizard of Oz* (1900) and its sequels as key markers of the rise of consumerism at the beginning of the twentieth century. Characterizing Baum's book as a sort-of American feel-good fairy tale that lacks the darkness of its European predecessors, Leach notes the way in which the positive tone of the book assured its early readers that the dramatic changes occurring around them should be welcomed, rather than feared. Moreover, though some have seen the book as a critique of capitalism, Leach sees no trace of such critique in a book that "far from challenging the new industrial society, endorsed its values and direction" (251).[9] The Wizard himself is a sham and a humbug whose power arises not from genuine magic but from the kind of chicanery that is the stuff of advertising, promotion, and, of course, window dressing. But the Wizard is ultimately a positive figure; he rules the Emerald City wisely and well, and he is able to help Dorothy and her entire entourage achieve everything they wish for. The

Emerald City itself is a bit of fakery: everything in it appears to be the color of money, but only because the entire population has been tricked into wearing green glasses at all times. But no matter. The illusion is a benevolent one that helps the inhabitants to have happier lives. The message seems to be clear: the new prosperity of American consumer capitalism may be partly a matter of smoke and mirrors, but those who go along with the deception can have wonderful lives.

Baum's message was well received. His book was vastly popular and spawned a whole series of such books, continuing the feel-good message that all you have to do is believe in yourself and believe in the system and all will be well. Granted, Dorothy does, in the first book, seem to prefer the drab grayness of Kansas to the lure of the Emerald City, but later in the sequence she abandons this attitude and moves once and for all to the consumerist utopia of the green metropolis, taking Uncle Henry and Auntie Em along with her. Once there, they live in splendor, all their dreams fulfilled. Then, in 1939, Baum's work became a central icon of American popular culture once and for all, with the release of a lavish Technicolor film version (directed by Mervyn LeRoy) that contrasted with the bleakness of the Depression in much the same way that the Emerald City contrasted with the drabness of Kansas. The reassuring intentions of this film are clear, and they are effectively achieved, which may be why the film is still much viewed and much beloved.

The fictional worlds of Burroughs were not quite so rosy. John Carter on Mars and Tarzan in darkest Africa must struggle a bit more than Dorothy or the Scarecrow to achieve their goals. Yet their goals are achievable with sufficient effort (and sufficient violence), which sets them starkly apart from such high-culture protagonists as Jay Gatsby, Frederic Henry, or Thomas Sutpen, whose mighty efforts (often aimed at overcoming class inequality) are doomed to failure. Moreover, Burroughs himself was a sort of one-man embodiment of the new ethic of consumerism, producing long sequences of books, such as the Tarzan series and the Martian series, in assembly-line fashion. Both of these series were vastly popular, allowing Burroughs to become a wealthy man, following his fellow Chicagoan Baum to Southern California, where the two of them pursued their own private utopias, becoming members of a vanguard that would soon make Los Angeles and its environs the locus classicus of the modern American dream, consumer-style. Both of Burroughs's series derived their popularity from pure fantasy value, allowing their readers to imagine lives of romance and adventure no longer available in the routinized world of consumer capitalist America.

Both of Burroughs's series, in short, were designed to allow readers to imagine the reopening of the now-closed American frontier, but without the real dangers and hardships that life on the actual frontier had posed. In some sense, then, Burroughs's work is critical of capitalism, because it implies the desirability of an escape from the modern capitalist world.

Tarzan, for example, is presented as noble primarily because of his superior English aristocratic bloodlines. The rightful Lord Greystoke, he is inherently superior not only to the savage cannibals he constantly encounters in Africa but also to the vulgar capitalists he encounters in America. He is interested in truth, justice, and honor but remains safely aloof from and above the workaday world of the scramble for money. He thus represents idealized standards of conduct (and racial superiority) that look back to precapitalist times, while at the same time enacting the strain of nostalgia for British aristocratic splendor that, as Christopher Hitchens documents, informs the American popular mind throughout the twentieth century, helping to fill the need for a usable glorious past that America's own history, informed by a rejection of tradition and cult of the new, cannot provide.

The Tarzan books also suggest a nostalgia for empire. For one thing, the idea of imperial expansion offered an obvious possibility for renewal of the frontier and thus a presumed resuscitation of the American spirit. For another, it was the empire that made Great Britain great, and, if America looked to Britain for models of glory, then the notion of empire was necessarily central to those models. Of course, the Africa patrolled by Tarzan was already thoroughly colonized by European powers, leaving no room for American expansion there. In fact, by the time of Burroughs's first Tarzan novel (1914), there were few places on the entire earth still available for colonization. For that, Burroughs had to look beyond earth. The Mars stories are even more overtly imperialistic than the Tarzan stories, and, in them, Burroughs "projected the American imperial (and protective) zeal into outer space, making of Mars what Theodore Roosevelt had made of the western hemisphere, a ward of the United States" (Seelye xiii).

However horrific the racism, sexism, and violence of Burroughs's fiction, the very popularity of that fiction suggests that it purveyed a point a view not that far outside the American mainstream. Slotkin, in his study of the role of the frontier in the American imagination, sees Burroughs's work as paradigmatic of American attempts to deal with the late nineteenth-century closing of the frontier. In particular, he notes that Burroughs, in books such as *A Princess of Mars* (first published in serial form in 1911), essentially adapted the format and ideology of the Western to a Martian context, complete with the attendant glorification of violence and (white) racial purity (195–211).

If Burroughs's fiction contains a strong utopian element built on the romance of male adventure, the violence, racism, and sexism of that fiction make its utopianism highly problematic, as does its backward-leaning nostalgia for aristocracy. Of course, given the realities of American history, it should come as no surprise that some of the most popular and compelling utopian ideas to have been produced in American culture should be centrally informed by images of the violent extermination of racial others and the masculine domination of alluring, but submissive females.

Burroughs's Martian novels maintain an important place in the history of American science fiction, though he is most widely remembered for his Tarzan books, or at least for the screen adaptations of those books. As with *The Wizard of Oz*, the Tarzan movies gained great popularity during the Depression years of the 1930s, when their presentation of escapist adventure similarly provided fantasy relief from the exigencies of everyday life in Depression-era America.[10] In fact, the Depression, oddly enough, triggered a temporary resurgence in utopian thought in America. Or perhaps it wasn't odd. With the consumer capitalist revolution temporarily derailed by the Depression, it became much easier to envision alternatives to the radically anti-utopian ideology of consumerism. Much of this new utopianism, of course, was the pure escapism of Hollywood cinema, in which all problems were easily solved and everyone lived happily ever after. From *Tarzan the Ape Man* to *The Wizard of Oz*, from Busby Berkeley musicals to screwball comedies, audiences, often sitting in lavish movie palaces, could enjoy fantasy resolution of all sorts of problems in the movies, including economic problems associated with the Depression, as in *Gold Diggers of 1933* (1933), directed by LeRoy. Little wonder, then, that Bloch saw Hollywood cinema as a corrupt perversion of the utopian impulse and thus as one of the objects of his greatest contempt. Though Bloch sees great potential in film as an art form, he concludes that

thanks to America the film has become the most desecrated form of art. The Hollywood cinema does not only supply the old kitsch: the sloppy kiss-romance, the nervebasher, where there is no longer a difference between enthusiasm and catastrophe, the happy end within a completely unchanged world; without exception it also uses this kitsch for ideological stupefaction and fascist incitement. (410).[11]

It is certainly the case that spectacles such as *Gold Diggers*, which is dominated by three lavish Berkeley-choreographed musical performances (including one in which female dancers cavort about the stage to the tune of "We're in the Money," clad in scanty costumes seemingly made only of coins), served as virtual dramatizations of consumerist desires. Even this film, however, could not conceal a certain anxiety. The last production number ends with the memorable "Forgotten Man" sequence. Here, the performers wear costumes simulating poverty and sing of the hardships of the Depression, with an emphasis (inspired by the 1932 Bonus Army march on Washington) on the failure of America to live up to the promises made to the soldiers who fought in World War I. Particularly striking is a sequence showing a troop of soldiers proudly marching off to war, then staggering back, wounded and bleeding, then standing in line at a soup kitchen. The film ends, without commentary, as the number closes, but the implications of the sequence are powerful, especially when read against the opening sequence and the romantic resolution of the plot, both of which this last number tends to undermine.

It would be a mistake to make too much of the implications of this number within the context of a film clearly designed for pure entertainment. Still, the "Forgotten Man" sequence provides one of the central examples of the occasional attempts by Hollywood (especially in the Warner Brothers "social problem" films) in the 1930s to comment on problems associated with the Depression—in carefully packaged ways and without suggesting radical solutions. Indeed, what is consistently striking about such social problem films is the extent to which they criticize the current system without suggesting any systemic alternatives. The gangster films of the early 1930s, the classic Universal monster movies, and such social-problem films as Mervyn LeRoy's *I Am a Fugitive from a Chain Gang* (1932), William Wellman's *Heroes for Sale* (1933) and *Wild Boys of the Road* (1933), Fritz Lang's *Fury* (1936), and William Wyler's *Dead End* (1937) suggested that all was not right in consumer land. Even mainstream comedies such as the Marx brothers' *Duck Soup* (1933) and Charlie Chaplin's *Modern Times* (1936) contained implicit criticisms of modern capitalism. But none of these popular films really suggested that capitalism per se was the problem.

Even King Vidor's *Our Daily Bread* (1934), which seemed rather clearly to suggest socialism as a viable alternative, did so in an oddly nostalgic, backward-looking way. There was a genuinely radical American cinema in the Depression years, though films such as Ralph Steiner's *Pie in the Sky* (1934), Herbert Kline's *Heart of Spain* (1937), Joris Ivens's *The Spanish Earth* (1937), and Elia Kazan, Robert Stebbins, and Jay Leyda's *People of the Cumberland* (1938) struggled against a woeful lack of funding and could not compete for audiences with the slick productions of Hollywood. Moreover, even these radical films tended to focus more on critiques of the ills of capitalism than on the presentation of revolutionary alternatives. Somewhat more successful (largely because it required less in the way of financial resources) was the proletarian literature movement that flowered briefly during the 1930s. Indeed, such works of proletarian fiction as Agnes Smedley's *Daughter of the Earth* (1929), Mike Gold's *Jews without Money* (1930), Myra Page's *Gathering Storm* (1932), and Jack Conroy's *The Disinherited* (1933), written largely in a realist vein, contained the strongest suggestions of possible utopian alternatives to capitalism that have ever appeared in American literature.[12]

These writers did not, themselves, reach particularly large audiences, but their work significantly influenced a number of better-known writers. Left-leaning works such as Dos Passos's *U.S.A.* Trilogy (1930–1936), John Steinbeck's *The Grapes of Wrath* (1939), and Richard Wright's *Native Son* (1940) have become recognized classics of modern American literature. Hemingway, in *To Have and Have Not* (1937) and *For Whom the Bell Tolls* (1940), also showed the influence of this movement. Fitzgerald moved to the left as well, though he was in decline and produced only one novel that was clearly influenced by leftist ideas, and that one was unfinished: *The Last Tycoon* (published posthumously in 1941), a critique of the Hollywood Culture Industry. Indeed, of the major American writers of the 1930s, only Faulkner seemed essentially oblivious to the politics of the decade (making him a principal object of contempt on the part of leftist critics at the time), and even he was more socially engaged than his contemporary reputation indicated.

Even the proletarian works of the 1930s were relatively mild in their call for revolutionary change, however, and such calls were diluted even more by the turn to the Popular Front late in the decade. The movement then collapsed altogether in World War II, with no chance for rebirth in the postwar climate of the Cold War. Any genuine spirit of utopianism also had little chance for rebirth in that climate. Leftist writers continued to write and to publish but were radically marginalized. Moreover, in the long 1950s, even the works of leftist writers tended to lack utopian energy, as these writers seemed to suffer from a collective lack of any ability to imagine genuine alternatives to the current capitalist reality. This phenomenon, in fact, can be taken as one of the surest signs of a national failure of utopian thought in the Cold War climate of the long 1950s.

The rejection of specifically socialist forms of utopian thought during the long 1950s was a matter of official public policy, but it was also consonant with more subtle ideological messages that tended to dismiss any sort of public (political) solutions in favor of the promotion of private (individual) solutions, whether they involve psychotherapy or simply a retreat into the private sanctuary of family and home. For example, Elaine Tyler May has documented the extensive complicity between the anticommunist hysteria of the Cold War years and the official glorification of family life during the same period. Meanwhile, May also notes the extent to which consumerism was at play in this phenomenon as well, as the official rhetoric of the period, with its special emphasis on home ownership and on household products and appliances, tended to transform the domestic sphere into a privileged locus of consumption.

Such retreats into the privacy of the commodity-laden suburban home helped to contain any potential subversive energies and to keep them out of the potentially dangerous public sphere. The culture of the long 1950s, with its consistent rejection of utopian ideas, tended to reinforce this phenomenon, whether intentionally or not. Chapter 1 of this study focuses on the canonical "literary" novels of the long 1950s, concentrating especially on the work of Nabokov. Not surprisingly, the canonical novels of the decade tend to be constructed according to a modernist aesthetic, which, through its exploration of stylistic and technical alternatives, contains an inherent utopian dimension. Chapter 2 looks at the leftist novels of the long 1950s, which tend to be constructed according to a realist aesthetic but which contain an inherent utopian dimension through their nominal understanding that there are systemic alternatives to capitalism. Chapter 3 then considers the possibility that utopian energies might be found in the popular fiction of the long 1950s, including a brief consideration of the Western and science fiction genres but focusing primarily on crime fiction, especially on the novels of Thompson. Chapter 4 extends this exploration to the realm of film, concentrating especially on the films of Hitchcock and Disney during the long 1950s.

All of these examinations lead to the conclusion that the utopian energies residing in these various kinds of works are extremely weak and that, in fact, the works tend to dismiss utopian thinking as naïve or even sinister. This weak utopianism, or even anti-utopianism, can, I argue, be related to the Cold War context in which these works were created and initially received. Moreover, the weak utopianism in these works tends to be reflected in characteristics—such as in the inability (or unwillingness) to sustain coherent narratives and an accompanying fragmentation in textual form in the psyches of characters—that have been widely described as central to postmodernism. This phenomenon suggests a close interrelationship between the Cold War and the rise of postmodernism, as opposed to the suggestions by critics such as Alan Nadel that postmodernism runs contrary to the mind-set of the Cold War and that postmodernism arose in the early 1960s to mark the end of the peak Cold War years.

## Chapter 1

# "Soiled, Torn, and Dead":
# The Bleak Vision of American Literary
# Fiction in the Long 1950s

In many ways, the long 1950s was not a particularly rich time for the American novel. Granted, important novels were published during the period, but the most respected novel published during the decade, *Lolita*, could not even initially be published in America due to its "shocking" subject matter. And, however American the texture of its evocation of cross-country car trips through a landscape saturated with the products of a pervasive Culture Industry, *Lolita* was written by a Russian émigré who fled back to Europe at the first economic opportunity, escaping what he clearly saw as the vulgarity of America. Other respected novels of the long 1950s were written by more "authentically" American writers, though many of those writers were cultural outsiders, such as the African Americans Ralph Ellison and James Baldwin, the Southerner Catholics Flannery O'Connor and Walker Percy, and the Jewish writers J. D. Salinger, Normal Mailer, Saul Bellow, and Joseph Heller. Partly as a result of the ethnic marginality of the writers, no novels of the decade have really gained the canonical status of, say, *Moby-Dick* or *The Great Gatsby*. Many readers are still uncomfortable with the subject matter of *Lolita*, while Ellison's *Invisible Man* (1952) has always been seen more as an African American classic than an American classic, and Heller's absurdist *Catch-22* (1961) is often seen as representing a particular (urban Jewish) reaction to a special moment in American history.

*Lolita*, *Invisible Man*, and *Catch-22*, arguably the three most important American novels of the long 1950s, are very different works, though all are linked by the fact that they are written in a modernist vein, a fact that is not surprising given that the extended decade of the long 1950s was the great era of modernist canonization. From this point of view, the literary production of the long 1950s might actually be seen as extremely impressive, the period having produced, after the fact, the golden age of the American modernist novel, even though the texts involved (most centrally the novels of that American trinity, Faulkner, Fitzgerald, and Hemingway) were mostly written and published in the interwar period. In any case, the critical turn toward modernism during the 1950s was so powerful that it was difficult for any new texts produced during the period to be regarded as seriously literary unless they were at least vaguely modernist in style and form.

There were, of course, respected literary novels of the long 1950s that were not modernist. Indeed, the earliest novel of the period subsequently to achieve at least semicanonical status was Norman Mailer's *The Naked and the Dead* (1948), a gritty, naturalistic account of an American assault on a Japanese-held island in World War II. In keeping with the typical skepticism of naturalist novels, *The Naked and the Dead* is anything but a triumphant account of the Allied victory in the war. Indeed, while World War II looms over much of the American fiction of the long 1950s, this fiction is surprisingly gloomy in its depiction of the American war effort, which is virtually never seen as sweeping American society toward a brave new utopian postwar world. In this sense, *The Naked and the Dead* is particularly pessimistic. In it, for example, the standard wartime motif of individual sacrifice in the interest of the common good is replaced by the depiction of an American army torn by internal strife as the alienated individuals who make it up fail to overcome their class and ethnic differences, even in the face of a battle to the death with their Japanese enemies on the Pacific island of Anopopei. Meanwhile, standard army discipline becomes an image of routinization that the book fears will be extended forward into postwar American society.

Thus, the book suggests that figures such as the neofascist General Cummings represent a dangerous element that threatens to ride the military victory in World War II to power in postwar America. This motif is profoundly anti-utopian. Far from suggesting alternatives, it suggests the lack of alternatives, the powers that be in America not being all that different from their fascist opponents. As Cummings's aide, the left-liberal Lieutenant Robert Hearn, puts it in one of his periodic political debates with the General, "You people can't lose the war either way" (176).[1] Meanwhile, if *The Naked and the Dead* suggests that certain powers within the military-industrial complex were ideologically similar to America's enemies in the war, it also suggests that many of the individual soldiers in the book are outsiders in America and thus have much in common with the Japanese against whom they are fighting, who serve as such obvious images of Otherness.

The essentially naturalistic style of *The Naked and the Dead* would quickly go out of fashion with the enthusiastic canonization of modernism in the 1950s, and Mailer would eventually be better known for his personal antics than for his first novel. The decade's other important naturalist war novel, James Jones's *From Here to Eternity* (1951), got even less critical respect. Jones's book has had its critical proponents, but has never quite been regarded as great literature, despite (or perhaps because of) its success as the leading fiction bestseller of 1951. The book is now best known through the greatly attenuated film version, which provided American culture with one of its most remembered images, a scantily clad Burt Lancaster and Deborah Kerr making love on the beach, while waves break over them.

Tellingly, the World War II novel of the long 1950s that would ultimately achieve the loftiest critical reputation was *Catch-22*. Published in 1961 (though begun in 1953), Heller's book serves as an appropriate conclusion to the literary production of the 1950s, especially if one views that production as beginning with *The Naked and the Dead*, a book that has a surprising amount in common with *Catch-22*, despite the dramatic stylistic and tonal differences between the two novels.[2] Alan Nadel sees *Catch-22* as a marker of the beginnings of a postmodernist revolt against the containment mentality of the peak Cold War years. He argues, for example, that both Heller's novel and the near-contemporaneous Bay of Pigs fiasco demonstrated the collapse of the authority of metanarratives. I agree, to an extent, but would characterize the phenomenon slightly differently. In particular, I would see *Catch-22* not as a turn away from the cultural dominants of the 1950s but as the culmination of postmodernist trends that had been building throughout the Cold War. *Catch-22* is, in fact, very much a novel of the 1950s, despite the fact that it reached its peak in popularity in the mid- to late 1960s, when it came to be regarded by many (including Heller) as a sort of prescient critique of the American military involvement in Vietnam.[3] Yet Heller also suggested that the book, which ostensibly focuses on the American bombing and invasion of Italy late in World War II, could be read as a comment on the Korean War.[4] In any case, whatever the innovations of its seemingly postmodern absurdist style, the book's central thematic concerns are very much the concerns of 1950s fiction as a whole.

The central object of critique in *Catch-22* is the military bureaucracy, which, in its insane enforcement of regulations, becomes a dystopian image of 1950s routinization pushed to an absurd extreme. Hilfer points out this emphasis, noting that the book is primarily a satire of the "insane logic of the rationalized world" (113). In the book, the insanely routinized military bureaucracy clearly stands in for government as a whole. Most specifically, many elements of the book seem designed specifically as a critique of the McCarthyite anticommunist purges, sometimes quite explicitly, as when Captain Black, one of the text's bureaucrats, launches a loyalty oath crusade in an attempt to purge the army of communists (122–25).[5] Even more generally, the military bureaucracy of *Catch-22* stands in for all of the forces that sought to enforce normality, routine, and regimentation in American society in the 1950s. Through its mode of absurdist satire, the book seems to reverse the central values of the decade, thus demonstrating that the decade's strict polar opposition between the sane and the insane, the normal and the abnormal could not stand very much scrutiny. But one could argue that the 1950s craze for normality was as strong as it was precisely because of anxieties over the stability of the normal–abnormal opposition. It is certainly the case that the forces of normality in *Catch-22* are consistently presented as crazed, while the forces of abnormality, centrally represented in the text by the protagonist, Yossarian, are presented as sane and sensible, even if they must struggle mightily to preserve this sanity in the face of the insane forces that are arrayed against them.

In a similar deconstruction, Yossarian, though the book's central figure, is very much an Other. Ethnically, he was originally conceived by Heller as Jewish but became in the published version an "Assyrian," thus preserving his Semitism but aligning him with no specific group in the modern world. More importantly, Yossarian refuses to accept the logic of his routinized world, thus remaining marginal to that world's centers of power. Yet he remains very much the center of Heller's book. A character who behaves insanely, receiving medals, sitting in trees, and marching backward, all while nude (in a rejection of the routinization represented by his uniform), Yossarian is clearly the sanest character in the book. Indeed, in one of the book's various manifestations of the bureaucratic clause from which it takes its title, Yossarian, a bombardier desperate to avoid flying any further missions, is told that he cannot be grounded due to insanity unless he himself asks to be grounded but that, if he asks to be grounded, then he must obviously be sane and therefore cannot be grounded (54–55). It is against such impossible restrictions that Yossarian protests in his various instances of seemingly insane behavior. Eventually, however, he concludes that the bureaucracy cannot be dealt with, so he decides to run away, perhaps to Sweden, where his former comrade, the pilot Orr, has reportedly gone.

In addition to its critique of bureaucratic routinization, *Catch-22* also includes overt criticisms of the workings of the capitalist system, most obviously in its depiction of the (largely successful) attempts of mess officer Milo Minderbinder to use his position in the war to build a giant corporate syndicate, quickly expanding from operations in Italy to cover the entire Mediterranean and, eventually, the globe. This syndicate, M & M Enterprises, clearly functions as a stand-in for capitalism as a whole, and Milo's willingness to do anything and everything to expand his operations and thus grow his profits is a dark commentary on the capitalist mind-set. Indeed, at one point, Minderbinder even contracts with the Germans to use American planes to bomb their own base at Pianosa. Caught in the act, Minderbinder and his syndicate seem to face sure doom, until he opens his books, reveals the huge profits he is making, and reminds all concerned that they own shares in the syndicate and thus are making profits themselves. In that case, of course, all is forgiven, except by a "few embittered misfits" who do not feel that the pursuit of profit justifies bombing and strafing an American base inhabited by American soldiers (269).

Given the overt critique of capitalism and the only slightly more oblique critique of McCarthyism that inform *Catch-22*, Heller's book is one of the most openly political of the canonical American literary novels of the 1950s. Thus, Brian Way sees the book as a work of social protest in the American tradition of Dreiser, Dos Passos, Farrell, and Steinbeck, its stylistic shift from naturalism representing a change in critical strategies necessitated by changes in the workings of the official power to which the book is opposed. Way's argument sheds important light on the book, but it fails to acknowledge the most important weakness of *Catch-22* as a political novel: its almost total lack of any utopian dimension that might present an alternative to the insane capitalist system it criticizes. Yossarian's eventual solution to his dilemma is pure escapism. Even if he does make it to Sweden, he will certainly find no utopia there, even though the Swedes did manage to avoid direct involvement in the conflicts of World War II. Granted, Sweden did become the most socialist of Western nations during the long 1950s, beginning when the Social Democrats took power in 1946, so one is tempted to see the book's potential identification of Sweden with utopia as a possible Aesopian nod toward socialism as an alternative to the capitalist West. Yossarian is heading for a Sweden in which the Social Democrats have yet to assume power, but, in a nonrealist book like *Catch-22*, we should not worry too much about that minor detail. Nevertheless, if Heller's Sweden is meant as a subtle endorsement of socialism, it is so subtle that few readers would be likely to pick up on it and thus not very effective as a political statement.

If Yosssarian must go away to Sweden to seek utopia, other literary protagonists of the long 1950s had to seek happiness in even more exotic places. Thus, Saul Bellow's *Henderson the Rain King* (1959) is a very typical work of the era, featuring an alienated protagonist who is driven from the comfort of his affluent American home in search of the obscure object of desire that is indicated by his inner voice, which insistently cries, "I want." "I want," of course, is the official mantra of a 1950s America in which individuals were inundated with a barrage of signals that encouraged a consumerist desire that consumption could never quench. Yet Bellow's lumbering protagonist, however emblematic he may be of contemporary angst, is an essentially comic, even carnivalesque figure,[6] bringing to life the stereotype of the ugly American as he blunders about Africa, meaning well but generally wreaking havoc because his physical power is rivaled only by his cultural ignorance.[7] Given the comic tone of the book, one is tempted to read it as a sort of parody of Conrad's *Heart of Darkness*. After all, Henderson repeats many of Charlie Marlow's Africanist clichés almost exactly, while his eventual status as the Sungo (rain king) of the Wariri recalls Kurtz's rise to power among the primitive tribesmen who inhabit the jungles around the Inner Station.

The problem is that Bellow does not really challenge the Conradian stereotypes that he repeats, other than instilling them with comedy. One could argue that Bellow's comic rendition of the condition of Africa is even more insulting and demeaning to Africans than was Conrad's achingly self-serious portrayal. One might, for example, object to the somewhat comic treatment of Henderson's destruction of the water supply of the peaceful (and vaguely utopian) Arnewi, noble savages all. This destruction will no doubt bring horrific suffering, if not death, to the entire tribe, yet Bellow at least leaves open the option of reading this event almost as slapstick. Note, for example, Gloria Cronin's characterization of this tragic (for the Arnewi) event as "hilarious" (270).[8] Bellow spares us the jungle motif, placing his book in arid East Africa, and he mercifully does not claim that the Wariri or other Africans in the book are cannibals. Nevertheless, his book contains enough racist clichés and stereotypes to fill a Disney film. For one thing, there are all those lions and all those lustfully naked dancing and gyrating African women. For another, everything in Africa, we are told, is primitive and ancient, and Henderson feels, as he moves into the interior, Marlow-like, that he is nearing the "original place," entering "the past—the real past, no history or junk like that" (46–47).

Bellow does essentially nothing to disabuse his readers of this Hegelian picture of Africa as a primitive land without history. Granted, Bellow seems to mock Henderson's expectations of African primitivism by having him encounter the sophisticated Dahfu, Western-educated king of the Wariri. But the Westernness of that education is precisely the point. Bellow's Africa is less primitive than Conrad's, but only because Westerners have brought civilization to the dark continent. Bellow presents Dahfu's education and sophistication as vaguely comic, but the comedy seems to derive less from the ridiculousness of Dahfu's Reichian viewpoint than from the incongruity of an African being educated at all.[9] Meanwhile, this incongruity, which also includes the Westernized character of the Wariris as a whole, bespeaks the common 1950s fear that the Other is no different from Us. In the particular case of Africa, this ultimate sameness destroys the whole justification for colonialism, though Bellow shows absolutely no awareness of the political realities of colonial Africa, making no mention whatsoever that Henderson's journey is to East Africa, site of the recent Mau Mau rebellion, or that the Africa Henderson visits is in the midst of an anticolonial movement that will soon lead to independence.

Of course, Bellow's novel is not about Africa but about the American Henderson, just as *Heart of Darkness* is about Marlow and his European culture. But this continuing ability to use Africa simply as an allegorical backdrop for the existential adventures of Westerners (while ignoring the reality or humanity of Africans) is part of the problem with Bellow's book, as if we had learned nothing in the 60 years of history that fell between the two novels. Granted, Henderson is at least a bit more self-conscious about his predicament, as when he explains to his guide, Romilayu, that he is only one of a literal horde of Americans who have spread out across the world seeking wisdom in light of the fact that all of the big battles have already been fought and won back home in America (276–77). In short, Henderson and these other Americans are engaged in a flight from routine (described by Henderson as the death of the soul) in an American society that has settled into comfortable sameness, the frontier having long been conquered, without utopia having been achieved. In particular, Henderson nostalgically figures World War II as the last great adventure, an attitude he shares to some extent with Sloan Wilson's gray-flannel-clad Tom Rath, whose military and sexual adventures during the war have been replaced by the routine of job and family.

Conrad's Marlow, incidentally, also figures European society as routinized, with its smug businessmen performing their daily monkey tricks on tightropes, "each moored with two good addresses, like a hulk with two anchors, a butcher round one corner, a policeman round another, excellent appetites, and temperature normal" (48). Indeed, both Marlow and Henderson are, in a sense, seeking fresh perspectives through their encounters with the Other of Africa. Marlow returns from Africa with a disgust rivaling that of Swift's Gulliver as he returns from the land of the Houyhnmhnms, having learned nothing of the truth but having confirmed that his society is based on a texture of lies. Henderson, on the other hand, returns invigorated, cavorting joyously in the fresh air of Newfoundland on his way back to New York, clutching a young Persian boy (an Other whom, like the caged lion cub that he also brings back from Africa, he can safely dominate and control) to his breast and feeling that he has discovered a great secret. Unfortunately, Bellow never really specifies what that secret is, and many critics have concluded that Henderson has learned nothing.

In fact, Henderson's trip to Africa is rather pointless, and it is frankly hard to find much of a point, certainly not a political one, to Bellow's novel, which was, of course, very much to its advantage in the 1950s, when books with political points were out of fashion indeed. It is no accident that the canonization of modernism occurred during this same Cold War period. For one thing, it was possible to read most modernist works as apolitical attempts at aesthetic innovation, regardless of the original intentions of the authors, which were often subversive and anti-bourgeois, even if not overtly pro-socialist. Works that were too avowedly political to meet this criterion (such as John Dos Passos's left-leaning *U.S.A.* trilogy, probably the greatest work of American modernist fiction) largely missed out on the modernist bandwagon of the long 1950s. Meanwhile, William Faulkner, whose works could fill the apolitical bill, though partly because their canonization as works of universal genius stripped them of the specificity of their Southern context, suddenly became perhaps the greatest modern American novelist. Lawrence Schwartz has chronicled the fact that the rise in Faulkner's critical reputation during the long 1950s needs to be understood within the context of a Cold War cultural campaign to delegitimate the left-leaning social and proletarian realism that thrived in the pre-Cold War United States. Within this context, Schwartz notes, Faulkner was lionized as a formerly misunderstood genius who, when read properly, emerged as "an emblem of the freedom of the individual under capitalism" (4).

Faulkner effectively met the need for a new, distinctly "apolitical" and purportedly authentic "American" novelist amid efforts to retool the American canon to fit the needs of the Cold War attempt to present American culture as more authentic, sophisticated, and legitimately "artistic" than Soviet socialist realism, though it is certainly the case that most of his critical proponents did not see their celebration of Faulkner's work as a direct contribution to Cold War propaganda. Indeed, many of the proponents of modernism—and detractors of realism—no doubt believed their own arguments that they were simply making objective aesthetic judgments and that such judgments really could be separated from ideology. One might note here Lukács's argument, made in 1953, that the intellectual climate of the postwar West was dominated by a rejection of the rationalist tradition of the Enlightenment so profound and thoroughgoing that alternatives to this rejection were extremely difficult to entertain. For him, "the protection of abstract, i.e., consciously anti-human and anti-realistic art by leading circles in America is … no accident, and only snobbery *as well* on the surface. It is no more of an accident than the persecution and suppression of realism" (*Destruction* 817).

However nonaccidental these phenomena, they were also not necessarily conscious on the part of those involved. In many cases, however, the canonization of modernism during the Cold War was more overtly and consciously political. For example, Serge Guilbaut, in *How New York Stole the Idea of Modern Art*, convincingly argues that the rise of abstract expressionism in the United States after World War II was less the result of a spontaneous shift of aesthetic sensibility on the part of artists and critics than the product of a self-consciously political drive to decanonize the old Popular Front realism of the 1930s and replace it with a depoliticized art compatible with the U.S. imperial elite's new image of itself as the guardian of aesthetic culture. And Frances Stonor Saunders has demonstrated that the canonization of abstract expressionism was at least partly the result of carefully calculated (and well-funded) efforts on the part of the American Central Intelligence Agency (CIA) to promote such modernist movements as evidence of American cultural superiority to the Soviets.

Of course, this canonization of modernism as anti-Soviet art was in some ways conditioned by the earlier official rejection of modernism by the Soviets themselves. Relevant as background here is the now notorious speech delivered by Karl Radek at the important 1934 Congress of Soviet Writers, in which he criticized Joyce for concentrating in his writing on linguistic (and scatological) trivialities while ignoring the issues that are truly important for worldwide revolution. To Radek, Joyce's view is so narrow that "for him the whole world lies between a cupboardful of medieval books, a brothel and a pothouse" (154). Radek grants Joyce's prominence by calling him (along with Proust) a "hero of contemporary bourgeois literature" (152), but he makes his own attitude quite clear when he goes on to suggest that Joyce's work, especially *Ulysses*, resembles a "heap of dung, crawling with worms, photographed by a cinema apparatus through a microscope" (153). Such statements (largely taken out of context) have helped to make Radek's analysis a sort of minor classic of Joyce criticism, serving in particular as a paradigm of the supposedly narrow-minded, short-sighted, and dogmatic rejections of Joyce's work among Marxist (especially Soviet) critics of the 1920s and 1930s.[10] Yet Radek himself went on to acknowledge that Joyce's focus on such details is simply an aspect of naturalism, noting that "a heap of dung is in the same way a part of reality as the sun, a drop of dew in which the sun is reflected. A heap of dung can be a component part of the great picture" (179).

If this conflation of modernism and naturalism seems surprising, one need only point to the *U.S.A.* trilogy, which is able to integrate the two modes so seamlessly and seemingly without effort. Meanwhile, the close link between naturalism and modernism is also emphasized by Georg Lukács, probably the best known of the numerous Marxist critics who have seen modernism as a mere product of bourgeois decadence. In essays such as "The Ideology of Modernism" (included in *The Meaning of Contemporary Realism*), Lukács extends his earlier critique of naturalism to modernism, which he sees as the immediate successor to naturalism and even as essentially a subspecies of naturalism that is even more decadent and less able to represent reality accurately than naturalism proper had been. Lukács bitterly criticizes modernist formalism and subjectivism as retreats from any genuine engagement from historical reality that deprive literature of any potential to oppose the bourgeois status quo. He believes that the formal fragmentation of modernist texts participates in the process of reification that is itself central to the fragmentation of social life under capitalism. Moreover, he sees in the dazzling verbal constructions of modernist writers a tendency toward the kind of reification and fragmentation that he finds rampant in modern capitalist society.

For Lukács, modernist writers like Joyce and Kafka pay a huge price when they make technique an end in itself, without regard to the human realities that this technique is supposed to convey. For Lukács this "negation of outward reality" is a central project of modernist writing, which represents a turning away from the world and a retreat into an aesthetic realm divorced from social reality. This disengagement is in direct complicity with the main cultural thrust of bourgeois society, which seeks to isolate art in a separate realm and thus deprive it of any potentially subversive political force. Modernist texts are thus for Lukács not progressive documents, interacting with history in a positive and productive way. Instead, they are sterile artifacts, divorced from history and totally caught up in the inexorable drive of capitalist society to convert all it touches into mere commodities. Ultimately, for Lukács, "modernism leads not only to the destruction of traditional literary forms; it leads to the destruction of literature as such" (*Meaning* 45).

For Lukács, modernist decadence is the culmination of a long historical process in which the peak achievements of nineteenth-century bourgeois realism, strongly "interlarded with utopian elements," gradually lose their utopian energies (*Meaning* 61). By the time of modernism, these utopian elements have been lost almost entirely, leaving a literature that may express antibourgeois sentiments but that is too cynical to believe that a better alternative might be possible. Thus, for Lukács, the modernist worldview "connives at that modern nihilism from which both Fascism and Cold War ideology draw their strength" (*Meaning* 63). Lukács was, in fact, one of the first Marxist critics to remark a complicity between modernism and Western strategies during the Cold War.

Granted, modernism had its proponents on the Left, even during the peak years of the Cold War. In fact, it was not just paid CIA operatives but also many Western Marxists who declared modernism the epitome of aesthetic achievement in literature during this period. Perhaps the central figure here is Theodor Adorno, who saw in modernism not a simple retreat from historical reality but a refusal to accept the historical reality of growing capitalist dominance. Indeed, for Adorno, modernist aestheticism, by refusing to enter into contaminating negotiations with capitalist reality, inherently suggested the possibility of an alternative order. Thus, as Albrecht Wellmer notes, for Adorno the work of art, through the arrangement of its formal elements, "*reveals* the irrational and false character of existing reality and, at the same time, by way of its aesthetic synthesis, it *prefigures* an order of reconciliation" (48).

In an American context, nominally leftist support for modernism came from the New York Intellectuals, but the canonization of modernism was furthered first and foremost by the institutionalization of the New Criticism as the official critical style of the American academy. This institutionalization itself greatly furthered the Cold War project of discrediting Soviet socialist realism and, with it, the American proletarian culture of the interwar years, even if the original New Critics themselves were only marginally less hospitable to communism than they were to modern industrial capitalism. In any case, given the anti-utopian tenor of the long 1950s, it should come as no surprise that a great deal of energy was devoted by critics of a variety of political persuasions to the enshrinement of modernist texts themselves, while focusing in particular on the anti-utopian aspects of those texts. Thus, Hemingway became best known not for the images of Spanish Republican solidarity in *For Whom the Bell Tolls* but for the gloom and despair of his early novels, as exemplified by Frederic Henry's sense of emptiness and hopelessness as he staggers out into the rain at the end of *A Farewell to Arms* (1929), his dream of a perfect life with Catherine Barkley having been destroyed. In addition, while one could locate utopian energies in the stylistic experiments of a modernist such as James Joyce (whom Hemingway so greatly admired), Hemingway's style, with its famous journalistic economies, clearly lacks the Menippean exuberance found in the style of Joyce. Fitzgerald's style is not especially exuberant either, its achievement lying more in careful control than in expansive energy. And Fitzgerald's finest work, *The Great Gatsby* (1925), is first and foremost a chronicle of the death of the American dream. For one thing, Fitzgerald's novel, often seen as a crucial social document of American life in the 1920s, depicts that decade as the culmination of the previous three decades of explosive growth in American consumer capitalism. It is a negative culmination indeed. As Malcolm Bradbury puts it, *Gatsby* is "the story of a gross, materialistic, careless society of coarse wealth spread on top of a sterile world; on it is cast an extraordinary illusion, that of the ex-Jay Gatz, the self-created Gatsby. A man whose poor past and corrupt economic supports are hidden in his own glow, Gatsby likewise decorates his entire world through his love for Daisy Buchanan" (87).

Most important, for my purposes here, *The Great Gatsby* carefully depicts America as a land whose once-limitless utopian promise has collapsed beneath the weight of the rampant commodification of everything via the growth of modern consumer capitalism. On the one hand, Gatsby's ultimate failure to overcome his class-based distance from Daisy demonstrates the fictionality of the American myth of unlimited upward mobility. On the other, Daisy herself becomes a fiction, commodified in Gatsby's fantasies as simply another object of consumerist desire. Meanwhile, Nick Carraway, in closing his narration, notes that the New World of America had once served as a powerful locus of utopian dreams, dreams that have now been swept away in much the same way as Gatsby's dream of possessing Daisy. Moreover, the death of the American dream announces, for Carraway, the death of utopian dreams altogether. Looking over a Long Island now blighted by capitalist development, he notes that

its vanished trees, the trees that had made way for Gatsby's house, had once pandered in whispers to the last and greatest of all human dreams; for a transitory enchanted moment man must have held his breath in the presence of this continent, compelled into an aesthetic contemplation he neither understood nor desired, face to face for the last time in history with something commensurate to his capacity for wonder. (189)

The elegiac tone and sense of loss in this passage are clear. In this sense, *The Great Gatsby* has a great deal in common with Dos Passos's *U.S.A.* trilogy, which so explicitly thematizes the death of utopian dreams in modern America. Unlike the works of Hemingway and Fitzgerald, Dos Passos's sequence *can* rival the great European modernist novels in its formal and stylistic richness and energy. But the utopian promise of the book's style is seriously muted by its overtly anti-utopian subject matter. The trilogy begins, in *The 42nd Parallel* (1930), with a vision of a Wobbly-led revolutionary fervor that is beginning to sweep across America in the early years of the twentieth century. It suggests, in *1919* (1932), the decline of that fervor (and of the idealism that drove it) in conjunction with the American participation in World War I and the consequent suppression of radical movements. By the third volume, it depicts a defeated Left and a broken American dream, anticipating Dos Passos's own later move to the Right. The very last segment of the trilogy focuses on "Vag," an allegorical all-American figure, driven to vagrancy by poverty and defeat, yet still taunted by consumerist desire, as "wants crawl over his skin like ants" (1240). But these wants will never be met: Vag walks the roads of America with no real place to go, with no real hope that the promises made to him in all the ads touting America as the land of unlimited opportunity will ever be kept.

Faulkner is the other American modernist novelist whose works seem to contain considerable utopian promise at the level of style and form, Faulkner's experiments suggesting new possibilities for narrative that, by extension, conceivably suggest new possibilities for history. Faulkner may also be the single American author whose reputation gained most from canonization of modernism, partly because of his relative obscurity prior to World War II and partly because his works were far less directly critical of modern American capitalism than those of Fitzgerald, Hemingway, and Dos Passos. It also helped greatly that his work had effective New Critical champions such as Cleanth Brooks. After all, most of Faulkner's books are set in the relatively agrarian South, so any potential social criticism contained in them could be safely interpreted as a critique of the failure of that region to get with the capitalist program. Even if one saw Faulkner's books as favoring Southern agarianism over modern American capitalism (as did Brooks), the alternative they suggested was at least an American one, not to mention the fact that it was too impractical and unrealistic to pose a threat to the capitalist order. Indeed, even Brooks could not take this alternative seriously; he thus de-Southernized Faulkner by attempting to portray him as a universal and transcendent genius.

Of course, Faulkner, in the Cold War years, profited considerably from the fact that leftist critics in the 1930s consistently expressed contempt for his work, characterizing him as politically irresponsible (at best) or downright fascistic (at worst).[11] Given this rejection of Faulkner by critics on the Left, it is perhaps not surprising that he is one of the modernist writers whose work best illustrates Lukács's vision of modernist pathological subjectivism. Indeed, leftist critics from the 1930s, such as Philip Rahv, sounded very much like Lukács in their assessment of Faulkner as more concerned with psychopathology than with the workings of history. A key figure here is Quentin Compson, whose obsession with the past—and with the sexuality of his sister, Caddy—helps drive him to suicide in *The Sound and the Fury* (1929). Quentin's retarded brother, Benjy, represents another of the version of the "abnormal" psychology with which the modernists, according to Lukács, are consistently fascinated. And Jason, the other brother, is the quintessential small-town capitalist, driven by greed and reducing all personal relationships to economic transactions. Meanwhile, the fragmented, nonlinear form of the book gives it a spatial form that lacks the forward temporal drive of the narratives of the great realists, such as Balzac, and thus strips it of any ability to suggest the forward movement of history. Yet even *The Sound and the Fury* has its utopian elements, most specifically in the figure of the long-suffering Dilsey, whose Christian faith helps her to endure (and accept her servitude), in spite of it all.

The subject matter of Faulkner's subsequent novels, *As I Lay Dying* (1930) and *Sanctuary* (1931), is, if anything, even more pathological. Darl Bundren, in the former, is a sort of lower-class version of Quentin, though in a sense he acts to escape from the past by burning down the barn containing the decaying body of his mother. That act, however, lands him in an insane asylum—while still failing to destroy the body. Yet the Bundrens, like Dilsey, somehow survive, and the book ends in standard comic-romance fashion, with Anse, the mean-spirited patriarch, taking a new wife. *Sanctuary* is famed as the most debased and degenerate of all of Faulkner's novels, with Popeye, the subnormal murderer and corn-cob rapist, serving as one of the most pathological of all of Faulkner's characters. But even this text features at least one vaguely positive character, the well-meaning lawyer, Horace Benbow. *Light in August* (1932) is even more reminiscent of *The Sound and the Fury;* it features the pathologically alienated Joe Christmas, staggering toward tragedy in a blighted modern wasteland, but still features a utopian (if stereotypical female) figure in Lena Grove, whom, according to Brooks, Faulkner uses "to affirm a kind of integrity and wholeness by which the alienated characters are to be judged" (68–69).

None of these vague utopian images in Faulkner's work posed any real threat to the status quo, because they failed to posit anything like a viable alternative social order. Thus, the utopian energies in Faulkner's work, like that in many modernist works, tend toward Eagleton's "bad" utopianism, encouraging quietist fantasy, rather than active participation in history. Faulkner's characters grasp not for the future but for the past, and thus have little chance to contribute to positive social change—or to expectations of positive social change on the part of Faulkner's readers. Faulkner is thus the perfect Cold War writer, complex and sophisticated enough to make social realist novels look simplistic by comparison, cynical enough not to appear naïve to a skeptical decade, and (once universalized and stripped of his regionalism) safely lacking in any real political vision in a decade suspicious of all "ideologies." Thus, by 1950, the once underappreciated novelist and largely unsuccessful screenwriter had risen to the towering heights of the Nobel Prize, securing a niche in the pantheon of great American writers.

Faulkner went on to produce a solid body of work in the coming decade or so, though novels such as *Requiem for a Nun* (1950), *A Fable* (1954), *The Town* (1957), *The Mansion* (1959), and *The Reivers* (1962) would never gain the critical respect of his earlier work. Still (perhaps in an indication of Faulkner's generally ascendant critical reputation), *A Fable* and *The Reivers* netted Pulitzer Prizes, while both *The Town* and *The Mansion* (which complete a trilogy begun with *The Hamlet* in 1940) have garnered substantial critical attention. However, the trilogy, which focuses on the nefarious and opportunistic Flem Snopes, is decidedly dystopian in its orientation, suggesting, among other things, the disastrous consequences that ensue when members of the Southern lower classes rise above their station to gain social, political, and economic power for which they have not been prepared by their white-trash origins.[12] Indeed, Robert H. Brinkmeyer, Jr., notes this orientation, suggesting that *The Hamlet* "is perhaps best understood as Faulkner's *It Can't Happen Here*" (89). And, should the ultimate conclusion of the trilogy (in which the radical Linda Snopes Kohl triumphs over the murdered Flem) be taken as utopian, Faulkner has Linda announce her victory with the purchase of a shiny new Jaguar, indicating her inability to escape the lures of modern consumer capitalism, despite her longtime espousal of nonconformist views.[13]

Ultimately, in Faulkner's work as a whole, the principal setting of utopia is the past, even if continued efforts to cling to a lost past are frequently criticized in his work. Ironically (given the fact that the 1950s as a decade would ultimately become the locus of so many nostalgic visions), this motif of a lost golden past is, in fact, quite common in the literature of the long 1950s. However, if Faulkner's work is in this sense typical of the 1950s, it is also the case that, despite his critical apotheosis during this period, none of Faulkner's works are typically thought of as landmark novels of the decade. J. D. Salinger's *The Catcher in the Rye* (1951) is a signature novel of the 1950s that similarly locates its utopian energies in a lost past. However, whereas Faulkner's vision of a lost past is a historical one, Salinger exercises a more personal view, locating utopia in the idealized world of childhood. *The Catcher in the Rye* is a coming-of-age story that clearly depicts the attainment of maturity as a loss of innocence. The book takes place during one crucial weekend in the life of Holden Caulfield, its 16-year-old narrator and protagonist. Holden comes from a wealthy white Christian family and is thus very centrally placed in American society. But that centrality itself is a problem, threatening to drag him into the heart of a commodified conformist society he regards as utterly "phony."[14]

Holden's alienation from this society is clear, despite his social position. He is, after all, a teenager, and he experiences all the normal adolescent feelings. No one understands him; in fact, he doesn't even understand himself as he battles against the adolescent changes that move him closer and closer to the phoniness of adult bourgeois conformity. Thus, Holden spends most of the weekend on the run in Manhattan, avoiding his status-conscious parents, who must eventually be told that he has been expelled from still another school, where he has once again been unable to adjust to the routine. Meanwhile, he concocts a variety of unrealistic schemes for escaping his looming bourgeois fate altogether, imagining various scenarios through which he might run away to pursue a nonstandard life that escapes routinization, including going away to live in the woods in a vague imitation of Thoreau. In the end, of course, Holden returns home and takes his medicine, which includes the obligatory 1950s course of psychoanalysis, a procedure apparently designed to help snap him back into conformity. Psychoanalysis, in fact, functions quite frequently in the culture of the 1950s as an emblem of conformism, apparently based on the fear that universal psychotherapy would be a powerful force for routinization, enforcing conformism by smoothing out the psychic rough edges that are the stuff of individual variation. Holden, however, dismisses the therapy as useless because the psychiatrist keeps asking him whether he is going to "apply" himself in the next school term, even though Holden is so alienated from himself he has no idea *what* he is going to do. The talking cure has no appeal for Holden, only helping to convince the alienated youngster that one shouldn't "ever tell anybody anything" (216).

*The Catcher in the Rye* focuses on Holden's position throughout and features no prominent characters who are outside the mainstream of American society. Of course, to the alienated Holden, almost everyone is Other, except perhaps his younger sister, Phoebe. One reason he can relate to Phoebe, though, is that she is prepubescent and has thus not yet entered the corrupting world of sex, in which girls function for Holden as extremely alien creatures. "Sex," he tells us, "is something I just don't understand," and the same certainly goes for all members of the opposite sex (64). Girls, he concludes soon afterward, "can drive you crazy" (74). Meanwhile, in the course of coming to grips with his emerging sexuality,

Holden repeatedly attempts to assure us (and himself) that he isn't really crazy and that his sexual urges are entirely normal, though he is forced to admit that, in terms of his thoughts, if not his actions, "I'm probably the biggest sex maniac you ever saw" (63). Indeed, despite Holden's expressed desire to escape the bourgeois mainstream, he desperately wants to be sexually normal; he thus generally includes in his visions of alternative lifestyles a thoroughly conventional bourgeois sexuality. After all, he does not want to be suspected of being one of those "flits," whom his acquaintance Carl Luce can so expertly identify.

In short, rebel though he may like to think he is, Holden Caulfield desires nothing more than to be normal, and one feels at the end of the novel that he is very likely to succeed, especially given his social and economic position. The eponymous protagonist of *Invisible Man* has far fewer advantages but is surprisingly similar to Caulfield in his desire to fit in. Indeed, Ellison's protagonist is not nearly as far outside the mainstream as a superficial look at his story might suggest. Granted, the African American perspective of the book means that the past is not seen as a preferable alternative to the present. But the book does little to point toward a better future, either. Indeed, *Invisible Man* introduces, then undercuts both black nationalism and communism as possible solutions to the dilemma of the black man in America, thus undermining the two principal utopian alternatives to the dystopian present detailed in the book.[15]

In the weakness of its utopian imagination, *Invisible Man* is a typical 1950s novel. It is typical of 1950s American culture in other ways as well. For example, Ellison's book supplanted Richard Wright's *Native Son* as the most canonical African American novel partly because of its fashionable modernist aesthetic and partly because it replaced Wright's former pro-communist viewpoint with a highly convenient rejection of communism, the ultimate mainstream position to take in the 1950s. Meanwhile, Ellison presents his protagonist, however central race might be to his predicament, as a quintessential alienated individual, somewhat in the mode of Dostoevsky's Underground Man but with a better excuse for his bitter feelings of alienation. Indeed, Ellison's book may have succeeded largely because it was a virtual catalog of fashionable 1950s motifs. Further, as Lloyd Brown noted in a contemporary interview in *Masses and Mainstream*, the book's critique of American racism has no political punch because Ellison's protagonist reserves his bitterest feelings of alienation for the African American masses, making him a representative not of his race but of the one-man-against-the-world theme that was so popular in the decade.

Ultimately, in fact, Ellison's book assures white American readers that its nameless narrator/protagonist is just like us, even as it demonstrates that Ellison can write just like a white modernist. Of course, we are all, according to the dictates of individualist ideology, supposed to be unique. Therefore, in order to be just like us, Ellison's eponymous protagonist must be like no one else, a position he assumes when he tells us near the beginning of his narrative that all of the experiences he is about to relate contributed to one central realization: "That I am nobody but myself" (13). Nevertheless, at the end of the narrative, he asks his readers whether his existential predicament of radical alienation is really so different from their own. "Who knows," he wonders in the book's final sentence, "but that, on the lower frequencies, I speak for you?"

There is, of course, a hint of warning about this question, and Ellison is enough aware of the problematic American attitude toward the Other that he knows it will not necessarily be comforting to white Americans to learn that African Americans are just the same as they are. If, in some obvious ways, this identity between the races makes African Americans seem less sinister and threatening, it is also the case that, if the races are really the same, then African Americans must be granted the same rights and privileges as everyone else, increasing competition for jobs and other resources. Moreover, if African Americans are just like white Americans, then American history looks baleful indeed, slavery and other forms of racist oppression having had no legitimate basis whatsoever.

Meanwhile, Ellison's invisible narrator ends his narrative with a thoroughly conventional complaint about the dangers of the thoroughly conventional, warning against the tide of conformity in America by extolling the richness that is provided by diversity. "America is woven of many strands," he announces with no hint of irony. "I would recognize them and let it so remain. ... Our fate is to become one, and yet many" (435). This "one and yet many" is not only one of the central clichés of bourgeois ideology but a central expression of the existential predicament of the American psyche in the 1950s: conformism and routinization demand that we all be alike; alienation and individualism demand that we all be different.

If Ellison views the alienation and routinization that informed American life in the long 1950s from a special perspective because of his status as an outsider, then the same can certainly be said for Nabokov, though it might also be said that, despite his status as an outsider (or perhaps because of it), Nabokov might have been the most typical American novelist of the decade. For one thing, Nabokov would ultimately emerge as the most respected modernist stylist of the decade. For another, his works are resolutely anti-utopian, rejecting with equal venom all of the major political solutions of the century, from fascism, to American consumerism, to Soviet communism. The first novel Nabokov wrote in America (published in 1947, near the beginning of the long 1950s) was *Bend Sinister*, which joins the earlier *Invitation to a Beheading* (1938, English translation 1959) as a central example of the use of complex modernist literary technique to produce an overtly dystopian political novel. Both novels focus on language and technique (as do all of Nabokov's novels), but both depict fictionalized carceral societies in which individual freedom has been brutally suppressed by a new totalitarian regime. In both cases, the central conflict is between the social demands of an oppressive state and the unique desires of specific individuals, thus placing the novels very much in the dystopian tradition.

Of course, Nabokov consistently claimed for himself a fashionable New Critical formalism; he denied that his work had any social or political relevance whatsoever and claimed to despise literary works that sought such relevance. Thus, in his introduction to *Bend Sinister*, he notes his lack of interest in the "literature of social comment" (vi). He goes on to acknowledge that *Bend Sinister* has much in common with the earlier *Invitation to a Beheading* and to note that *Invitation* has been compared to the work of both Kafka and Orwell. However, he disclaims any similarity between his books and "Kafka's creations or Orwell's clichés" and goes on to argue that *Bend Sinister*, despite appearances, is not a commentary on Stalinism or fascism:

The influence of my epoch on my present book is as negligible as the influence of my books, or at least of this book, on my epoch. There can be distinguished, no doubt, certain reflections in the glass directly caused by the idiotic and despicable regimes that we all know and that have brushed against me in the course of my life: worlds of tyranny and torture, of Fascists and Bolshevists, of Philistine thinkers and jack-booted baboons. No doubt, too, without those infamous models before me I could not have larded this fantasy with bits of Lenin's speeches, and a chunk of the Soviet constitution, and gobs of Nazist pseudo-efficiency. (vii)

Nabokov goes on to explain that his book is not about political ideology or about "life and death in a grotesque police state." It is, instead, concerned with the genuine humanity of its protagonist, Professor Adam Krug, and with the depiction of its characters, even the dictator Paduk, as true individuals rather than "types": "The main theme of *Bend Sinister*, then, is the beating of Krug's loving heart, the torture an intense tenderness is subjected to" (viii).

Nabokov would appear to be the quintessential bourgeois artist, not only accepting the estrangement between art and reality promoted by bourgeois society but, in fact, reveling in it. In High Modernist fashion, he seems to want to present art itself as a utopian alternative to the debased world of reality and politics. He proudly proclaims his art to be about not public concerns but the private feelings of an unusual individual, precisely the kind of focus that led Marxist critics such as Lukács to reject modernist art as decadent and hopelessly bourgeois. Indeed, Nabokov's work is, in many ways, a veritable catalog of the negative modernist characteristics outlined by Lukács: consistently concerned with the marginal attitudes of pathological individuals, Nabokov quite overtly retreats from history into a world of style. On the other hand, one might argue that Nabokov protests a bit too much in proclaiming the irrelevance of his fictions; it is noteworthy that he himself should call attention to the many obvious parallels between the "Ekwilists" of his book and the German Nazis or the communists of Soviet Russia. And, when Nabokov goes on in this introduction to mention that the language spoken by the inhabitants of his fictional country is a combination of "Slavic and Germanic," the suggestion that both Hitler and Stalin are implicated in his book seems rather clear. Moreover, Nabokov elsewhere openly acknowledges the political orientation of his dystopian novels, describing the protagonist of *Invitation to a Beheading* as a "rebel" who has been imprisoned by a "Communazist state" (*Conclusive Evidence* 217) and describing both *Invitation* and *Bend Sinister* as "absolutely final indictments of Russian and German totalitarianism" (*Strong Opinions* 156).

In his foreword (written in 1959) to the English translation of *Invitation to a Beheading*, Nabokov acknowledges the echoes of both communism and fascism in his work but suggests that these echoes are not really the point:

I composed the Russian original exactly a quarter of a century ago in Berlin, some fifteen years after escaping from the Bolshevist regime, and just before the Nazi regime reached its full volume of welcome. The question whether or not my seeing both in terms of one dull beastly farce had any effect on this book, should concern the good reader as little as it does me. (5)

Interestingly, Nabokov here slyly indicates that he *does* see communism and fascism as similar "beastly farces" and that this attitude *does* inform his book, even as he advises readers not to be concerned with this fact. Boyd thus follows Nabokov in emphasizing the parallels between the absurd dystopian world depicted in *Invitation to a Beheading* and real-world events in Nazi Germany and Soviet Russia, noting that "[i]t is no accident that Nabokov began *Invitation to a Beheading* while Goebbels as Minister of People's Enlightenment and Propaganda was striving to make all German culture Nazi 'culture,' or while Stalin's grip on the Union of Soviet Writers and on everything else in the Soviet Union was becoming still tighter" (*Russian Years* 411). Nabokov, in fact, consistently tends to link German Nazism with Soviet communism, thus repeating one of the favorite (and weirdest) clichés of Western Cold War propaganda, while at the same time ignoring the radical ideological opposition between fascism and communism and effacing the historical fact that the fascists were defeated in World War II primarily by the Soviet Red Army.

Nabokov's emphasis on the poignancy of Krug's individual suffering in *Bend Sinister* goes directly to the heart of what provides the main energy of dystopian fiction in general—not allegorized accounts of specific political structures but dramatized depictions of fictional people in fictional pain that gain power because of their parallels to the real pain of real people in various modern societies. It is, in fact, largely this vividness and particularity that give dystopian fiction a potential political force that the theoretical ruminations of cultural critics lack. Of course, Nabokov's denial that his work has any real social and political relevance, combined with the ideological confusion of his conflation of fascism and communism, threatens seriously to mute the political force of his work. In particular, the inability to distinguish between such polar opposites as fascism and communism suggests an inability to imagine utopian alternatives of any kind. Nabokov at times seems to want to suggest the world of art as a utopian alternative to the real world of politics, but the alternative is a feeble one. For one thing, people cannot live in the world of art; for another, this notion seems dangerously similar to the aestheticization of reality identified by Walter Benjamin in "The Work of Art in the Age of Mechanical Reproduction" as a central political strategy of the German Nazis.

In *Invitation to a Beheading*, the protagonist, Cincinnatus C., is an outcast whose only crime is being different in a strictly conformist society: "From his earliest years Cincinnatus, by some strange and happy chance comprehending his danger, carefully managed to conceal a certain peculiarity" (32). But this concealment finally fails, and he is imprisoned by the oppressive regime of the book for the crime of "gnostical turpitude"—as an unusual individual he is unable passively to accept the officially approved version of reality. During most of the book Cincinnatus sits in his cell awaiting execution, though it is clear that the absurd prison in which he is incarcerated serves as a mirror of the carceral society outside. This world is, in short, a classic dystopia, and Cincinnatus's arrest and imprisonment represent a classic dystopian motif, as does the public execution to which he is condemned. In this sense, Nabokov's book clearly echoes Zamyatin's *We* (a book Nabokov had recently read when he was writing *Invitation to a Beheading*), as does the suppression of imagination by the book's dystopian regime. *Invitation* also resembles other absurdist dystopias of the 1930s, such as Ruthven Todd's *Over the Mountain* (1939) and Rex Warner's *The Wild Goose Chase* (1937).

On the other hand, both *Over the Mountain* and *The Wild Goose* are overtly antifascist works that derive their ideological perspectives from the politics of the Popular Front, while the political perspective of *Invitation to a Beheading* is much more ambiguous. As a result, *The Wild Goose Chase*, in particular, is able to suggest socialism as a significant utopian alternative to its fascist dystopia, while *Invitation to a Beheading* has essentially no utopian dimension, except perhaps for the modernist artistry of the text, and even that is called into question by the fact that this very artistry seems suspiciously similar to the aestheticization of politics practiced by the book's dystopian regime. *Invitation to a Beheading* comments on the blatant manipulation of reality in totalitarian societies by employing an array of outrageously artificial, defamiliarizing literary devices to depict a society that is itself outrageously artificial.

The book's totalitarian government presents a bizarre staged reality that has much in common with modern absurdist drama. Stuart appropriately notes the theatrical quality of the entire book, suggesting that it is a "staged drama which happens to appear, misleadingly, in the outward form of what one is used to call a 'novel'" (58). Importantly, though, the theatrical quality of *Invitation to a Beheading* mirrors the world that it depicts — this is a society in which all the world is indeed a stage. It is a world of impersonations, gimmicks, and theatrical props, most of them poorly performed or badly made. Nabokov leaves no doubt that the official literarization of reality in this society leads not to enrichment but to impoverishment. The powers that be in this society serve as playwrights and stage directors, but their desire for conformity and fear of imagination make them bad writers and directors who can produce only the cheapest and most tawdry of dramas.

Against the inferior official artistic production that is the reality of this society, Nabokov sets his own virtuoso performance. Much of the activity of Cincinnatus C. as he awaits execution consists of his attempts to express himself in writing, and his difficulty in finding a way to convert his vague emotional impressions into words becomes a sort of allegory of the tribulations of writers in general. His special circumstance as a condemned prisoner also addresses the particular difficulties faced by writers under totalitarian regimes. Yet, despite his frustration and feeling of almost Beckettian futility, Cincinnatus, through his literary ruminations, sometimes soars to the heights of lyricism in ways that seem intended to indicate the power of literature to suggest alternatives to the status quo. Thus, Alter argues that the ostentatious artifice of *Invitation to a Beheading* does not represent an attempt to escape reality so much as a specific strategy of political engagement. Alter, in fact, sees the book as a clear attack on totalitarianism: "By emphasizing an elaborately self-conscious art both as its medium and its moral model, the novel affirms the tough persistence of humanity in a world that is progressively more brutal and more subtle in its attempts to take us away from ourselves" (59).

This attempt to argue the political power of Nabokov's fiction may be a bit of a stretch, but it does recall the work of Adorno, who so strongly believed in the political power of art that refused the contamination of direct negotiations with the real, famously preferring, for example, the absurdist drama of Samuel Beckett to the more obviously engaged drama of Bertolt Brecht. *Bend Sinister* continues in the modernist vein, though it is substantially more realistic in its depiction of political oppression than *Invitation to a Beheading* had been. Like its predecessor, *Bend Sinister* is filled with instances of sudden arrests, including that of Krug himself, while the horrifying death of Krug's son, David, foreshadows the abominations of Orwell's Ministry of Love. As in *Invitation to a*

*Beheading* the Ekwilist regime of *Bend Sinister* brutally suppresses any individual deviation in favor of strict conformity. This conformism leads to a mob mentality that Nabokov satirizes through his depiction of the communal spirit of a group of criminally insane patients. Presented by their keepers with a potential victim and led by a "representative" or "potential leader," these inmates organize their attack on the victim in a manner that clearly functions as a comment on the behavior of conformist (especially collectivist) populations everywhere: "It was interesting to observe how the 'gang' spirit gradually asserted itself. They had been rough lawless individuals, but now something was binding them, the community spirit (positive) was conquering the individual whims (negative)" (219).

Emboldened by the "positive" strength of their communal bond, these lunatics then murder the victims presented to them, including David Krug. Nabokov thus suggests that the suppression of individuality in favor of community is insane and leads to horrific results. Indeed, the absolute insanity of totalitarian regimes is a central theme of both *Invitation to a Beheading* and *Bend Sinister*. *Invitation to a Beheading* is not only absurdist but rather comic, taking a tone that is perhaps made possible by the fact that it was composed before the worst excesses of both the Stalinist and the fascist regimes that it satirizes. The later *Bend Sinister* is much darker but maintains an absurd and grimly comic tone. For example, the sudden arrests of both Krug and his friend Ember are slapstick scenes of the kind that might seem perfectly at home in a play by Beckett or Ionesco, with the arresting agents engaging in pratfalls and sexual shenanigans that may de-emphasize the horror of the arrests but that add extra emphasis to the absurdity of Paduk's Ekwilist policies.

This emphasis on insanity, especially the use of a carceral insane asylum as a microcosm of the society at large, anticipates a number of commentaries from later in the long 1950s, including such works of social science as Erving Goffman's *Asylums* (1959) and Michel Foucault's *Madness and Civilization* (first published in French in 1961 as *Histoire de Folie*), novels such as Ken Kesey's *One Flew over the Cuckoo's Nest* (1962), and films such as Samuel Fuller's notorious *Shock Corridor* (1963). The motif also resonates strongly with the popular concerns of American society in the long 1950s, which often focused on questions of mental health and insanity. In fact, a close look at Nabokov's dystopian fictions, especially *Bend Sinister*, suggests that Nabokov's political satire is aimed not just at Nazi Germany and the Soviet Union but at the United States as well. For example, the concern with conformism in *Bend Sinister* echoes one of the central fears of Americans in the long 1950s, while the aesthetic strategies of the book can be taken as an indirect commentary on the decline in aesthetic value amid the rampant commodification of everything in American society after World War II.

Much of the dystopian vision of *Bend Sinister* has a specifically postmodern quality. In particular, the text shows a strong skepticism toward the kind of historical metanarratives (such as Marxism) that facilitate the imagination of a better future. For Nabokov, events of the twentieth century suggest that history is governed by no rational metanarrative whatsoever, an attitude he expresses in *Bend Sinister* through the introduction of a character who is a Professor of Modern History. This professor explains that

to try to map our tomorrows with the help of data supplied by our yesterdays means ignoring the basic element of the future which is its complete nonexistence. The giddy rush of the present is mistaken by us for a rational movement. ... the past offers no clues, no *modus vivendi* — for the simple reason that it had none itself when toppling over the brink of the present it eventually filled. (45)

This philosophy, labeled by the book's Professor of Economics as "pure Krugism," serves as an obvious attack on the Marxist vision of dialectical history as well as anticipating the work of postmodern thinkers such as Foucault, for whom history is discontinuous and inexplicable.

History, for Nabokov, is chaos, to which he opposes the order of art, echoing the attitudes of earlier conservative thinkers such as T. S. Eliot, even though Nabokov would later express contempt for Eliot in works such as *Lolita*. *Bend Sinister* firmly situates itself in the world of literature through its frequent allusions to other literary texts. But even these allusions can have political significance. For example, cataloguing some of the book's allusions to classical texts from Rome and Egypt, Larmour argues that these allusions reinforce the book's critique of the Soviet system (170). The most vivid confrontation between art and politics in *Bend Sinister* occurs in Chapter 7, in which Ember, a translator of Shakespeare, complains to Krug about a production of Shakespeare with which he is currently involved. Just as the Communists in the Soviet Union (or the leaders of Zamyatin's One State) sought to harness literature in the interest of official power, so, too, does Paduk's Ekwilist regime seek to appropriate (and distort) *Hamlet* for its totalitarian ends. The production is based on a book by one "Professor Hamm," who reads *Hamlet* as a "tragedy for the masses," as the story of a decadent democratic Denmark that is saved from itself in the nick of time when Fortinbras ascends to the throne at the play's end. Fortinbras, for Hamm, is a sort of ideal Aryan hero and leader, a "blooming young knight, beautiful and sound to the core" (108). Fortinbras's new regime is, of course, a thinly veiled suggestion of Paduk's, and the Ekwilist producers of the play are willing to distort it in outrageous ways in order to reinforce their pro-Paduk message. The ghost becomes the father not of Hamlet but of Fortinbras, the gull Osric becomes a brilliant spy for Fortinbras, and so on.

Ember's story clearly emphasizes the lack of appreciation of Shakespeare among Paduk and his followers. Meanwhile, Krug responds with his own anecdote about a planned American movie version of *Hamlet* that turns out to be equally distorted, with every possible cheap film device employed to make the play appeal to a mass audience. This chapter thus serves to suggest that both totalitarianism and American popular culture run counter to the creative spirit of art as Nabokov perceives it. Meanwhile, Nabokov opposes the aesthetic quality of his own fictions to the debased aestheticism of the dystopian regimes depicted in them. Of course, within the context of the cultural debates of the long 1950s, it is also the case that this opposition tends to become that between "high" art and "low" popular culture. Nabokov himself frequently railed against the philistine vulgarity, or *poshlost,* of the Soviet regime and of popular culture in general. Boyd, meanwhile, suggests that the satire of *Bend Sinister* is directed as much against American mass culture as against Hitler and Stalin. Noting that the book was written after Nabokov became familiar with American popular culture, Boyd argues that "*Bend Sinister* defends the freedom of the individual mind not only against dictatorships abroad but against the coercion of mass culture or mass mobilization at home or anywhere else" (*American Years* 96). The later *Lolita,* in which Charlotte and Dolores Haze are mesmerized by advertising and movie magazines, presents an even stronger condemnation of the mind-numbing effects of the American Culture Industry, though, in fact, Nabokov had begun his attack on the seductions of popular culture even during his Russian novels of the 1930s. In *The Gift,* written during 1935–1937, Nabokov describes the false idealizations of advertising:

Thus a world of handsome demons develops side by side with us, in a cheerfully sinister relationship to our everyday existence; but in the handsome demon there is always some secret flaw, a shameful wart on the behind of this semblance of perfection: the glamorous glutton of the advertisement, gorging himself on gelatin, can never know the quiet joys of the gourmet, and his fashions (lingering on the billboard while we move onward) are always just a little behind those of real life. (25)

Such attacks on the *poshlost* of modern mass culture are also central to *Invitation to a Beheading* and *Bend Sinister,* in which the dystopian regimes are largely characterized by their philistinism. Thus, Stanley Edgar Hyman suggests that the theme of both books might be summarized as "the vulgarity of power" (60). In perhaps the most extensive published discussion of the political relevance of Nabokov's dystopian fiction, Rampton suggests that Nabokov's two-pronged attack on the tyranny of totalitarianism and the vulgarity of American popular culture undermines the effectiveness of his criticism of either (42-43). Further, Rampton suggests that Nabokov's contempt for popular culture reveals a cultural elitism probably related to his aristocratic Russian background. Meanwhile, Alter acknowledges that *Invitation to a Beheading* equates totalitarianism with the vulgarity of *poshlost* but argues that this move represents much more than a simple suggestion that totalitarianism is in bad taste. He usefully notes that Nabokov's point is not that regimes like those of Stalin and Hitler have historically shown bad taste, but that their lack of appreciation of art is part of a general suppression of all things genuinely human in these societies. *Poshlost* is thus "an indispensable principle of such regimes, a necessary expression of their inner nature" (55). Of course, one is tempted to see in Nabokov's comparison of the atrocities of totalitarian governments with the banality of mass culture a conventional elitist bias in which he presents his work as a "high" art alternative to such philistinism. Moreover, if Nabokov in this sense again recalls Adorno, who (along with Bloch) tended to see extensive parallels between the ideologies of American popular culture and German Nazism, it is also the case that Nabokov lacks the hopefulness of Bloch and is, in fact, far more skeptical and cynical than even the famously pessimistic Adorno. Thus, Adorno is able to maintain a vision of socialism as a preferable alternative to Nazism and consumer capitalism, while Nabokov tends to see all three as appallingly dystopian.

Nabokov is also more skeptical than Adorno with regard to the utopian potential of the aesthetic. It is worth remembering that, in *Lolita*, where Nabokov conducts his most powerful and overt assault on American popular culture, he specifically refuses to identify "high" culture as an alternative. The Hazes have had their minds so thoroughly shaped by popular culture that they are seriously hampered in their dealings with the real world. But Humbert Humbert, whose mind had been equally informed by "literature," is, if anything, even more seriously crippled (Booker, *Literature* 70–89). In either case, it is not the kind of culture to which the characters respond that leads to dire consequences: it is the *way* they respond. Characters who accept any fictionalized version of reality uncritically and unquestioningly (like citizens who accept the dictates of politicians without challenge) are rendered incapable of effective action in the real world. By consistently emphasizing the fictionality and literariness of his own creations, Nabokov seeks to avoid contributing to this problem by refusing to have his own work taken as an authoritative statement about reality.

*Lolita*, if only because it is so focused on American culture, is clearly the most "American" of Nabokov's novels from the long 1950s. The vivid depiction of the American countryside, as Humbert and Dolores Haze travel about from one cheap motel to another, reads almost like a travelogue, enhancing the American feel of the book. After all, the content of these descriptions derives from Nabokov's own yearly cross-country auto trips from his residence in New York to Colorado, where he hunted butterflies. At the same time, these cross-country trips also suggest the growing homogenization of America, as Humbert and Dolly continually encounter the same ads, the same brands, and the same attitudes wherever they go. Meanwhile, the book draws much of its material from contemporary American popular culture, depicting both Lolita and her mother, Charlotte, as bovarystes held in thrall by movie magazines and radio ads. Indeed, I have argued elsewhere that Nabokov's depiction of the construction of the Hazes by American popular culture (and of Humbert by European high culture) has much in common with Louis Althusser's elaboration of the concept of interpellation, through which bourgeois ideology constructs individual subjects in its image, thus assuring that those subjects will find bourgeois points of view natural and unavoidable. Similarly, I have noted that Nabokov's critical treatment of American popular culture in the book has much in common with the critique of Horkheimer and Adorno in their famous elaboration of the concept of the mind-numbing (and thus routine-enforcing) "Culture Industry."[16]

Such similarities to neo-Marxist critiques of Americanism, especially coming from a Russian, might seem to set *Lolita* very much outside the mainstream of American culture in the Cold War 1950s. However, Nabokov was redeemed by his expressed contempt for the Soviet Union and his seeming nostalgia for the good old days of czarist Russia. Meanwhile, the social commentary of *Lolita* is couched within a plot so titillating and a text so stylistically brilliant that very few readers really noticed the book's critique of consumer capitalism. When the book was finally released in the U.S. in 1958, it became an immediate bestseller, attracting an extremely diverse audience, ranging from those who sought pure sexual stimulation (having heard all sorts of rumors about the book), to those who simply wanted to demonstrate their cultural sophistication and superiority to such lurid concerns by reading the book for its style and literary allusions, all the while presumably ignoring the plot. In this sense, *Lolita* was in many ways the perfect book for the literary culture of the 1950s, dominated as that culture was by New Critical formalism, with its emphasis on style and technique and its insistence that what books were actually about didn't really matter, because all books ultimately turned out to be about books.

*Lolita* is quite overtly about books. Not only is Humbert's dazzling style highly allusive, but his vision of Lolita herself is extremely literary. *Lolita* was also a quintessential 1950s American novel through its individualist emphasis on a single, highly alienated protagonist. Humbert is, in many ways, a quintessential example of alienation. To begin with, he is a European who never feels quite at home in America. He is also an intellectual, tapping into the decade's suspicion that intellectuals (especially European ones) are ideologically dangerous, tending toward either sexual perversion or communism or both. In the psyche of the 1950s, they amount to pretty much the same thing. Meanwhile, as much as he attempts to present his lust for young girls as a matter of art, rather than sex, Humbert is perfectly well aware that his sexual inclinations mark him as a pervert outside the norm in an American society that places a huge premium on normality, despite its supposed celebration of individualism. He places a particularly 1950s spin on this motif by calling attention to his contempt for the Freudian psychoanalysis that has marked him as a pervert and that was such a fad in 1950s America.

Humbert's (and Nabokov's) mockery of psychoanalysis, like much of the book, is highly comic, as is Humbert's alienation itself, at least on the surface, though it has an abject core. *Lolita* may, in fact, demonstrate more than any other book of the decade the distinctive sort of comic alienation that characterizes the literature of the decade. Characters in the 1950s are at least as alienated as the protagonists of the High Modernist classics of the 1920s. However, in the 1950s, only characters who are marginalized by age and ethnicity seem to be able to take their own alienation seriously, perhaps because it is now so difficult to imagine the utopian alternative of *not* being alienated. A white male in his late 30s, like Humbert, might still suffer from alienation but now attempts to cope with it through irony, absurdism, and comedy, taking it for granted that alienation cannot be overcome. Thus, while Humbert's plight may be poignant and painful (and Lolita's is an absolute nightmare), *Lolita* is narrated in a mode of comic exuberance so compelling that numerous readers were able to sympathize with Humbert and to follow him in viewing little Lo not as a person but merely as an aesthetic artifact. In any case, even the daring Nabokov, with his contempt for American vulgarity, seems to nod to American conformism in the end, largely redeeming Humbert by having him feel genuine remorse, then turning him into an avenging angel who takes vengeance on the even weirder Clare Quilty. On the other hand, all of this is complicated by the fact that we ostensibly get the story from Humbert, who is on trial for Quilty's murder and thus may have his own good reasons for expressing a remorse that he does not really feel. In any case, while the text certainly does not endorse Humbert's sexual exploitation of the helpless Lolita, it is also the case that she is ultimately killed not by the perversions of Quilty or Humbert but by a childbirth resulting from her thoroughly conventional marriage to young Dick Schiller.

Meanwhile, Humbert is unable, by killing Quilty, to restore Lolita's (or his own) lost childhood. In *Lolita*, what is lost can never be recovered; what is broken cannot be mended. This theme of irretrievable loss pervades a novel that is thoroughly anti-utopian from the outset: both Humbert and Dorothy Haze are already dead when the text begins, so that there is no question of hope for either of them. Indeed, by killing off both of the central characters in Dr. John Ray's foreword, Nabokov forecloses any future whatsoever, confining all of the action in an irreducible anteriority. This notion is made explicit in the text in a number of ways, as when Humbert and Lolita drive across America, and the girl (in a quin-tessential American moment) suddenly notices that the odometer is roll-ing over into the next thousand. "When I was a little kid," she tells Hum-bert, "I used to think they'd stop and go back to nines, if only my mother agreed to put the car in reverse" (221). Odometers do not run backward when cars are in reverse, of course, just as time itself never runs back into the past.

The theme of loss in *Lolita* is established early on, as Humbert, the narrator and putative author of the text, outlines the background of his love for nymphets, which arises from his abortive love for the girl Anna-bel Leigh, taken from him in childhood after an abortive courtship in a fairy-tale "princedom by the sea" (11). Humbert then spends the rest of his life in a futile quest to recover the joys of his childhood passion, pri-marily through the pursuit of young girls who remind him of his lost childhood love and can thus restore his own childhood, which seems, he says "to fly away from me in a flurry of pale repetitive scarps like those morning snow storms of tissue paper that a train passenger sees whirling in the wake of the observation car" (17). He can never, of course, gather those scraps and restore them to wholeness, because he cannot reverse, or even arrest, the flow of time, however much he tries. In this attempt, Humbert is the quintessential postmodernist author, at least as described by Jameson, refusing any sense of historical progression and attempting to spatialize time itself, a project he openly acknowledges, noting his tendency to "substitute time terms for spatial ones," as when he envi-sions the age limits of nymphethood (9 to 14) as analogous to the boundaries of "an enchanted island" (18).

When Humbert finally meets Lolita, he immediately identifies her as the reincarnation of his Annabell Leigh, not to mention Petrarch's Laura and Dante's Beatrice, and thus as a potential focus for the restoration of his lost ideal love. In this sense, of course, one is tempted to read the text as an allegory of the European encounter with America, that New World in which European explorers sought a renewal and restoration of soured Old World dreams. Humbert, a Swiss citizen of mixed French and Aus-trian heritage, with "a dash of the Danube" in his veins," is, after all, a sort of all-purpose allegorical European, somewhat in the mold of Con-rad's Kurtz (11). Moreover, Humbert seems at times to want to see America in Edenic terms, describing the American wilds he encounters on his car trips with Lolita as "heart-rendingly beautiful ... with a quality of wide-eyed, unsung, innocent surrender that my lacquered, toy-bright Swiss villages and exhaustively lauded Alps no longer possess" (170). The contrast here between the freshness of the American wilderness (and Lolita) and the decadent exhaustion of a hyper-civilized Europe (and Humbert) is unmistakably reminiscent of the contrast Humbert sees be-tween the purity and vitality of nymphets and the gross physicality of mature women, who serve for him as walking intimations of mortality.

Of course, Humbert's distinction between nymphets and "real" women is that of a lunatic and is clearly undermined in the text. Lolita is just as much a living, physical creature as is her mother, and she is not all that innocent to begin with. Conversely, the bovarystic Humbert is in many ways incredibly naive, deriving many of his fantasies from hopelessly idealized visions in European literature. Meanwhile, the American wilderness is not all that Edenic. Whereas, according to Humbert, Old World mountainsides at least provide comfortable mossy beds for romantic trysts, the wilder wilds of America are not so hospitable to the would-be lover: "Poisonous plants burn his sweetheart's buttocks, nameless insects sting his; sharp items of the forest floor prick his knees, insects hers; and all around there abides a sustained rustle of potential snakes" (170).

But the real serpent in the American garden is the popular culture of consumer capitalism, a culture toward which Humbert feels very much the same revulsion that he experiences in the presence of a naked adult woman. Thus, when it occurs to him that Lolita might be trying to accumulate enough cash to finance an escape from his clutches, he imagines her fleeing to Broadway or Hollywood (or maybe a dismal ex-prairie state), chief iconic settings of the culture he so abhors, where everything is "soiled, torn, dead" (187). Hollywood is, in fact, a consistent focus of Humbert's distaste for American culture, much of which is focused on film. For example, his extended summary of the American genre films ("musicals, underworlders, and westerners") for which the young Lo has such a passion suggests his contempt for the medium (172). On the other hand, it also suggests his complete lack of sophistication as a film critic: the description is accurate as far as it goes but completely superficial. Then again, Humbert generally pays very little attention to the films he attends with Lolita, devoting his attention instead to an attempt to cop secret feels in darkened theaters.

Humbert is consistently appalled by Lolita's cultural tastes, a fact that also becomes clear in his extended catalog of the contents of the teen magazines she leaves in his car after decamping with Quilty (256). This catalog, reminiscent in many ways of Joyce's lampoon of the discourse of women's magazines in the "Nausicaa" chapter of *Ulysses*, mocks the magazines primarily as a marketing tool of consumer capitalism, as a collection of "ads and fads." It is, in fact, advertising for which Humbert reserves his strongest contempt, a fact that reinforces the anti-utopian texture of the book, given that advertising was probably the central locus of utopian images in American culture of the long 1950s, however packaged and commodified those images might have been. Realizing, for example, the barrage of advertising discourse to which the young Lolita has been subjected throughout her lifetime, he attributes the vulgar aspects of his young love to her exposure to the "snub-nosed cuteness of ads and magazine pictures" (46). Later, when he meets the pregnant Lo, metamorphosed into womanhood by pregnancy and the passing of time, he dismisses her ultraordinary new life as like something from a "beer ad" (275).

On the other hand, Humbert is not above using the power of advertising to his own advantage. He soon realizes, for example, that the immersion of the Americans he meets in the discourse of advertising might make them putty in his hands. After all, this discourse is specifically designed to render malleable the desires of its consumers, and Humbert (who works as an ad copywriter when he first arrives in America) presumably understands the discourse well. Thus, when he decides to seduce Charlotte Haze, he models his speech on the discourse of advertising; for example, he invents, when she asks about them, a catalog of former lovers, the diversity of which is derived from "the rules of those American ads where schoolchildren are pictured in a subtle ratio of races" (82). On the other hand, he soon grows weary of her tendency to see everything through the optic of expectations derived from advertising, soon complaining of her tendency to see the two of them as a "pretty ad for the Traveling Agency" (92).

The younger Lolita, having lived her entire life in a fully functioning consumer capitalist society, is even more a product of advertising than is her mother. "She it was," Humbert concludes, "to whom ads were dedicated: the ideal consumer, the subject and object of every foul poster" (150). Again, however, Humbert attempts to use this fact to his advantage, assuming that Lolita's desires are thereby easily manipulated. And this is especially the case after he discovers, affixed to the wall over her bed, an ad from a "slick magazine" that depicts a handsome "conquering hero," whom Lolita has labeled "H. H." His distaste for advertising (and his sardonic description of the ad) notwithstanding, Humbert accepts the association, acknowledging the resemblance (71).

It is here, however, that Humbert reveals himself as even more naïve than Lolita. Her desires may have been formed by advertising, but she is still able to perceive a difference between the world of ads, movies, and magazines and the real world in which she lives. Humbert, his own desires having been constituted by his exposure to European idealist literature, does not seem able to make such a distinction and literally attempts to act out desires that, for Lolita, remain mere fantasies. In addition to being reduced, via Humbert's solipsism, to a literary artifact, Lolita is also the book's central utopian image, Humbert having seemingly convinced himself that, if he can only have her, his tortured life will be restored to wholeness and tranquility. Thus, the crazed nature of Humbert's desire for Lolita can be taken as an oblique suggestion of the craziness of utopian thought in general.

If there is a genuine utopian element in *Lolita*, it would have to be located in the bravura style, much in the way that Jameson has seen modernist style in general as a "Utopian compensation for increasing dehumanization on the level of daily life," even if modernism also represents a reification of style, per Lukács (*Political* 42). Moreover, the style of *Lolita* is a little *too* good, a little too exaggerated, a little too literary, so that the virtuoso style of *Lolita* functions, in the other direction, very much like the junk style of Dreiser. By calling attention to its own reification and commodification, it potentially critiques those phenomena, especially when combined with the thematic critique of consumerism that provides so much of the content of the book.

Unfortunately, Nabokov seems unable to take his own bravura style seriously, undermining any such potential protest. Even the book's numerous passages of great lyrical beauty are problematic, somehow inappropriate to the story being told. And Humbert pokes fun at the excesses of his own style, calling attention to its self-parodic nature, when he notes as his narrative begins that "you can always count on a murderer for a fancy prose style" (11). This self-consciousness indicates an attitude far more pessimistic than that of Dreiser. In Dreiser, a banal style announces the difficulty of transcending banality amid the rampant commodification under way as consumer capitalism begins its rise to dominance in America. Nabokov's spectacular verbal fireworks, on the other hand, demonstrate that, even if one can transcend banality in style, it does no good, leaving one still trapped within the confines of commodification.

Give the self-dismantling nature of the style of *Lolita*, it might be appropriate to regard the book as postmodernist, rather than modernist. But it is certainly the case that the book is post-utopian. It contains certain utopian gestures but then becomes self-conscious about those gestures, quickly undermining them. Like its great modernist predecessors, it contains a style that sets it apart from the routine and that announces a certain alternative to the mundane interchangeability of the commodity, but this alternative collapses in self-parody. Moreover, within the context of the canonization of modernism in the 1950s, the modernist style of *Lolita*, unlike that of, say, *Ulysses*, is no longer startling but merely ordinary. Indeed, perhaps the simplest way one can distinguish between modernist and postmodernist works (which often use pretty much the same stylistic resources) is that the first can still shock, achieving a powerful defamiliarization, while the second cannot, modernist style having now been safely appropriated by the literary establishment. The canonization of modernism was, in short, one of the central contributing factors to the emergence of postmodernist works in the long 1950s.

From this point of view, the self-parody of *Lolita* can be taken as a protest against this appropriation, while the content can be taken as an attempt to recover the shocking power of the pioneering modernist works of previous decades. But the critical and commercial success of the book suggests that the book was still easily absorbed into the consumer capitalist mainstream. By the time of *Pale Fire*, Nabokov's style has become even more obviously postmodernist, and the self-parody has become entirely dominant. The post-utopianism is more evident, and any protest that the book attempts to mount against the status quo is correspondingly weaker.

In particular, the book derives its principal energies from a complex entanglement of different ontological levels, in the gesture that Brian McHale has seen as perhaps the central postmodernist motif. But this postmodernist collapse of ontological boundaries is profoundly anti-utopian. If, in Nabokov's earlier work, there is little to distinguish fascism from communism from consumer capitalism, now there is little to distinguish truth from fiction or even life from death. If even these kinds of fundamental distinctions do not hold, then it is difficult to see how any imaginative alternative, utopian or otherwise, can be sustained as anything other than an illusion, or perhaps delusion.

Like *Lolita*, *Pale Fire* is a technical tour de force. The book resembles *Lolita* in other ways as well, while at the same time serving as a sort of literary bite of the critical hand that had been feeding Nabokov's reputation ever since *Lolita* was published. Indeed, much of *Pale Fire* serves as a sort of parody of literary scholarship and of the ability of literary scholars comfortably to appropriate all that is written to their own doctrine. Perhaps proving the point, critics have typically loved *Pale Fire*, as when Brian Boyd calls it perhaps "the most perfect novel ever written" (*American Years* 425). Of course, it is something of an aficionado's book, far more popular with critics, who enjoy the gamelike attempt to untangle its complexities, than with general readers, who have little patience with the slow pace, however gamelike, and seem to have been little amused by the academic satire.

However, the perfection of *Pale Fire* does not include any attempt to instill utopian hopes in its readers. Again, the book begins by announcing that a central figure, the poet John Shade, has died even before the narration begins, thus eliminating one important avenue of hope. Then the narrator/commentator, Charles Kinbote (like Humbert, a foreigner and sexual "deviant"), proceeds to annotate Shade's last poem, driven by a Humbertesque solipsism that causes the commentary to drift consistently off-course, telling us far more about Kinbote and his background than about the poem.[17] This background has a vaguely utopian (or at least nostalgic) flavor, hinting at Kinbote's former status as King Charles II (aka Charles Beloved) in the golden land of Zembla, where he not only enjoyed the usual trappings of monarchy but also profited from a permissive environment in which his homosexual proclivities were perfectly acceptable.

Unfortunately, King Charles, like his British predecessor and namesake, is unseated by a revolution and forced to flee the country. Much of Kinbote's narrative, in fact, details the king's flight to America and his pursuit by the assassin Gradus, who ends up accidentally shooting Shade instead. Or so Kinbote says. The problem, of course, is that his narrative is highly suspect. Not only does the text make it fairly clear that Shade was shot by an escaped American mental patient, not a hired Zemblan assassin, but it also seems to suggest that Kinbote's entire story is a fabrication (or delusion), Zembla itself having apparently been invented from the whole cloth. In short, the utopianism of *Pale Fire* is doubly problematic, doubly subjunctive, to use Eagleton's term: not only is it nostalgic, pointing backward rather than forward, but it points back to something that never existed in the first place. This sort of double-layered nostalgia is highly postmodern and is central to what Jameson calls the "nostalgia for the present" and identifies as a central element of postmodernist thought. It is a central post-utopian gesture as well, suggesting a double separation from any ability to construct a utopian vision in which one can truly believe. Put differently, *Pale Fire* suggests a nostalgia for nostalgia, a desire to be able to remember something worth being nostalgic for.

*Pale Fire* thus participates in the turn to aesthetics and the concomitant collapse of utopian vision that is central to mainstream American literary fiction in the long 1950s. If the same can be said for all sorts of cultural products of the decade, the trend culminates in the work of E. L. Doctorow, who began his career late in the decade with the 1960 publication of *Welcome to Hard Times*, a novel in which the modernist novel, the leftist novel, and the Western all converge.[18] This may, of course, be another way of saying that Doctorow's novel announces the arrival of full-blown postmodernism: the collapse of distinctions between genres and, especially, between high and low culture, is one of the classic characteristics that various commentators have associated with postmodernism.[19] Given the general weakness of utopian imagery in both the Westerns and the leftist fictions of the long 1950s, it should come as no surprise that neither the genre of *Welcome to Hard Times* nor Doctorow's own leftist sympathies can rescue the book from the loss of utopian energies so typical of American culture of the period. In Doctorow's novel, as in *The Treasure of the Sierra Madre*, gold mining is hard work that does not necessarily pay off. Moreover, Doctorow's miners are employees of a capitalist corporation, removing the last vestige of individualist romance from the quest for gold. The very title of the book is anti-utopian, suggesting not only a failure of utopian dreams but potentially, through the apparent allusion to Dickens, suggesting that the failure of utopia can be attributed to the expansion of capitalism into the once-wild West. It is, in fact, the machinations of the capitalist mining corporation, not the harsh Dakota climate or savage redskins, that ultimately destroy the book's utopian dream, which involves the founding of a new town in the Dakota territory in the late nineteenth century.

The townspeople are led by "Blue," the book's narrator and the town's unofficial mayor. As the book begins, a fledgling town is already in existence, made economically viable (barely) by its proximity to a meager gold mine in the hills north of the town. The inhabitants of the town have come there by various paths, all hoping to build a new and better life. Many, for example, have been drawn by reports that, in this new land, "water flows from the rocks, game will nibble at your back door, and if you're half a man you can make your life without too much trouble" (28). Of course, this "half a man" designation suggests that a certain amount of struggle (and perhaps violence) might be necessary to succeed even in this idyllic environment. Meanwhile, this masculinist notation tells us nothing about the possibilities offered to women. As it turns out, the only significant female characters in the text are prostitutes, while the men find that success in the West is far harder to achieve than they had hoped.

Indeed, Blue's own activities inherently contradict the notion of frontier romance. He records the story of which the novel consists as part of his passion for record keeping, a passion that can only contribute to an increasing routinization that is antithetical to romance. Meanwhile, the primacy of violence in this Western environment is brought home in the very beginning of the book, as an ultraviolent "Bad Man from Bodie" (aka Clay Turner) rides in from the surrounding plains, terrorizes the residents, and sets the town afire, burning most of it to the ground. He then rides away toward the mining operation to the north. Several residents are killed in this attack, and most of the others leave afterward. Blue, however, stays on to try to rebuild the town, dubbing the reborn entity "Hard Times" to acknowledge his recognition of the difficulty of the task that faces him.

The structural opposition between Blue and the rather allegorical Bad Man challenges numerous conventions of the Western genre and suggests crucial contradictions in the logic of that genre. Blue, as the representative of civilization and routinization, is the protagonist and "hero," though he is an ineffectual hero who is entirely unable to stand up to the Bad Man during the initial attack on the town. The Bad Man, meanwhile, is both the embodiment of evil violence and the epitome of the mysterious Western individualist, a sort of pre–Clint Eastwood Man with No Name. Thus, according to the normal conventions of the Western, the Bad Man, who resists routinization, should logically be the hero, while Blue, whose efforts would strip life of romance and adventure, should be the villain. This reversal serves as a reminder of the damned-if-you-do and damned-if-you-don't contradiction that destabilizes Western romance as a whole: the West promises the possibility of a better life because it offers a chance for adventure and romance that is no longer available in the civilized East; in order to achieve that better life, new settlers in the West must impose civilization and thereby destroy the very chance for romance that brought them West in the first place.

Given this contradiction, it is not surprising that Blue's attempts to found a town ultimately fail, despite early signs of potential success. The first inhabitants of his rebuilt town barely survive their first harsh Dakota winter, but, once spring comes, the town begins to grow rapidly. It becomes far larger than it had been before its initial destruction, built largely by cannibalizing lumber from a nearby ghost town and propelled partly by rumors that the Eastern mining corporation that runs the mine north of the town is planning to build a new road through the town of Hard Times to facilitate the transport of gold ore from the mines to a new mill on the other side of the town.

But this success has a downside. Overcrowding soon leads to increasing tensions among the new inhabitants, who find themselves competing for increasingly scarce resources. Blue struggles to initiate various projects that might generate jobs and income for the growing population of the town, but these projects (dubious to begin with) collapse when word comes that, far from building a new road through the town, the mining company is closing down the nearby mine altogether. The newly unemployed miners, accompanied by the Bad Man himself, stream into the town, which erupts in an apocalyptic riot. In the end, only Blue and a madwoman are left alive in the town. He considers setting fire to the ruins of the town to drive off the buzzards that are gathering to feed on the corpses that litter the streets but opts not to. In a final surge of hope, he decides that the wood might be valuable to some future settlers, who might come this way someday, hoping to build still another new town. There is, however, nothing in the text to suggest that this future town will fare any better than its predecessors.

Having deconstructed the myth of the Old West in his first novel, Doctorow would then proceed, in his subsequent novels, to deconstruct twentieth-century American history as well. In particular, Doctorow's novels as a whole tend to document, in fictionalized form, the modern historical phenomenon of the demise of the Left as a force in American society and politics. As Jameson puts it, Doctorow is "the epic poet of the disappearance of the American radical past" (*Postmodernism* 24). Indeed, both Nabokov's seeming nostalgia for a better past and Doctorow's exploration of a failed past place the authors in a position similar to that of American leftists in the long 1950s, many of whom were nostalgic for the earlier days of the 1930s (when the Left was a far more viable force in American society) but many of whom also saw 1930s proletarianism as a failed and misguided project. From this point of view, perhaps it is not surprising that even the leftist novel of the 1950s was relatively weak in utopian energy, which was somewhat ironic given that much of the overtly anti-utopian tone of the American literature of the decade came from the fact that utopian alternatives to the problems posed by modern capitalism essentially came to be equated with "ideology," one of the decade's code words for communism. Within the Cold War paradigm, this ideology was regarded as a synonym for simplistic didacticism and thus the opposite of real literature, which was, by this model, supposed to indicate the aching complexity of the modern world, a complexity that seemed to ensure that no clear solutions could ever be found to life's problems. In this context, even leftist novels showed a strong skepticism toward the class-based premises of the proletarian literature of the 1930s. In the next chapter, I turn to a consideration of American leftist novels of the long 1950s and to the loss of utopian energy in those novels relative to their leftist predecessors.

# Un-American Activities: American Realism and the Utopian Imagination of Leftist Fiction in the Long 1950s

In 1954, Herbert Biberman, Paul Jarrico, and Michael Wilson joined forces with the International Union of Mine, Mill, and Smelter Workers to make the film *Salt of the Earth*, still widely regarded as the greatest work of radical cinema to have been produced in America. The film was a genuine departure from the Hollywood norm, not only in its clearly leftist political stance but also in its attempt to give voice to the working-class Mexican Americans of New Mexico, a group that had previously received little attention in American culture, even in the culture of the American Left. *Salt of the Earth* also directly thumbed its nose at the anticommunist purges sweeping Hollywood at the time, a phenomenon that had already landed Biberman, Jarrico, and Wilson on the blacklist. Biberman, one of the Hollywood Ten, had even served time in the federal pen in Texarkana, Texas, as a political prisoner. Not surprisingly, retribution for this act of resistance was swift. One of the film's stars, Mexican actress Rosaura Revueltas, was deported to Mexico even before filming was completed. Meanwhile, the resources of corporate Hollywood, reinforced by the U.S. government, responded with a vigorous suppression of the finished film, organizing an official boycott that denied the film access to theater screens all over America.[1]

This effort at censorship and suppression was almost entirely successful. *Salt of the Earth* went virtually unseen and was soon almost forgotten. Luckily, the film was rediscovered in the 1960s, becoming a sort of cult classic on college campuses all over America. Granted, it is not at all clear that the largely middle-class white audiences who saw the film in this way were entirely capable of understanding the real conditions of the struggle that the film depicts and of which it became a part. Nevertheless, the film was saved from oblivion and remains, if nothing else, available on video (it was released on DVD in 1999) and therefore accessible to future audiences.

*Salt of the Earth* narrates a successful strike of Mexican American zinc miners, with strong support from their wives and families. It is a testament to the power of collective action to oppose economic, political, and racial oppression and, in that sense, contains some of the most powerful utopian energies to be found anywhere in American culture in the long 1950s, even if it stops short of imagining a systemic alternative to capitalism. The suppression of the film thus indicates, among other things, the suspicion and fear with which utopian ideas were regarded in the decade, thereby indicating some of the obstacles faced by leftist writers of the period and providing at least a partial explanation for the noticeable decline in utopian energy in the fiction they produced. Of course, American leftist writers of the long 1950s were doubly out of fashion. In addition to the obvious problems associated with their politics in the era of the McCarthyite purges, such writers also wrote primarily in a realist vein in an era when critical fashions shifted dramatically in favor of modernism. These two phenomena were not unrelated. The critical turn away from realism in the long 1950s can surely be interpreted, at least in part, as a repudiation, within the difficult climate of the Cold War, of both Soviet socialist realism and the American proletarian fiction of the 1930s. Even leftist writers, in a sense, repudiated their proletarian past, intentionally attempting to move in directions that distanced them from their now-unfashionable predecessors in the 1930s. This attempt, which made it impossible for leftist writers of the long 1950s to imagine radical systemic alternatives to capitalism, had profound consequences. Though leftist writers of the period certainly maintained a utopian vision that was superior to that of their bourgeois contemporaries, even the leftist utopian vision of the long 1950s was decidedly weak and uncertain. In fact, one of the crucial markers of the loss of utopian imagination during this period is the decline of utopian energies in American realist fiction, even in fiction produced by writers working from an openly leftist perspective, especially as evidenced in a loss of focus on class as the central category of social inequality.

A virtual horror of the very idea of class is one of the central characteristics of American thought from the 1940s onward. Thus, Constance Coiner, in her introduction to the 1997 republication of Alexander Saxton's 1948 novel *The Great Midland* (an introduction tragically cut short by Coiner's untimely death aboard TWA Flight 800 in July 1996), praises the book as being unusual for its sophisticated handling of the issue of class in modern American society. For Coiner, Saxton, who published a total of three novels from 1943 to 1959, thus differs from most of his contemporaries among American writers. He also offers an important object lesson to American literary scholars, who, Coiner suggests, continue, even in the supposedly politicized teaching and criticism of the 1990s, to treat class as "the last taboo, the Great Unmentionable" (xi). Coiner is right, of course. The specter of institutionalized New Criticism (without the anticapitalist passion of the original New Critics themselves but with a subtext of Cold War anticommunist hysteria) continues to haunt English departments all over America, typically in the guise (sometimes naïvely sincere, sometimes simply disingenuous) of rescuing the beauties of art from the ugly clutches of (leftist) politics. While American literary critics have, in recent years, begun to surmount the ostensibly complete rejection of politics (which really amounted to a rejection of *leftist* politics) that marked the criticism of the decades immediately after World War II, they have continued to avoid class as an analytical focus, preferring to concentrate instead on the more fashionable categories of race and gender, which critics have not been conditioned to abhor by a half century of Cold War propaganda but which also do not require the imagination of systemic utopian alternatives to capitalism.

The new "postMarxism" of theorists such as Ernesto Laclau and Chantal Mouffe, highly influential in recent leftist literary studies, epitomizes this turn away from class even by leftist political thinkers. Of course, literary scholars are not alone in avoiding the topic of class. For example, sociologist Paul Blumberg, in a 1980 study of economic inequality in America, notes that class remains "America's forbidden thought," while cultural critic Paul Fussell begins his study of class in America by noting that he was made to feel, while writing the book, as if he had been "writing a book urging the beating to death of baby whales using the dead bodies of baby seals" (1). The effacement of class in literary studies is, however, an especially striking phenomenon, if only because American literature and American literary scholars have, at times, been so intensely aware of class. Obviously, the turn from class in literary studies does not begin with postMarxism. Indeed, a review of American cultural history in the last half of the twentieth century shows that the effacement of class, even in leftist thought, begins with the Popular Front of the late 1930s and then intensifies in the embattled Cold War climate of the years immediately after World War II. One aspect of this phenomenon is the decided lack of emphasis on class in the thought of the so-called New Left in America.[2] But this phenomenon can perhaps be seen most clearly in the drastic difference between prewar leftist fiction, with its strong emphasis on class, and postwar leftist fiction, which is far less focused on the issue of class. The specific reasons for this dramatic turn surely lie in the historical circumstances of the Popular Front and World War II battle against fascism and in the political pressures of the subsequent Cold War, which is another way of saying that the effacement of class in contemporary leftist thought has roots in the antifascist compromises of the Popular Front and the anticommunist hysteria of the immediate postwar years and should therefore be looked upon with considerable suspicion in the very different circumstances of the early years of the twenty-first century.

The postMarxist emphasis on race and gender, rather than on class, is clearly reminiscent of the oppositional political movements of the 1960s but has roots that go back to the long 1950s, when the climate of the Cold War made genuine, class-based Marxist critique anathema in the United States. But, as Fredric Jameson has argued, the "categories of race and sex as well as the generational ones of the student movement are theoretically subordinate to the categories of social class, even where they may seem practically and politically a great deal more relevant" (*Signatures* 37). Jameson here is responding precisely to "postMarxist" thinkers such as Laclau and Mouffe, and his argument obviously deserves some serious consideration amid the postMarxist drift away from class as the central category of social analysis and critique. Among other things, the context of Jameson's argument identifies postMarxism as a holdover from the 1960s, with attendant doubts as to its ultimate political power. Jameson's argument also has extremely serious implications for contemporary literary studies in general, which have largely heeded Jameson's own arguments about the centrality of history and politics to any adequate understanding of culture but have done so in a decidedly 1960s sort of way, finding topics such as race and gender far more attractive and "relevant" than that of class, the very mention of which by now has an old-fashioned, even Stalinist ring to it.

Jameson's emphasis on class here should be placed within the context of his own continuing call for serious critical attention to the utopian dimension of literature and culture. Elsewhere, Jameson notes the close interrelationship between class and utopia: "*All* class consciousness — or in other words, all ideology in the strongest sense, including the most exclusive forms of ruling-class consciousness just as much as that of oppositional or oppressed classes — is in its very nature Utopian" (*Political* 289).

One can, of course, envision forms of utopianism that are not based on class, but the elimination of class inequality must surely be central to any utopian vision that places itself in the Marxist tradition. Thus, the decline in class consciousness in leftist culture of the long 1950s can be interpreted as part and parcel of the general decline in utopian thought during that period. Unable any longer to think confidently in terms of class, leftist thinkers were simultaneously unable to imagine genuine alternatives to the class inequality of capitalism. This loss is a crucial one. Any effective oppositional project, for Jameson, must include a utopian suggestion of alternatives to the status quo. Utopianism is thus not escapism but stubborn resistance: "The Utopian idea ... keeps alive the possibility of a world qualitatively distinct from this one and takes the form of a stubborn negation of all that is" (*Marxism* 111).

Of course, American leftist literary scholars maintained at least some awareness of class even during the darkest days of the anticommunist hysteria of the Cold War, though the work of scholars such as Bruce

Franklin and Michael Folsom in his area received very little attention. Now, in the post–Cold War era, such studies are beginning to achieve more visibility. In addition to Coiner's own work, recent publications by such scholars as Barbara Foley, Cary Nelson, James Bloom, James Murphy, Douglas Wixson, and Walter Kalaidjian have recently called important attention to the task of recovering the American radical literary tradition, with its often militant treatment of the issue of class, from the dustbin of history, into which it had been swept beneath a constant barrage of anticommunist propaganda during the Cold War. Such scholars have begun to make significant inroads into the hegemony of the key Cold War notion that political art, shackled by the insistent demands of the party line, is diametrically opposed to "genuine" art, in which the mind of the individual artist roams free, soaring to heights of creativity and innovation and flying by the nets of ideology.

This work has, with good reason, tended to focus on the proletarian literature of the 1930s. After all, there is no question that such works of proletarian fiction as Mike Gold's *Jews without Money*, Jack Conroy's *The Disinherited*, John Steinbeck's *The Grapes of Wrath*, Richard Wright's *Native Son*, Agnes Smedley's *Daughter of the Earth* (1929) and Myra Page's *Gathering Storm* (1932) represent a distinct historical moment in the literary treatment of class never equaled in American literature before or since. Yet, this moment is now more than half a century in the past, while this critical focus on the 1930s to the exclusion of later leftist culture threatens, in subtle and unintentional ways, to reinforce the widely accepted notion that the interwar proletarian movement was a brief flowering that was soon extinguished, discredited by such subsequent historical events as the 1939 Hitler–Stalin pact and the resurgence of American capitalist affluence after World War II. In particular, an exclusive focus on the proletarian fiction of the 1930s tends to make that fiction look like a dead end that held nothing of value for subsequent generations of American leftist writers, if indeed those subsequent generations even exist.

As Catharine Stimpson notes, in an extremely telling survey of American postwar radical literature, it is now "conventional" to argue that "literature as radical statement did not exist in the 1940s and 1950s" (1063). Stimpson actually suggests that this account is at least partly accurate, but Coiner's identification of the important connections between Saxton's work and the radical literature of the past suggests that literature as "radical statement" did, in fact, exist in the 1940s and 1950s. Saxton is not merely the exception that proves the rule. Contrary to popular perceptions, American leftist culture in the dark decades immediately after World War II continued to function and to produce numerous works of its own while also exerting considerable influence on mainstream American culture. An identification of the extensive ways in which the radical culture of the 1930s continued into the culture of postwar America has been at the heart of the recent work of such scholars of leftist culture as Alan Wald and Michael Denning. These scholars have convincingly demonstrated that American leftist culture continued to thrive during the Cold War years, though often in a different and more subtle key than in the more confrontational days of the 1930s. Wald, paying special attention to the works of African American, Jewish American, and other "ethnic" writers, has emphasized the ways in which leftist literature after World War II tended to be dominated by writers who emphasized forms of oppression other than those based on class. Wald also notes that postwar radical writers have tended to shift to production in such popular genres as science fiction and detective fiction, continuing to convey leftist political messages in these new forms but in a more oblique fashion than that which characterized the proletarian fiction of the 1930s. In this sense, Wald's work accords particularly well with that of Denning, who presents detailed arguments for a continuing powerful presence of the Popular Front culture of the late 1930s in American popular culture of the decades since World War II.

The work of scholars such as Wald and Denning is useful in a number of ways. For one thing, this work convincingly demonstrates that the models of cultural history that held almost universal sway in the West during the Cold War were not only wildly inaccurate but inaccurate in politically motivated ways that should (but no doubt won't) put to rest once and for all the silly, but amazingly durable, notion underlying such models of an incompatibility between art and political commitment. Meanwhile, reminders that American leftist culture was not quite as thoroughly routed during the Cold War as most cultural historians have come to believe can be heartening to those of us who firmly believe that culture makes its most important contributions to the betterment of human life not when it ignores reality in favor of spectacular formal high jinks and pointless aesthetic preciosity but when it addresses, in a politically responsible way, the real problems of social injustice and economic exploitation that plague the physical and psychic lives of the vast majority of the world's inhabitants.[3]

The demonstrations of Wald and Denning that American radical culture extends beyond the 1930s not only call needed attention to postwar radical culture but reemphasize the value of 1930s radical culture as well. After all, if the project begun in the 1930s still has such powerful ramifications, then surely the proletarian writers of the 1930s were not nearly so misguided as many have wanted to believe. On the other hand, honesty demands that we not ignore the potential negative implications of the information unearthed by scholars like Wald and Denning in recent years. For example, it may well be that the proliferation of ideas and techniques from the proletarian culture of the 1930s into the popular culture of the 1950s and beyond suggests the continuing power of proletarian culture. It may also be that American popular culture, which is even better than early Christianity at appropriating opposing ideas and making all that is written conform to its own doctrine, has simply absorbed the energies of proletarian culture for its own bourgeois purposes. Here, one might compare Matei Calinescu's observation that avant-garde artistic strategies, once designed to shock and outrage, had by the 1960s become standard fare in advertising and popular culture, thus robbing those strategies of any scandalous power they might have had: "Ironically, the avant-garde found itself failing through a stupendous, involuntary success" (121).[4] The same might be said for the somewhat less radical, but still decidedly high-tech, aesthetic strategies of modernism, a once marginal movement that was, during the Cold War 1950s, suddenly adopted as the official high culture of the West so that it could be set in diametrical opposition to both Western proletarian literature and Soviet socialist realism, which were then declared to be clunky, simplistic, and (horror of horrors!) "ideological" in comparison. Thus, in one fell swoop, modernism was deprived of whatever subversive energies it might once have had, and proletarian literature was consigned to the realm of the inartistic, both subsequently to be recycled for use as raw material for the mills of the culture industry in the production of a safely pro-capitalist postmodernism and a whole range of images and attitudes for the commodified productions of television and film.

If we need to be careful to avoid a premature celebration of the existence of continuing echoes of 1930s proletarian culture in contemporary popular culture, then we need to be even more cautious in assessing the full implications of the turn, emphasized by Wald, to ethnicity as a category of resistance in postwar American fiction of the Left, if only because that turn is in so many ways such an obviously positive development. One might include gender in the same category, and it is indicative of more than her own background that Stimpson, in her survey of postwar "radical" literature, restricts her discussion mostly to feminist texts, even while acknowledging that "after 1945, blacks were America's most formidable voices of protest" (1063). There can be no doubt that gender and race are crucial categories of oppression in American society and that a socially responsible literary criticism needs to address these categories. Indeed, the American Left has a proud heritage of resistance to oppressions based on gender and race. Moreover, a scholar such as Wald, with his encyclopedic knowledge and understanding of American leftist culture, is perfectly aware that oppressions based on race, gender, and class are closely intertwined. But not everyone is so knowledgeable, and there is no doubt that a focus on categories such as race and gender alone tends to work in complicity with the effacement of class that is one of the central underpinnings of the American myth of equal liberty and justice for all, a myth that successfully obscures the ruthless viciousness with which capitalism does its work. After all, if women, African Americans,

Hispanics, and other identifiable "minorities" tend to have less income and access to positions of power than do white males, then this situation would seem a specific problem in social attitudes that can be addressed without making any fundamental changes in the economic structure of capitalism. On the other hand, capitalism, by its very nature, requires inequalities based on class, so any challenge to class-based inequities is, at least potentially, a fundamental challenge to capitalism itself.

If the work of scholars such as Wald and Denning on American postwar leftist culture threatens inadvertently to reinforce the effacement of class in American society, it is also the case that American literary critics of the long 1950s made far more fundamental contributions to this trend with their almost unanimous acceptance of the notion that art and politics were inherently inimical. Most critics during this period ignored political fiction altogether, not only rejecting leftist works produced during the decade as somehow less than literary but also scrupulously repressing their memories of the leftist tradition inherited from prior decades. When such repression was not possible, critics attempted to recuperate and rehabilitate certain texts by depoliticizing them, as in the case of *The Grapes of Wrath* (1939).

Even critics who acknowledged the existence of political art in the long 1950s tended to do so in ways that effaced the issue of class. At the time it was published, Walter Rideout's *The Radical Novel in the United States* (1956) was unusual, even courageous for its suggestion that there is much of value in the tradition of radical American fiction. Yet Rideout accepts without question the anticommunist premises of the Cold War, suggesting that attempts to squelch radical literature were reprehensible primarily because they were "an unconscious assumption of the doctrinaire Communist's position, as so many attacks on freedom turn out to be" (289). Then, foreshadowing many leftist critics of the 1990s, Rideout proclaims that "the future of the radical novel ... lies almost wholly with the independent radical" (290). Independent radicalism means, of course, a rejection of communism in favor of a particularly enthusiastic endorsement of the individualist rhetoric of Americanism. It means, in short, a focus on individuals, rather than classes, as the agents of history, as if an isolated individual, alone, could ever determine the course of public events.

Even Daniel Aaron's *Writers on the Left* (1961), recently reissued and now much admired by many on the Left, accepts the fundamental premise that communist commitment is inimical to artistic creativity. Despite the rejection of Aaron's book by *Partisan Review* critics such as William Phillips, Aaron's book, in fact, portrays the history of the literary Left within the confines of Manichean models of literary history that had long been promulgated by critics associated with *Partisan Review* and the New York Intellectuals, most of whom, if they talked about class at all, did it in ways that disdainfully portrayed the working class as an uncouth and undifferentiated, unwashed mass.[5] As Schaub puts it, the work of figures such as Harry Levin, Lionel Trilling, Daniel Bell, and Irving Howe often focused on "the erosion of classes and of 'class conflict' as meaningful concepts for understanding culture" (189).[6] In any case, Aaron's book, published, we should recall, by Clinton Rossiter's Fund for the Republic specifically as a work of anticommunist propaganda, does not treat literature of the long 1950s but assumes that American leftist culture essentially came to an end with the arrival of World War II.

Subsequent critics of the literature of the long 1950s, even those who have tried to emphasize the political power of radical art, have continued to contribute to the effacement of class through celebrations of works that avoid any real engagement with class. Stimpson's survey of "literature as radical statement," as a chapter in the *Columbia Literary History of the United States*, has something like official status as a statement on the matter. Yet Stimpson mentions only five novels from the long 1950s, none of which focus on working-class experience or class at all. Moreover, none of these novels are written from a theoretically coherent leftist perspective. Her list includes B. F. Skinner's *Walden II* (1948), which she describes as an example of the utopian imagination but which, in fact, combines an anticommunist subtext with an overt glorification of interpellation by official ideology to produce a vision of society that many would regard as distinctly dystopian. She also includes William S. Burroughs's *Naked Lunch* (1959), in some ways the ultimate 1950s individualist alienation novel, and three books that center on gender as a source of alienation, Gore Vidal's *The City and the Pillar* (1948), Sylvia Plath's *The Bell Jar* (1963), and Mary McCarthy's *The Group* (1963).

Stimpson, of course, is not alone. Consider, for example, Frederick Karl's far-ranging *American Fictions, 1940–1980* (1983), which seems promising in its inclusion of a chapter on "The Political Novel: 1950s and After" but then describes this chapter as "mainly a celebration of *Henderson the Rain King*," a book it characterizes as "so fine a political novel because politics, narrowly, is not its base" (255). This indication of Bellow's avoidance of politics is, of course, another way of saying that the book does little to suggest utopian alternatives to the status quo. While Karl mentions a number of other novels in his chapter, he manages to ignore, with the exception of some of Norman Mailer's early work, the dozens of genuinely leftist novels that were produced in the long 1950s. Meanwhile, if Bellow is, in some ways, the definitive "political" novelist of this decade, one could also point to that other widely celebrated "political" novel of the 1950s, Ralph Ellison's *Invisible Man* (1952), which certainly expresses black rage and alienation in a powerful and poignant way but which, we should be willing to admit, owes much of its near-canonical status to its self-indulgent modernist form and self-serving anticommunist politics, both of which contribute to its nicely safe conclusion, foreshadowing Laclau and Mouffe (and Rodney King), that we should reject both communism and black nationalism in favor of a "can't-we-all-just-get-along" pluralism.

Bellow and Ellison are major figures of 1950s literature partly because their central thematic emphasis on alienation as an existential, rather than Marxist, category corresponded to the seemingly inexplicable anguish so many readers were feeling in that supposedly idyllic decade of capitalism's Golden Years; at the same time, both writers scrupulously avoid any suggestion that this anguish might be a fundamental and inevitable product of capitalism itself. A similar turn to existential anguish (along with explicit renunciations of his communist past) may have saved the literary reputation of Richard Wright, which was nearly extinguished during the long 1950s but which returned with a vengeance after the 1960s, when African American culture began to receive serious critical attention at last. Of course, it also helped that even *Native Son*, surely Wright's greatest work and one of the finest leftist novels ever to have been produced by an American writer, could be safely recuperated by a sufficiently myopic reader as being about race rather than class. One could even argue (by ignoring the book itself and concentrating instead on Wright's later trajectory) that *Native Son* was actually anticommunist. Thus, in the *Oxford Companion to African American Literature*, another semi-official text, the entry under Wright bizarrely describes the transparently pro-communist *Native Son* as an attempt to "instruct the party about its failures in addressing African Americans, thus implying its pathetic lack of knowledge and understanding of black history, culture, and life" (Gibson 794).

Wright, of course, contributed to such readings of his work with his diatribes against his own former communism in his contribution to Richard Crossman's anthology *The God That Failed* (1949), perhaps, along with J. Edgar Hoover's Mein Kampfesque *Masters of Deceit* (1958), one of the two greatest classics of American anticommunist propaganda of the long 1950s. Yet Wright remained, through the remainder of his life, more ambivalent about communism — and more antagonistic toward American capitalism — than is usually acknowledged by those who would trot him out as an anticommunist spokesman. Still, the apostasy of Wright and Ellison (who had also flirted with the Left in his younger and presumably more naive days) is central to one of the standard cultural stereotypes from the long 1950s — the notion that African Americans, during this period, thoroughly rejected communism as just another white man's grab for power.

Another central figure in this narrative is Chester Himes, whose *Lonely Crusade* (1947) has been almost universally regarded as a bitter denunciation of communism, even by critics sympathetic to communism, such as Foley in *Radical Representations*. Himes's novel certainly shows a great deal of skepticism concerning the American Communist Party, and this skepticism is surely related to Himes's own rejection of the attempts of the party to recruit him during his years in Los Angeles. On the other hand, a careful reading of the book shows that it does not reject the basic premises of communism, especially the notion of class struggle, nearly as thoroughly as most critics have assumed. The book ends with a workers' demonstration in which union leader Joe Ptak is beaten into unconsciousness by deputies who are attempting to quell the demonstration. Ptak drops his union banner, and, for a moment, the workers are stymied, but then protagonist Lee Gordon (generally seen as an anticommunist figure based partly on Himes) rushes forward to Ptak's side, takes up the banner, and bears it onward as the book ends.

Importantly, Gordon's heroic final action is immediately motivated by his own realization, as he watches the gathering workers, that black and white workers are really in the same class situation and that their racial separation only serves to facilitate their own oppression by the forces of capitalism: "They were bound together by their own oppression rendered by the same oppressors—their fears and their superstitions and their ignorance indivisible. Only their hatred separated them, like idiots hating their own images" (392). Meanwhile, he realizes that the gathering workers are a potentially powerful, even revolutionary force, held in check by the official repression of the line of deputies, "cutting off the success of the rally, the future of the union, the movement of the working people of the world" (397). *Lonely Crusade* thus ends on a note that is highly reminiscent of the endings of many proletarian novels from the 1930s. Lee's final "conversion" does not occur on impulse. For one thing, he has been almost desperately seeking throughout the book to be able to overcome his radical alienation through a utopian longing to become a part of something larger than himself. His race, the party, the union, his marriage, and his relationship with Jackie have all failed to fill this role adequately, but he is able at the end finally to identify the working class as this larger entity to which he can genuinely belong. Moreover, this realization is prepared by his encounter with the Jewish communist Abe Rosenberg shortly before the rally. The compassionate Rosenberg belies any notion that *Lonely Crusade* is either antisemitic or unequivocally anticommunist. Moreover, his long, impassioned discourse to Lee on the importance of Marxist dialectical materialism as the key to understanding social and historical reality (despite his own recent expulsion from the Communist Party) is clearly meant to be convincing, to both Gordon and the reader.

Other African American writers of the long 1950s remained enthusiastically devoted to the Left and to proletarian class struggle as the key to black liberation. Lloyd Brown's *Iron City* (1951), based on a real 1941 case in which Willie Jones, an African American, was framed for murder and then executed, shows white communists in the forefront of efforts to achieve justice for Lonnie James, the black protagonist based on Jones. *Iron City* is a strongly pro-communist work that provides important reminders of the party's long legacy of antiracist activism. *Iron City* also responds to works such as *Native Son* (which is, in fact, alluded to in Brown's book) and Himes's *If He Hollers Let Him Go* (1945) in that it shows African Americans not simply as victims of racial oppression but as taking positive collective action to battle against their oppression.

John O. Killens's *Youngblood* (1954) features a vivid evocation of African American life in the South in the early part of the twentieth century. It is also one of the finest and most committed works of leftist literature to have been produced during the long 1950s. Wald rightly identifies *Youngblood* as one of the most underappreciated works of modern American literature, calling the book a "neglected masterpiece" and describing it as "a stunning dramatization of the complex interactions among class, gender, and race worthy of the 1960s, even the 1990s. It is a work expressing a rich, Fanonian view of nationalism as a stage to internationalism, climaxing in a powerful deconstruction of the myth of biological 'race'" (*Writing* 119). Wald's enthusiasm for the book is well placed. Few works of modern American fiction detail the lives of specific characters in more vivid and compelling ways, while at the same time making clear the historical and social context in which these lives occur. In its sophisticated understanding of the economic foundations of both racism and sexism and in its rousing endorsement of collective class action as the key to overcoming oppression based on race and gender, as well as class, *Youngblood* is one of the most effective political novels to have been produced by an American writer. The book addresses a number of crucial issues related to race and gender, though Killens insists, via a variety of strategies, that class is the most important and fundamental social category in America. For example, he emphasizes the common economic exploitation shared by blacks and poor whites in the South, noting the way in which race has been used to separate these groups and thus prevent them from making common cause against the rich bosses who take advantage of them both.[7]

Killens, despite the achievement of *Youngblood* and of his long and productive career as a writer and scholar, was virtually ignored by critics during the long 1950s. Brown received even less recognition. Yet neither was a minor figure, and their work indicates that the relationship between African American writers and the Left in the long 1950s was far more complex and extensive than has been emphasized in most accounts of American literary history. Wright, Ellison, Himes, and others have been widely promoted as anticommunist spokesmen, presumably embittered by the "betrayal" of African Americans by the Communist Party.[8] Writers such as Brown and Killens, who could not be read as anticommunist spokesmen by any stretch of the imagination, have been either ignored altogether or, at best, treated as writers concerned primarily with the issue of race, rather than class. It is, in fact, true that the best leftist fiction of the long 1950s often features race and ethnicity in important ways, partly because race and ethnicity are, in America, inseparable from class.

Indeed, some of the most impressive efforts of the literary Left during this period were devoted precisely to an exploration of relationships between class and ethnicity. The two largest-scale works of American leftist literature during the long 1950s explore this topic: W.E.B Du Bois's *Black Flame* Trilogy, comprising *The Ordeal of Mansart* (1957), *Mansart Builds a School* (1959), and *Worlds of Color* (1961); and Philip Stevenson's *The Seed*, the collective title of a series of novels that includes the published volumes *Morning, Noon, and Night* (1954), *Out of the Dust* (1956), *Old Father Antic* (1961), and *The Hoax* (1961). That both of these impressive sequences are now virtually unknown is indicative of the deafening critical silence with which leftist works were greeted in the long 1950s, even though they were produced by a writer of the fame of Du Bois.

The very fact that Du Bois could maintain such fame as a spokesman for African Americans, while his leftist inclinations were virtually forgotten, is one of the most telling instances of the suppression of class in favor of race in American culture in the long 1950s. One of the intellectual giants of modern global culture and leading figure in African American social, political, and intellectual life, Du Bois was one of the founders of the National Association for the Advancement of Colored People (NAACP), the longtime editor of the journal *Crisis*, and a leading spokesman for African American rights for more than seven decades.[9] As a historian, journalist, and essayist, he was the author of a number of the most important works of modern African American culture and, indeed, of American culture as a whole. *The Souls of Black Folk* (1903) remains his best-known work. Other crucial nonfiction works include *The Suppression of the African Slave-Trade to the United States 1638–1870* (1896), *John Brown* (1909), *The Negro* (1915), and *Black Reconstruction in America* (1935). In 1951, Du Bois, long identified with leftist causes, ran afoul of the anti-communist purges sweeping America at the time and was indicted as an unregistered agent of a foreign power for his involvement in the Peace Information Center, which he chaired. Unlike many others who were, in fact, convicted for similar activities, Du Bois had his case thrown out of court. His experience with the indictment is described in *In Battle for Peace: The Story of My Eighty-Third Birthday* (1952). Through the 1950s, Du Bois continued to battle against repression in America, but, in 1959, he emigrated to Ghana, where he became a citizen and renounced his U.S. citizenship. He also became a member of the Communist Party, formalizing an intellectual position toward which he had leaned throughout most of his career.

In Ghana, Du Bois worked on an encyclopedia of African culture and completed the last volume of *The Black Flame*. He had earlier published two other novels, *The Quest of the Silver Fleece* (1911) and *Dark Princess* (1928); he was, in fact, an accomplished novelist, even if his accomplishments in other areas tended to overshadow his work as a writer of fiction.[10] *The Black Flame* is a sweeping, encyclopedic account of American history from the mid-1870s to the mid-1950s, related from a radical African American perspective. The trilogy focuses on a single figure, Manuel Mansart, an African American intellectual of considerable, if not spectacular, talents and achievements, but it also introduces most of the major real-life figures and events that played roles in American history during the 80 years covered by the narrative. The trilogy calls attention to both the importance of racism in modern American history and the prominence of African Americans in battling against racism. But the real focus of the trilogy is not on race but on class, and Du Bois consistently presents racism as a strategy designed by capitalists to divide the working class and to make it easier for capital to exploit labor all over the world.

*The Ordeal of Mansart* begins in 1876 as Tom Mansart, a former slave who has now been elected to the state legislature, visits Colonel John Breckinridge in an attempt to negotiate a political alliance between his black constituency and the former Southern aristocracy of large planters. Mansart hopes thereby to stave off attempts of the emergent white bourgeoisie to strip African Americans of the new political power they have gained in the wake of the Civil War. A strong believer in the importance of organized labor in the effort to achieve true democracy, Mansart attends a black labor meeting, which is attacked by a mob of poor whites who do not realize that their class interests are the same as those of the poor blacks they so despise. In the ensuing confusion, Mansart attempts to save Mrs. Breckinridge, who has come to the meeting thinking her husband, John, will be there. Mansart is then set upon by the mob, accused of abducting the white woman, and lynched on his own doorstep. At that very moment, his wife is inside giving birth to their son, Manuel.

Manuel is thus born under allegorical circumstances that suggest the textual mechanics of the entire trilogy, in which the experiences of individual characters represent not just the stories of individuals but the experience of large segments of the African American population. These characters are, in short, "typical" in the sense indicated by Georg Lukács in relation to the best historical novels of the early nineteenth century. Indeed, *The Black Flame* as a whole is an impressive historical novel that in many ways epitomizes the standards described by Lukács for the most effective historical fiction, even as it introduces antiracist and anticolonial elements that are not central to Lukács's discussion. Du Bois is clearly more interested in presenting history in a compelling and accessible fashion than in creating clever fictional narratives. As he points out in a postscript to the first volume, he wrote *The Black Flame* as a novel rather than as conventional history partly because it was faster, and he knew that his own time was growing short. (The third volume was published when he was ninety-three, two years before his death.) Nevertheless, Du Bois indicates that he has based the books on historical reality as much as possible, employing his own vast knowledge to produce a work that is "more history than fiction, more fact than assumption, much truth and no falsehood" (*Ordeal* 316).

Most of the first half of *The Ordeal of Mansart* is concerned with the presentation of a vivid picture of the politics and economics of the Reconstruction South. The book then traces the late nineteenth-century rise of radical populist politics, led by Tom Watson and his black confederate, Sebastian Doyle.[11] It also follows the conspiratorial machinations of big business not only to squash this populist movement but also to drive a racist wedge between black and white workers and thus ensure the continued domination of both by capital. Meanwhile, the book follows Manuel Mansart as he grows to adulthood, becoming a promising student and managing to attend college at the all-black Atlanta University, a school at which Du Bois taught history and economics from 1897 to 1910. Indeed, Du Bois is represented in the text by James Burghardt, a black intellectual whose activities and attitudes clearly mirror Du Bois's own. Among other things, Burghardt is highly skeptical of the program set out by Booker T. Washington for the economic advancement of blacks. Burghardt also teaches at Atlanta University for several years (Mansart is one of his students) but then returns North, where he is instrumental late in *Ordeal* in the founding of the NAACP. By the end of the book, Mansart has completed his education and has become the principal of a large black school in Atlanta. He has considered going North, especially in the wake of the 1906 race riots that hit Atlanta, but he decides to stay in Georgia and apply for the newly vacated position of superintendent of Atlanta's black schools.

In *Mansart Builds a School*, Mansart gets the superintendent job and struggles for years to improve the black schools of Atlanta, despite the extremely meager support given these schools in comparison to white ones. He is aided, to some extent, by the support of his superior, Arnold Coypel, the sympathetic white superintendent of schools in Atlanta. Eventually, however, he moves on to Macon, where he becomes president of the new Georgia State Colored Agricultural and Mechanical College, founded there in 1920. In the meantime, he and his wife have three sons, Douglass, Revels, and Bruce, and a daughter, Sojourner. Coypel, now in charge of the state system of higher education, continues to offer his support, but Mansart nevertheless struggles with numerous social, economic, and political obstacles in his attempt to build the new college into an effective institution of higher learning. He is also joined at the college by a new secretary, Jean Du Bignon, a highly intelligent woman who is essentially white but who is considered black in the South because she had an African American great-grandfather. Jean has a doctorate in sociology from the University of Chicago, but because of the double onus of race and gender, she is unable to get the kind of professional position she deserves. However, she soon becomes indispensable to Mansart and is eventually named dean of the college. In the meantime, the story of Mansart, his family, and his acquaintances is again placed firmly within the context of history. Du Bois's evocation of the prejudice and persecution suffered by African American soldiers in World War I (in which both Douglass and Revels serve) is particularly powerful, thus reinforcing earlier leftist critiques of the U.S. involvement in that war, such as Dos Passos's *1919*.

Other important events during this period include the growth of the NAACP and its journal, *Crisis*, edited by Burghardt. Much attention is again given to the good-ole-boy maneuverings that constitute Georgia politics at this time, but Du Bois's focus remains principally economic, as capital continues to promote racism as a way of impeding the attempts of organized labor to oppose the exploitation of workers. The book ends in the early years of the Depression, which hits blacks particularly hard. Here, Du Bois introduces Franklin Delano Roosevelt, who is treated very positively in the text, and his important adviser, the socialist Harry Hopkins, who becomes the head of the new Works Progress Administration (WPA). By the end of the volume, Mansart, with Jean's help, is making real progress in Macon. Douglass, meanwhile, is a prosperous insurance man in Chicago, having devoted himself to the bourgeois ideal of making money. Revels has become a successful lawyer and judge in New York, while Sojourner is a promising and talented musician and student of African American music, married to Roosevelt Wilson, an ambitious minister. However, Bruce, once a talented young man with great promise, has been hanged in Kansas City after he is set on the road to crime by an ugly racial incident in which he is unfairly accosted by the Atlanta police and savagely beaten, never again to be the same.

The third volume takes the story of Mansart from the 1930s to the mid-1950s, in the meantime encompassing such historical events as World War II, the Cold War, and the McCarthyite purges in America, depicted by Du Bois as part of an ongoing capitalist conspiracy to disrupt the efforts of organized labor. The coverage in this volume becomes particularly global as Du Bois shifts his focus from African Americans to nonwhite peoples around the globe, indicating the tremendous potential for cooperative effort not only among Africans and members of the African diaspora but also India, China, and other nonwhite nations. Meanwhile, the Soviet Union, as the first nation officially to outlaw racism, also emerges as a powerful ally to these nonwhite nations—indeed as the leader of the effort to resist imperial domination of the globe by the white nations of Western Europe and North America. Early in the book, Mansart takes a European tour, during which he learns for the first time the true nature of the Spanish Civil War. He also visits Germany and observes Nazism firsthand, at the same time observing Jesse Owens's triumphant performance in the 1936 Olympic games in Berlin. He then moves on to the Soviet Union, where he is greatly impressed with the attempt to build socialism there. During the trip, he meets C.L.R. James and becomes aware of James's important book, *The Black Jacobins*. The book inspires him, after his return to Georgia, to encourage Jean to take a trip to the West Indies. She does so and is both surprised and inspired to learn of the important role played by the black peoples of the Caribbean in the history of the modern world. She learns, for example, a great deal about the late eighteenth-century slave rebellions in Haiti and of the crucial part played by Haiti in the French Revolution.

Back in America, however, Jean finds that some brief, sympathetic remarks she makes about communism to one of her classes, combined with her participation in a global peace movement, lead to her being charged as an unregistered agent of foreign powers—as was Du Bois, for his work in the interest of world peace. The charges are dropped after a key witness against her is exposed as an obvious impostor, but Jean is soon afterward dismissed from the college as a result of the charges, however unfounded. In this sense, her fate is portrayed as part of the increasingly sinister and repressive atmosphere in America after World War II. Among other things, powerful forces begin to conspire to remove Mansart from the presidency he has now held for more than a quarter of a century, fearing that he is becoming too influential in the post. Together, Manuel and Jean resist these attempts, but, after her dismissal, he, now a widower, eventually retires so that they can be married and spend the remainder of their lives together. Soon after their wedding, Mansart is brought up on charges of subversion for participating in some private political discussions, though Revels manages to get the charges dropped. Manuel and Jean then move to New York to stay with Revels and his family. There, Mansart, at seventy-eight, soon dies, after a final utopian vision of a future triumph of the non-Western world over the conspiratorial attempts of corporate capitalism to maintain its global hegemony.

Lily Wiatrowski Phillips suggests that the lack of critical attention received by *The Black Flame* over the years may arise from the fact that "its narrative logic is unfamiliar and off-putting to most of Du Bois's home audience." In particular, she concludes that the book derives its aesthetics largely from Soviet socialist realism (838). However, the book, though sympathetic to the Soviet Union and to communism, cannot rightly be considered a work of socialist realism because it does not deal with the historical construction of socialism. It is, in fact, more in the tradition of critical realism, even if its particular mixture of history and fiction makes it a highly unusual work in comparison to any tradition. Moreover, it should also be pointed out that the book has not been entirely without admirers. As Gerald Horne notes, many initial reviews of the volumes were extremely enthusiastic (271). For example, Sidney Finkelstein, in a review first published in the leftist journal *Mainstream*, calls the trilogy an example of unusually "serious and gifted" fiction. He also regards the novels as extremely important in the way they are able "to present not merely the real forces, economic, political, and social, operating in the world faced by his typical personages, but also something more difficult and complicated; namely, the growing consciousness by the people of what these forces are" (200). Later critics have also found much of value in the trilogy, as when Richard Kostelanetz calls it "a remarkable performance" that deserves far more attention than it has received (179). Keith Byerman, meanwhile, calls *The Black Flame* "perhaps the most complicated, if not sophisticated" of all of Du Bois's writings (138). Even Arnold Rampersad, while expressing a certain discomfort with the Marxist perspective of the trilogy, finds it an important work that can be regarded as the culmination of Du Bois's career (287). Because of the shortness of time left to the aging Du Bois, *The Black Flame* shows some signs of hasty construction, but it is nevertheless an impressive work that combines a coherent historical vision with encyclopedic historical knowledge and effective literary technique. It presents a compelling leftist survey of modern American history from an African American point of view while at the same time vividly presenting the participation of individuals in this history.

*The Black Flame,* sweeping in scope and peopled with characters who clearly derive their identities from their participation in the historical process, in many ways resembles the early nineteenth-century bourgeois historical novels praised by Lukács. The trilogy ends with the death of its protagonist, Manuel Mansart, but it also closes on a utopian note, providing a final glorious vision of a future triumph of the non-Western world over the conspiratorial attempts of corporate capitalism to maintain and extend its global hegemony. Nevertheless, the focus on African American history, from organized violence against blacks during Reconstruction, to the political persecution of civil rights activists in the 1950s, forces *The Black Flame* to be largely a dystopian story of oppression and abuse. Indeed, if Balzac and Scott document, in their novels, the sweeping historical victory of the European bourgeoisie, *The Black Flame* well indicates the difficulties faced by leftist historical novelists in the long 1950s, who have no such victory to document but can only, at best, attempt to maintain hope of future victories.

Stevenson's sequence, *The Seed*, is very much in the same situation. It focuses on the travails of Latino miners in New Mexico and is thus reminiscent of *Salt of the* Earth. Stevenson was a prominent communist writer and activist in the 1950s, closely associated, among other things, with the journal *California Quarterly*. However, Stevenson felt it necessary to publish the volumes of *The Seed* under the name Lars Lawrence after he was blacklisted following his refusal to name names when interrogated by the House Committee on Un-American Activities in 1951. The blacklist also brought an end to Stevenson's promising screenwriting career, which had already seen him script several films, including *The Story of G.I. Joe* (1945), for which Stevenson and cowriters Leopold Atlas and Guy Endore were nominated for an Academy Award for Best Screenplay. Based on events emanating from the Gallup Strike of 1933, all of the volumes of *The Seed* focus on the experiences of Mexican American coal miners in New Mexico in the 1930s, which Stevenson envisions as the potential beginning to revolutionary change, employing the title metaphor of the series in much the same way as Émile Zola in his classic 1885 strike novel, *Germinal*, which also centers on coal miners.[12] Stevenson was at work on a fifth volume of the series, tentatively entitled "The Sowing," when he died while touring the Soviet Union in 1965. [13]

*Morning, Noon, and Night* begins with an introduction of Reata (based on Gallup), an ugly coal-mining town set in the midst of great natural beauty. The town itself is populated mostly by Anglos, though much of the surrounding land is inhabited by Navajo, who remain very marginal to the society of Reata and to Stevenson's novels. The local economy derives a substantial amount of income from tourism but is dominated by coal mines on the mountain overlooking the town. Two miles up the slope from the town to the coal camp is the hamlet known as La Cieneguita, peopled by impoverished Mexican American coal miners and their families, who provide most of the manpower for the mines. The area is still tense from a recent communist-led strike in which the coal miners won numerous concessions, though many of the strike leaders have subsequently found themselves blacklisted and out of work. The remaining miners, meanwhile, have been manipulated into switching their membership to a new, more moderate union that is working in league with the mining company to try to eliminate communists as an influence on the miners. As the book opens, local politician Jacques Mahoney, who surreptitiously obtained title to most of the land on which La Cieneguita sits back in the 1920s, has begun evicting the blacklisted miners, who are unable to make payments on their meager housing because of unemployment. When Arturo Fernández and his family are evicted, Ramón Arce, one of the leaders of the strike, helps them to slip back into their house so they will have somewhere to stay at least for the night. However, this simple action sets into motion a chain of events that leads to the arrest of Arce and Fernández and to the subsequent assemblage, led by the half-Navajo Tranquilino de Vaca, of a crowd of Cieneguitans at the courthouse to attend the hearing of the two men and of Lugardito Destremadura, an old woman who was recently arrested for scavenging through the coal camp's garbage looking for food for her grandchildren. When Arce is taken out of the courthouse into the back alley, the crowd believes he is about to be beaten and rushes behind the courthouse to his aid. The sheriff and deputies begin to fire tear gas into the crowd; in the subsequent turmoil, gunshots are fired as well. The sheriff and one of the miners are killed by gunshots, while two deputies are wounded, as is another miner, who subsequently dies.

The crowd scatters, and Arce escapes in the confusion. The forces of official authority shift into high gear, declaring the event a riot and the sheriff's death a murder, though there are indications that he may have accidentally been shot by one of the deputies. Deputy Burns Bolling, a decent man caught up in difficult circumstances, deputizes large numbers of the local Anglos, who institute a reign of terror in the region, arresting, often with considerable brutality, virtually all of the denizens of La Cieneguita except for a few old men, women, and children. The prisoners are herded into squalid and crowded conditions in the city jail. De Vaca, a communist, is among the prisoners, as are most of the leaders of the local Communist Party, which had been largely responsible for galvanizing the miners in the recent strike. These include the section organizer Hamilton Turner, as well as such local leaders as the nurse Concepción Candelaria, the African American Moby Douglass, and Mike and Lydia Kovacs. Arce, however, remains free, the object of an extensive manhunt. Before going to jail, Lydia Kovacs manages to cable Los Angeles labor lawyer Frank Hogarth for help. As the book closes, the jail remains packed as the authorities ponder ways of dealing with so many prisoners. Hogarth is on his way to Reata by car, accompanied by his French wife Mignonne. Arce is still at large, headed for Mexico, though the authorities have just captured miner Woodrow Wilson Lucero, who collapses while fleeing on foot from motorcycle patrolmen who believe him to be Arce.

All of the events of *Morning, Noon, and Night* occur during a single day, and *Out of the Dust* picks up immediately afterward, at dawn the next morning. In an attempt to deal with overcrowding in the jail, the authorities, with the reluctant cooperation of Turner and the other leaders of the miners, process the prisoners quickly, giving them cursory preliminary hearings without the benefit of legal counsel. The majority, including all of the women and children, are released on their own recognizance, though most of these are ordered not to leave their homes. The remaining prisoners, 54 in all, are marched through town in chains, then put aboard a train and transported to the state's capital city, Hidalgo, where they are installed in the state penitentiary while awaiting trial. In an effort to help the local business community resume normal operations, the town newspaper, the *Lariat*, prints articles assuring all that peace has been restored to Reata, while at the same time continuing to carry incendiary articles concerning the nefarious contributions of "Reds" to the recent violence. Indeed, the suggestively named Damon McCarthy, editor of the *Lariat*, emerges in this volume as one of the central villains of the piece as he dreams of parlaying an anticommunist editorial campaign into personal gain. Meanwhile, various other members of the Anglo community attempt to deal with the aftermath of the recent violence, including Mayor Harriman, who ponders ways of making himself appear to be a strong leader during the crisis; Assistant District Attorney Ben Mallon, who assumes initial leadership in the prosecution of the prisoners; and District Attorney Luís Cortez, a sort of token Mexican American in the city administration, who returns after being out of town during the riot only to find that he must compete for jurisdiction in the case with state Attorney General Dewey Soames, who hopes to use his handling of the Reata Reds as a springboard to the governorship.

Arce remains on the run, while the prisoners remain in the pen in Hidalgo, with de Vaca providing leadership there. Lydia Kovacs, Connie Concepción, Ham Turner, and others spearhead a campaign among the free citizens of La Cieneguita to provide for the legal defense of the prisoners. Hogarth assumes a leading role in this effort after he arrives in town, though he first has to make his way through roadblocks that have been thrown up around the town to prevent the incursion of Red agitators. He also has to deal with the hostility of Cortez, Mallon, and McCarthy, who do everything possible to hamper his efforts. The book ends as the town authorities attempt to give a furtive burial to Crescencio Armijo, the first miner killed in the disturbance in the alley, hoping thereby to prevent his burial from becoming the occasion for a political demonstration. However, many of the locals manage to get to the event, including a number of Anglos and all of the women who have been ordered to remain in their houses. The burial ceremony becomes a beautiful and moving one, highlighted by a passionate, revolutionary oration by Miss Priscilla Armour, a wealthy old Anglo woman considered eccentric in the town for her sympathy with the cause of the miners. Looking on, Ham Turner realizes that his own revolutionary message is beginning to take root in the town, a conclusion confirmed when Richard "Witless" Watterson, the best student in the local high school, approaches him and asks for his guidance in learning about communism. Cheered by the request, Ham promises to provide some literature, then goes back to rejoin the people gathered for the burial.

*Old Father Antic* again resumes the narrative immediately after the end of the previous volume, as Frank Hogarth drives with Mignonne, Lydia Kovacs, and her son, Mikey, to Hidalgo to confer with the prisoners and to begin to make arrangements there for local efforts in their defense. Aided by Pansy Parmalee, a middle-aged woman doctor who sympathizes with the working class despite her own hopelessly bourgeois worldview, Hogarth finds several allies in Hidalgo, including Paul Schermerhorn, a local attorney who agrees to take the case so that he can officially invite Hogarth to join him. Leo Severance, an experienced labor lawyer called in by Ham Turner, joins the defense team as well. Much of *Old Father Antic* is devoted to descriptions of the bourgeois decadence of the various denizens of Hidalgo, many of them artists who have come there to enjoy its reputation as something of an artists' colony. This situation gives Stevenson an opportunity to comment on the political irresponsibility of many artists. The Hidalgo artists think of themselves as opponents of bourgeois conservatism and conformism, but they have largely lost touch with the problems of ordinary people and are unable to imagine their work as participating in a working-class struggle against the bourgeois order: "They had always thought of the role of art as being to shock, to startle, to épater the bourgeois, rather than defend his victims" (99).

First and foremost, *Old Father Antic* is a courtroom drama, and its central event concerns a preliminary hearing that is held in Hidalgo after District Judge Bernardo Becque, himself part Mexican American, declares the earlier hearings in Reata null and void. The prosecution, represented by Cortez, Mallon, Soames, and the scholarly Assistant Attorney General Arthur Levitsky, presents its case, which appears so weak that Hogarth, Schermerhorn, and Severance, representing the defense, decide to call no witnesses of their own but instead to rely on their cross-examinations of the prosecution witnesses. During the proceeding, the prosecution, knowing it has no evidence of conspiracy, shies away from presenting the disturbance in Reata as the result of a communist plot, but the defense lawyers, led by Hogarth, do attempt to link the case to a long history of legal persecution of radicals, from the trials of the Haymarket Square anarchists, to the recent cases of the Gastonia strikers and the Scottsboro boys. After the presentations are completed, Becque, struggling to reach a fair verdict that will nevertheless leave his own political ambitions intact, releases most of the prisoners, who now number more than 60 after several additional recent arrests. Becque does, however, order four defendants, including Tranquilino de Vaca, bound over on murder charges without bail. Six others are ordered to be tried for murder, but with bail set at $7,500 each. Three women, including Concepción Candelaria, are ordered to be tried for aiding in the escape of Arce, with bail set at $1,000 each. As the book closes, the freed prisoners are returned to Reata, where Moby Douglass is reunited with his daughter, Sugar. The girl begs him to take her away from Reata, where they are among very few African Americans; he agrees, insisting that they leave at once for the West Coast, where he can become a longshoreman and enjoy the effective union representation of the International Longshoreman's Association.

*The Hoax* opens the day after Becque's verdict and focuses on a trip made by Frank and Mignonne Hogarth, Ham Turner, and several others aligned with the defense team to Reata to gather evidence for the upcoming trials. They make little headway, however, meeting with considerable official resistance and with hostility from the local press. Meanwhile, they begin to receive threats, which culminate in the kidnapping of Turner and Hogarth by a gang of hooded thugs. The two are taken to a remote location and badly beaten, then abandoned with a warning not to return to Reata. Much of the book concerns their struggle to make their way back through the wilderness to the town, while the remainder of their party scrambles to search for them, even though they get no cooperation from the local authorities. With the help of some friendly Navajo, the two do make their way back, only to find that the authorities refuse to try to find their kidnappers. Indeed, Mallon has declared the kidnapping a communist hoax. The *Lariat*, of course, supports Mallon's position, but the national and even international press widely publicizes the kidnapping as an attempt to suppress defense efforts, which pressures the state authorities to begin at least a perfunctory investigation.

Aided by information supplied by Richard Watterson, who was losing his virginity with Laura-Jean Mangin in the woods at the time Turner and Hogarth were left there by the kidnappers, the two victims, accompanied by a party of friends, reporters, and state police, manage to retrace the route taken by the kidnappers and to gather a considerable amount of evidence. They then return to Reata, only to find that Mallon still maintains that the kidnapping was a hoax and meanwhile plans to impound the evidence they have gathered, probably to destroy it. Judge Becque again saves the day, impounding the evidence himself and having it sent to Hidalgo for safekeeping. The defense team then leaves Reata for Hidalgo, stopping on the way in the town of Compostela, where a large labor meeting is being held to support their efforts. Hogarth begins to speak at the meeting, impressed by the enthusiasm of his audience. However, the stresses of recent events finally catch up with him. A longtime sufferer of tuberculosis, he suffers a fatal attack and collapses on the stage. Turner takes over the podium while Hogarth looks on, knowing that he is dying but happy to see such a show of solidarity among workers.

The ending of *The Hoax* is especially poignant given Stevenson's own death (he had also long suffered from tuberculosis) soon afterward, but in general the book, though it has suspenseful moments, is the weakest of the four volumes of the series. In particular, it focuses on the activities of lawyers and other middle-class characters and tends to lose direct contact with the workers who had been so central to the earlier volumes. Nevertheless, *The Seed* as a whole constitutes the most extended example of class-conscious fiction to have been published in the United States during the height of the Cold War years. The series is especially good in its treatment of such issues as race and ethnicity as part of a larger context of class struggle. The Mexican American miners of Reata suffer special forms of oppression because of their ethnic backgrounds, but Stevenson makes it clear that their struggle is ultimately the struggle of workers everywhere.

*The Seed* is also strong in its treatment of gender. The various volumes pay significant attention to the special forms of oppression suffered by women in the region. Predictably, these include poor Chicanas such as

Cha-Cha Juárez, forced by economic pressures to become a prostitute, thus employing her only marketable asset as a means of survival. But they also include Anglo women such as a variety of abused wives and young Laura-Jean Mangin, who becomes involved with Richard Watterson only after she loses her virginity when she is raped by her boyfriend, Buddy Wedemeyer, when his passions are stirred by his service as a deputy during the roundup the night of the riot. Women, however, are not merely victims in the book. There are a number of strong female characters among the supporters of the miners, especially Lydia Kovacs and Concepción Candelaria. On the other hand, there are also villainous women in the book, just as there are villainous Mexican Americans. Even central protagonists such as Turner and Hogarth have their own human failings, while figures of authority such as Sheriff Burns Bolling are not entirely evil. Stevenson, in fact, neither idealizes nor demonizes his characters but instead presents a compelling, realistic picture of normal human beings caught up in a class struggle that moves them to take either heroic or villainous actions, depending upon the class with which they are aligned. Throughout *The Seed*, class, not ethnicity or gender, is the principal social category, a fact that, among other things, helps Stevenson to avoid falling into exoticism when depicting Mexican Americans.

In short, Stevenson's vision is complex and sophisticated, while maintaining a firm leftist stance—despite the widespread belief promulgated during the Cold War that such a stance must, by definition, be simplistic and doctrinaire. *The Seed* also contains both critical and utopian elements, suggesting that the injustices of capitalism are difficult to resist but not entirely irresistible, despite the failure of the Gallup Strike itself. That Stevenson had to reach back to the 1930s to recover such utopian energies may be telling, but his work suggests the continuing possibility of a leftist utopian imagination at the beginning of the 1960s.

Stevenson's emphasis in *The Seed* on gender as a special category of oppression that is nevertheless part of a larger phenomenon of class struggle builds upon a point made by any number of writers from the 1930s, many of them women. In the long 1950s, however, women writers, who had enjoyed an unprecedented prominence in the leftist literature of the 1930s, tended to recede into the margins. In fact, the paucity of leftist fiction by American women writers during the 1950s is striking in comparison to the prewar years. Tess Slesinger died at the beginning of the long 1950s. Agnes Smedley, at the very top of the list of American writers singled out as targets of the McCarthyite purges of the late 1940s, devoted the remainder of her life and career to the fight to build socialism in China. Of the major women leftist writers of the 1930s, some, following the trajectory of apostates like Wright, openly rejected their earlier political associations. Josephine Herbst drifted into a sort of leftist anticommunism, but the classic case is Grace Lumpkin, who authored two important proletarian works in the 1930s, the Gastonia novel *To Make My*

*Bread* (1932) and *A Sign for Cain* (1935). Yet Lumpkin, by the 1950s, had sunk into conservative Christianity and right-wing politics, serving as a key informer against her earlier communist acquaintances during the McCarthy purges.

If Lumpkin's career thus serves as a sort of mini-allegory of the demise of the American Left from its heyday in the 1930s to the dark days of McCarthyism, it is also the case that many women writers from the 1930s remained firm in their commitment to class struggle, but to little avail. Tillie Olsen and Meridel Le Sueur did important work in the 1930s but were virtually forgotten after World War II, largely as a result of official attempts to repress their work. Both would later reemerge in the 1970s as feminist icons, admired by a new generation of readers who often ignored their consistent devotion to class-based leftist politics. Myra Page, whose *Gathering Storm* and *Moscow Yankee* (1935) are two of the finest works of 1930s proletarian fiction, continued in somewhat the same vein in *With Sun in Our Blood* (1950), but with a focus on the life of a Tennessee mountain woman in the years leading up to World War I. The book was largely ignored when it was published. However, this book, like Le Sueur's *The Girl* and Tillie Olsen's *Yonnondio* (1930s novels not published in their entirety until 1978), would be reincarnated as a feminist work when it was republished as *Daughter of the Hills* in 1977 and again in 1986.

*With Sun in Our Blood* is, in some ways, a precursor to Harriette Arnow's fine, but less class-conscious, 1954 novel, *The Dollmaker*, which got a reasonable amount of recognition when it was published (it was runner-up to William Faulkner's *The Fable* for the 1955 National Book Award) but has become much more prominent after its rediscovery by feminist critics in the 1970s and its television adaptation (starring Jane Fonda in the title role) in 1984. *The Dollmaker*, which focuses on a Kentucky mountain family that moves to urban Detroit during World War II, shows Arnow's typical interest in the culture of the Cumberlands, but it also addresses a number of political issues (such as labor relations in the Detroit automobile plants) that relate directly to a tradition of leftist literature that grows out of the 1930s. Indeed, Glenda Hobbs suggests that *The Dollmaker* is really more a novel of the 1930s than the 1950s (161), while Denning calls the book "the last and perhaps the greatest proletarian novel of the age of the CIO [Congress of Industrial Organizations]" (467). However, the novel puts relatively little emphasis on proletarian labor struggles, concentrating instead on the domestic struggles of its protagonist, Gertie Nevels, who has much in common with Arnow, who herself having moved to Detroit with her husband in 1943.

*The Dollmaker* is an impressively comprehensive work that manages to include virtually all of the aspects of critique of consumer capitalism to be found in the modern leftist novel, even if some of them are in rather muted form. The book is particularly good in its evocation of the rampant commodification of modern American culture, as symbolized in the dolls and other carvings that Gertie first makes by hand as works of art but is then forced by economic pressures to mass-produce by machine as cheap trinkets. But class takes a back seat to gender and culture in the book, which emphasizes more than anything the individual strength and resourcefulness of its protagonist, a fact Arnow herself later emphasized in an interview when she insisted that "I don't like the term Marxist, any more than I like 'proletariat.' Neither term allows for the person's individual qualities to come through. When I write about poor people I don't want tags put on them or on me" (qtd. in Baer 60).

"*Ever*body's different," as Mama Gump says. But this emphasis on individual difference does little to promote collective action among those whose differences make them objects of oppression. Meanwhile, Arnow's rejection of class in favor of individualism shows the extent to which the effacement of class in postwar American culture goes beyond the attempts of critics to classify most leftist fiction as nonliterature, to salvage such works as *Native Son* and *The Grapes of Wrath* by divesting them of their class-based political content, or to argue that African American leftist fiction is really about race and women's leftist fiction is really about gender. In fact, leftist writers themselves have tended to shy away from class as their principal focus, beginning with the Popular Front turn to emphasis on antifascism instead of class struggle in the late 1930s. This effacement of class in American leftist culture was especially strong in the years immediately after World War II, when any American writer who chose to emphasize class struggle in his or her work would have been exposed to the threat of ridicule, blacklisting, or even imprisonment.

This situation impacted the work of American writers in a number of ways. One can cite numerous examples of writers who enhanced the reputations of their past writings (while ironically diminishing the quality of their subsequent writing) through an explicit turn away from communism in the long 1950s. John Dos Passos, who moved all the way from darling of the Left to darling of the Right during these years, is perhaps the most spectacular case, though his decline into conservative Republicanism was already under way in the 1930s and can be discerned in embryo in the gradual rightward slide of the successive volumes of the *U.S.A.* trilogy, a classic work of American leftist fiction nevertheless. Indeed, Dos Passos's Spanish Civil War novel, *Adventures of a Young Man* (1939), is already bitterly anticommunist. Almost as bad is Upton Sinclair, the grand old man of American leftist fiction, whose "Lanny Budd" series, a massive 11-volume chronicle of American history, begins in 1940 with early volumes that take a decidedly pro-Soviet leftist stance. Yet, by the final volume, *The Return of Lanny Budd* (1953), which takes the narrative to 1949 and the beginning of the Cold War, Lanny (who at one point in the volume is imprisoned in East Germany) battles for the American cause against the Russians.

Or one could cite the case of newcomer Norman Mailer, whose first novel, *The Naked and the Dead* (1948), showed a great deal of promise in its treatment of class, recalling predecessor texts of 1930s naturalism such as *The Grapes of Wrath* and *Native Son*.[14] But Mailer's novel has little in the way of a utopian dimension, confining its most radical political statement to a suggestion that it mattered very little who won World War II, because the two sides were not very different ideologically. Then one could trace Mailer's subsequent career through his next novel, *Barbary Shore* (1951), which includes a fairly sophisticated intellectual engagement with Marxist ideas about history but is strongly anti-Stalinist and oddly devoid of any real treatment of class. Again, the most radical statement is that the Soviets and Americans are pretty much the same, both being dominated by corporate routinization, whether the corporation be run by the private or government sector. In short, if *The Naked and the Dead* suggests that there is very little difference between a victorious America and its fascist foes from World War II, *Barbary Shore* tends to suggest that there is very little difference between late capitalist America and its Soviet Cold War opponent. Thus, Mailer's work of the long 1950s, far from suggesting utopian alternatives, goes almost as far as Nabokov's in suggesting that there *are* no real alternatives to the status quo. One could then follow the rest of Mailer's career, in which he tends to jettison Marxism altogether, pursuing an eccentric course of individualist leftism that leaves little room for any viable sense of classes as the collective agents of history but leaves a great deal of room for Mailer to be installed in the canon and embraced as a Great American Writer.[15]

Writers such as Dos Passos, Sinclair, and Mailer were presumably sincere in their turn away from Marxism, though one must wonder if such a turn, in the long 1950s, really demonstrated "independence" or whether it simply showed a capitulation, out of intimidation or indoctrination, to the anticommunist rhetoric that saturated Cold War America. Sometimes the pressure to conform to this rhetoric was quite direct. Even Saxton, in his 1959 novel *Bright Web in the Darkness*, gave in to the insistence of his publishers that he make this story of black shipyard workers more about race than class, meanwhile suppressing the fact that communist organizers had been central to the real events on which the book is based.[16] Saxton himself, however, remained loyal to his principles and to the working class, something that could not be said for other, more nakedly opportunistic, "reformed" leftist writers. One could, for example, cite such disgraceful examples as Budd Schulberg's *Waterfront* (1955), a novelization of the 1954 award-winning film *On the Waterfront*, scripted by Schulberg and directed by Elia Kazan. Like the film, the book focuses on the hardships faced by dockworkers but identifies a corrupt labor union, rather than an exploitative economic system, as the primary cause of these hardships. Neither film nor book suggests that the dockworkers can improve their lives through collective class action, both instead suggesting that villains such as the corrupt union can best be dealt with by government agencies. Accordingly, the works heroicize those who would contribute to the cause of justice by providing information to government investigators, who can then try to clean up the unions and meanwhile make sure that the frustrated workers are not driven into the seductive arms of opportunistic communists. In short, both book and film provide a rather transparent justification for the naming of names by both Kazan and Schulberg before the House Un-American Activities Committee (HUAC) a few years earlier, leading to lucrative subsequent careers for both, while their more principled leftist colleagues (many of whom they informed against) had their lives and careers maimed by imprisonment and the blacklist.

There are, fortunately, better books on this topic, including Howard Fast's *Silas Timberman* (1954) and Martha Dodd's *The Searching Light* (1955), both of which, perhaps because the authors themselves suffered persecution by the authorities, appreciate the human cost of the anticommunist terror that swept American campuses in the early years of the Cold War. Further, in their understanding of the fact that one need not actually be a communist to suffer from this terror, both books indicate the depth to which anticommunist terrorism penetrated American society at the time. *Silas Timberman* and *The Searching Light*, in dealing primarily with the tribulations of middle-class intellectuals, lack the intense dedication to the promotion of working-class solidarity that permeated the proletarian fiction of the 1930s and that was important in Fast's own *Clarkton* (1947), one of the rare old-style "strike" novels of the post–World War II years. Still, Dodd provides hints that English professor John Minot, her protagonist, may have the strength of character to oppose the loyalty oaths being imposed at Penfield University partly because of his own working-class background. And Fast at least gestures toward class in *Silas Timberman*, as when he indicates the working-class

Not quite as reprehensible as *Waterfront*, but still deeply troubling, is Mary McCarthy's *The Groves of Academe* (1952), another work from the New York Intellectual family of authors. In a sense, McCarthy's novel acknowledges the anticommunist purges that swept American college campuses in the early years of the long 1950s, ruining the lives and careers of hundreds of good and decent academics and putting a Cold War chill on academic freedom that has to this day not completely thawed.[17] For McCarthy, these purges are treated essentially as a joke.[18] Moreover, foreshadowing the recent right-wing furor over "political correctness," McCarthy suggests that some American universities were so careful to avoid persecuting leftist professors that a communist affiliation could even be an advantage, protecting otherwise unworthy academics from dismissal.[19]

background of his eponymous protagonist or when he shows that protagonist longing for the sense of belonging to a larger group (read class) that he associates with Mike Leslie, a union leader he meets in the course of his victimization by the anticommunist purges that sweep Clemington University. Fast's book is also particularly good in indicating the centrality to the anticommunist rhetoric of the period of the excoriation of class as a category that is somehow un-American.

In a somewhat similar vein, Abraham Polonsky, in *Season of Fear* (1956), shows the anticommunist purges on a college campus spilling over into the community at large. By focusing on the terror experienced by his protagonist, a perfectly conventional, apolitical engineer, Polonsky extends the literary exploration of the effects of the purges beyond the Left to provide important reminders that the repressive atmosphere of the 1950s meant that no American was entirely safe from political persecution, no matter how conventionally bourgeois his or her attitudes and lifestyle. Indeed, a critical response to HUAC and the purges of which it was a central part forms the basis of an entire family of leftist novels in the long 1950s, many of them written by victims of those purges. It is telling, however, that the novel that best integrates a critique of the anticommunist repression with a narrative of class conflict was written by an immigrant, Stefan Heym, whose own earlier experience as a refugee from Nazi Germany made McCarthyite America look all too familiar. Indeed, *Goldsborough* (1953), which effectively places its story of a coal miners' strike within the broader context of American politics in the early Cold War years, was published the year after Heym fled political persecution in the United States and returned to Europe to live and work in East Germany. In the book, anticommunist hysteria provides the most effective weapon used against the striking miners by their opponents in the local political machine, who seek to associate the strikers with antiAmerican communist agitation. Given Heym's personal background, it is not surprising that he links the repressive atmosphere of America in the McCarthy era with that of Germany under the Nazis.[20] As one of his characters, a lawyer who supports the strikers, puts it, the American tactic of branding political opponents as communists is "the new way of putting people into concentration camps. No barbed wire, no guard towers, just a word branded on their forehead" (451).

Alvah Bessie's *The Un-Americans* (1957), based on Bessie's experience with the HUAC investigations and his subsequent imprisonment and blacklisting, also links the paranoid politics of the purges to those of Nazi Germany, while effectively reaching back to the official U.S. policy of nonintervention in the Spanish Civil War as a key marker of the moral bankruptcy of American democracy. As with so many leftist novels from this period, *The Un-Americans* focuses more on intellectuals than on workers, though it is also the case that Benjamin Blau, its principal protagonist, is a dedicated communist who seeks to overcome his own bourgeois origins and to establish a genuine sense of solidarity with the working class. Bessie, who suffered imprisonment and blacklisting, understands the anticommunist purges firsthand, as does Carl Marzani, who, in 1946, was dismissed from the State Department on suspicions of communist sympathies, thus becoming the first government employee to be removed under the new McCarran rider to the Appropriations Bill of that year. He subsequently spent three years as a political prisoner, during which time he authored *We Can Be Friends*, a study of the origins of the Cold War. After prison, Marzani became an important leftist filmmaker and publisher, and his superb, but virtually unknown, 1958 novel, *The Survivor*, is one of the best existing accounts of the atmosphere of simultaneous hysteria and cold-blooded opportunism that was sweeping the U.S. government in the years immediately following World War II. *The Survivor* is also one of the most class-conscious novels of the long 1950s, showing a strong sense of solidarity with the working class.

In this sense, however, Marzani's novel is highly unusual, and most anti-McCarthy novels focus more on the tribulations of leftist intellectuals than on the working class, culminating in that eulogistic summa of the woes of the American Left in the long 1950s, Clancy Sigal's fine leftist road novel, *Going Away* (1961). Sigal's novels have been, with some justification, described by Fredric Jameson as being among "those rare cultural objects which can be said to have overt political and social content" (*Signatures* 23). Yet it is only in *Weekend in Dinlock* (1960), which is, tellingly, set in Britain (where Sigal spent decades in exile) rather than America, that class, especially the working class, is a major issue in Sigal's work. Meanwhile, though cultural objects with "overt political and social content" are not nearly as rare in the long 1950s as many might think, even works that overtly focus on working-class experience during the period tend to do so in ways that do little or nothing to encourage visions of collective working-class oppositional action. Many, such as Himes's *If He Hollers Let Him Go* (1945), Willard Motley's *Knock on Any Door* (1947), William Gardner Smith's *Anger at Innocence* (1950), Samuel Ornitz's *Bride of the Sabbath* (1951), and Warren Miller's *The Cool World* (1959), employ essentially naturalistic techniques to describe the grim horrors of poverty and alienation, often with central ethnic themes but seldom with any real focus on class consciousness or collective action toward the goal of utopian alternatives.

The classic case here might be Harvey Swados's *On the Line* (1957), which sympathetically portrays, through a series of vignettes, the hardships faced by workers in an automobile assembly plant in upstate New York but lacks any real sense that these workers might actually take collective action to improve their plight. The workers have very little in the way of class consciousness, and, though the plant is unionized, the union seems to be more of a nuisance to most of the men than a source of hope.[21] In fact, the only hope for improvement, however remote, that the book presents lies in escaping from the working class altogether.[22] In this sense, the book is a throwback to such classics of British "working-class" fiction as Thomas Hardy's *Jude the Obscure* or D. H. Lawrence's *Sons and Lovers*, while also echoing the more contemporaneous works of British authors such as Stan Barstow, John Braine, and Keith Waterhouse.[23] Meanwhile, the failure of *On the Line* to envision successful working-class collective action is probably indicative of Swados's own individualistic ideology, which emphasizes independence to the extent that collective action is rendered nearly impossible. The book, therefore, demonstrates, inadvertently, the limitations of independent radicalism (however popular it might be among many on the Left these days), which may allow for cogent critiques of the abuses of capitalism but can do very little in the way of mounting opposition to those abuses.

The "independent" orientation of the radicalism of Swados (and of so many other 1950s leftists, particularly the New York Intellectuals) leads quite naturally and directly into the particularly individualistic (and often incoherent) nature of the radical political movements of the 1960s.[24] More than one observer has noted that the recent turn toward politics in literary studies apparently has its roots in these very movements, in which so many leading intellectuals of the 1980s and 1990s participated as students. One could argue, though, that the radical activism of the 1960s, informed more by emotional reaction to oppression than thoughtful analysis of the foundations of oppression, provided a particularly poor political foundation for intellectuals. The classic literary expression of this phenomenon may be found in Thomas Pynchon's *Vineland* (1990), in which a group of radical students takes over a California campus in the 1960s and proclaims it the independent "People's Republic of Rock and Roll." Life in the new, presumably utopian, republic is informed by a great deal of "dissent from official reality," such as public sexuality and drug-taking, but little theoretical reflection. As Pynchon's narrator sardonically notes, "None of these kids had been doing any analysis" (205).

Pynchon also shows a good understanding, in *Vineland*, of the fact that the radical political movements of the 1960s were seriously hampered by their lack of connection to the class-based movements of the past, especially from the 1950s. Indeed, the American New Left was consistently more interested in being new than in being Left in those years. It is certainly clear that the political movements of the 1960s (recall all those television images of benighted hard hats jeering at, or even physically attacking, idealistic students) were particularly lacking in solidarity with the working class or understanding of class issues in general, however effective those movements might have been at calling attention to issues surrounding race and gender. Given this fact, the failure of 1960s-style politics to overcome the hegemony of bourgeois ideology is not very surprising, even without reminders by figures such as Jameson that "conscious ideologies of revolt, revolution, and even negative critique are—far from merely being 'co-opted' by the system—an integral and functional part of the system's own internal strategies" (*Postmodernism* 203). Actually, Jameson is here summarizing the conclusions of Jean Baudrillard, but Jameson himself consistently argues the same view, as when he notes specifically with regard to the 1960s that

> the values of the civil rights movement and the women's movement are thus preeminently cooptable because they are already--as ideals--inscribed in the very ideology of capitalism itself, . . . which has a fundamental interest in social equality to the degree to which it needs to transform as many [as possible] of its subjects or its citizens into identical consumers interchangeable with everybody else. (*Signatures* 36)

The ideals to which Jameson here refers are the ideals of the Enlightenment, and Jameson is perfectly aware that Marx himself was heavily influenced by these same ideals. Jameson thus notes that the "slogans of populism and the ideals of racial justice and sexual equality" so popular in the 1960s had been used centuries earlier by the emergent bourgeoisie as an ideological critique of the ancien régime in Europe but that these same notions are also central to the "socialist denunciation of capitalism" (*Signatures* 36). However, Jameson goes on to argue that Marxism, while including the ideals of the Enlightenment, goes beyond those ideals by grounding them in a "materialist theory of social evolution" that demonstrates the inability of the capitalist system to realize its own ideals of social justice (36–37). In short, however convenient racism and sexism might have historically been as props for certain capitalist practices, capitalism can, at least to some extent, absorb demands for equality on the basis of race and gender, because race and gender equality are not structurally incompatible with the workings of a capitalist economy, however effectively racism and sexism might have served as tactical weapons in the arsenal of bourgeois ideology.[25] Socialism, with its emphasis on the obliteration of class distinctions, is thus the only position that cannot be co-opted by capitalism, which must maintain class inequality in order to survive.

My readings of the leftist fiction of the long 1950s, most of which is realist in its orientation, show that this fiction is far richer than most critics have been willing (or able) to admit. We certainly need to do more to resurrect this culture. On the other hand, far more than simply celebrating the fact that writers such as Heym, Arnow, Killens, Marzani, Stevenson, and Du Bois were producing admirable works during the long 1950s, we also need to interrogate the shortcomings of the leftist fiction of this period. Among other things, the relatively weak treatment of class in the leftist fiction of the long 1950s shows that the erosion in the use of class as the central category of anticapitalist critique had begun by the end of World War II and can be attributed at least in part to the pressures placed on American leftist writers by the repressive climate of the early Cold War years. This drift away from a focus on class can, in fact, already be observed in the Popular Front culture of the late 1930s. This historical fact makes it clear that the recent postMarxist rejection of class is not simply an increase in sophistication and should give pause to those who have so enthusiastically jumped aboard the bandwagon of post-Marxism in recent years. This rejection of class not only grows directly out of the anticommunist hysteria of the Cold War but is also rooted in the conscious compromises made more than half a century ago to meet the crisis posed by the rise of European fascism. The origins of the work of postMarxists such as Laclau and Mouffe may thus be located not in the presumably emancipatory politics of the 1960s but in the repressive politics of the long 1950s and the crisis situation of the late 1930s and early 1940s.[26] To abandon class-based critique at this point in history is surely to ignore the obvious reality of continuing class inequality within the global system of late capitalism. It is also to perpetuate a trend begun in response to fascism and McCarthyism and thus to let these supposedly discredited and long-dead bogies rise from the grave to enjoy the last laugh, having posthumously completed their historical mission of destroying communism and making the world safe for an unfettered global capitalism.

As one would expect, the leftist fiction of the long 1950s certainly contains stronger utopian elements than the mainstream literary fiction of writers such as Nabokov. Still, the utopian energies of even leftist fiction are relatively weak during this period, as one might perhaps expect given the embattled status of leftist thought in general at the time. From that point of view, one might expect the era's most powerful utopian energies to reside not in "literary" works at all but in works of popular culture, American popular culture being the triumphant phenomenon of the decade. Granted, the utopian vision that resides in popular culture is almost by definition a form of commodified escapism, though it is telling that, idealized television sitcoms aside, the escape provided by popular culture in the long 1950s was often into a world even *worse* than the world of reality. This phenomenon might be the most telling of all commentaries on the loss of utopian energy in the long 1950s. In the next chapter, I discuss the utopian elements in the popular fiction of the decade, concentrating in particular on the pulp fiction of Jim Thompson, which typically provides visions not of an ideal suburban enclave of peace and prosperity but of a nightmare world of crime and violence.

# Monsters, Cowboys, and Criminals: Jim Thompson and the Dark Turn in American Popular Culture in the Long 1950s

Some of the weakness of the leftist realist fiction of the 1950s can be attributed to the fact, noted by Alan Wald in much of his work, that leftist writers were driven into popular genres in the decade to escape censorship and political persecution. But, again, the numerous works in popular genres from the long 1950s that have clearly leftist orientations tend to be weak in their treatment of class—and, correspondingly, in their suggestion of utopian alternatives to capitalism. The same can be said for the more mainstream popular fiction of the long 1950s as well, even though such fiction, almost by definition, contains strong elements of fantasy and romance that have considerable utopian potential. Drawing upon Max Weber's account of the routinization of life under capitalism, Fredric Jameson has suggested, in a variety of places, that the persistence of forms of romance in Western culture even into the twentieth century arises from a utopian longing for the absent magic that no longer exists in the modern world. In particular, Jameson argues that romance can offer utopian alternatives in a postmodern world in which realism, once itself potent as a social and political force has itself become reified, losing its utopian energy. In this case, for Jameson, romance re-emerges to "offer the possibility of sensing other historical rhythms, and of demonic or Utopian transformations of a real now unshakably set in place" (*Political* 104).

From this point of view, it perhaps comes as no surprise that the long 1950s saw a veritable explosion in the production and consumption of popular literature, though the emphasis in this literature was definitely more on demonic than utopian transformations of reality. During this period, realism was on the decline in terms of both production and critical assessment. Meanwhile, the critical establishment of the period turned its back on realism in favor of modernism, but modernism was of little uto-

pian value to the general population, if only because it was far too difficult (and, for most people, unpleasant) to read. Various genres of popular fiction then emerged to fill the void left by a now moribund realism,
though it should also be kept in mind that strong material and social
forces, such as increased literacy and more efficient techniques for the
production and distribution of cheap paperback texts, also contributed to
the proliferation of popular fiction in the long 1950s.

What is striking about the popular fiction of postwar years, however,
is the extent to which even it lacks utopian energy, no matter the specific
genre. In fact, while this literature consistently offers readers glimpses of
an alternative reality, this alternative is, if anything, typically *worse* than
the present-day reality of America. Works of what might be called popular realism occasionally pointed out social problems but suggested that
these problems could be overcome without fundamental changes to the
system. Thus, of the decade's two signature works in this category, *Peyton Place* (1956) assures us that suburban bigotry can be overcome by the
sufficiently virtuous, even without changing the structure of suburbia,
while *The Man in the Gray Flannel Suit* (1955) soothes us with a demonstration that it is possible to be happy without making any fundamental
changes to our system or its institutions. Meanwhile, genres such as science fiction and the Western flourished as never before during the long
1950s, but even these genres, which have a powerful inherent utopian
dimension, tended to be weak in utopian energies. The new worlds explored in science fiction tended more toward dystopia than utopia, while
the Western, while still sometimes reminiscing nostalgically about the
Old West, also began critically to interrogate former utopian visions of
life on the frontier.

In any case, it is telling that both of these classic American genres
were easily eclipsed in popularity by crime fiction, and a crime fiction
often so dark and brutal that the hard-boiled classics of the 1930s seemed
utopian by comparison. Meanwhile, all those embarrassingly popular
Mickey Spillane novels provide repeated evidence that the current system is fine, as long as we are willing to look the other way while tough
guys like Mike Hammer make short work of those who would threaten
the system. Indeed, despite his radical nonconformism and distaste for
bureaucracy, Hammer himself verifies the virtues of American individualism, while his evil enemies tend to be precisely the Others of whom the
1950s were so frightened: communists and psychopaths. They are, in
fact, generally communist psychopaths, communism itself being in Spillane a form of psychopathology, which explains why his communist
characters spend so much time (and take so much sick pleasure in) strip-
ping and whipping helpless females and also endorses Hammer's own
sadistic violence as a form of necessary therapy.

All of this is not surprising. One can certainly make a good argument
that the bestsellers of the long 1950s capture the mainstream sense of the

decade far more accurately than did the "literary" works of writers such as Nabokov, Bellow, and Heller. If the decade itself was bereft of utopian energy, one would expect that fact to be reflected in the decade's popular fiction. Granted there were popular works with genuine romance elements, but these generally contained utopian energies of the "bad," nostalgic kind. For example, the historical romances of Thomas Costain were wildly popular, suggesting the desire of many in the decade to retreat to an older, more heroic, and prenuclear time. But the best selling author of the decade (by a wide margin) was Spillane, whose brutal works provided an escapist framework within which readers (especially if they were male WASPs) could live out their fantasies of sex or violence or, even better, both at the same time. Thus, Geoffrey O'Brien concludes that, with Spillane, "the hardboiled novel comes full circle: a genre that originated in a concern for realism now provides the trappings for the wildest of fantasizing" (102).

Spillane's fantasies of violent retribution against criminals and communists participates in a skepticism about law enforcement that is echoed in any number of other products of American popular culture in the long 1950s. One recalls, for example, Will Kane's disgust at the end of *High Noon* (1952), when he demonstrates that, like the banditos of *The Treasure of the Sierra Madre* (1948), he ultimately has no need for a stinking badge, emblem of law, order, and capitalist routinization. Film noir may be the outstanding example of this phenomenon, but it is also reflected in the crime fiction of the decade, in which the line between law enforcers and law breakers was seriously blurred. This blurring is in keeping with a general postmodernist blurring of boundaries, but it is also a specific sign of the era's anxieties, emanating from Hiroshima and Nagasaki, that the black-and-white, good versus evil terms of wartime propaganda (building on the longtime national discourse of savage war) had been a radical misrepresentation of reality. Spillane's Hammer is an exemplary figure here. Seemingly desperate to restore a sense of stable polar opposition between good guys and bad guys, Spillane demonizes Hammer's psycho-commie criminal foes. However, in order to be able to cope with such savage opponents, Hammer is forced to resort to savagery himself, thus falling back into a long American tradition, outlined by Slotkin in *Gunfighter Nation*, of authorizing savage tactics in order to win savage wars. But Hammer may go a bit too far; in the long 1950s, the former confidence that such tactics really were authorized is seriously diminished, creating a constant air of anxiety.

Certainly, there were crime-solvers of the decade who continued in the relatively virtuous (if already morally ambiguous) footsteps of Dashiell Hammett's Sam Spade and Raymond Chandler's Philip Marlowe. For example, Ross MacDonald's Lew Archer was the centerpiece of a long sequence of novels that spanned the long 1950s (and would continue well beyond), from *The Moving Target* (1949), to *The Far Side of the*

*Dollar* (1964). Archer is a detective very much in the Hammett-Chandler hard-boiled tradition, walking a fine line between sin and redemption but ultimately providing a moral center (and thus a utopian dimension) in an otherwise corrupt world. In general, however, the private eyes or even the cops (as in the case of Chester Himes's Grave Digger Jones and Coffin Ed Johnson) became more and more like the criminals they pursued. Moreover, in an even more telling development, the crime fiction of the long 1950s often shifted away from a focus on cops and detectives, making the criminals themselves the central characters. For example, Patricia Highsmith was able to make her Tom Ripley, a psychotic killer, the "hero" of a sequence of novels, beginning with *The Talented Mr. Ripley* (1955). Ripley, in fact, is a crucial figure of the decade, not only because he is a criminal hero but because he is able, chameleonlike, to switch identities from one moment to the next, thus anticipating Jameson's later observations about the instability of personal identity in the postmodern age.

For Jameson, the loss of historical sense and psychic fragmentation of the individual subject under postmodernism lead to a schizophrenic experience of the world. Drawing upon the work of Jacques Lacan, Jameson sees schizophrenia primarily as a loss of any sense of temporal continuity. The schizophrenic, he says,

is condemned to live in a perpetual present with which the various moments of his or her past have little connection and for which there is no conceivable future on the horizon. In other words, schizophrenic experience is an experience of isolated, disconnected, discontinuous material signifiers which fail to link into a coherent sequence. The schizophrenic does not know personal identity in our sense, since our feeling of identity depends on our sense of the persistence of the "I" and the "me" over time. ("Postmodernism and Consumer Society" 119)

The serial identities of Highsmith's Ripley correspond well to this description, and it is clear that Ripley's murderous tendencies arise largely from this lack of any sense of the persistence of his identity over time. After all, he cannot be held responsible for any of his past actions if he is no longer the same person who committed those actions.

Ripley tends to travel in a relatively affluent world, but other crime novelists of the long 1950s, such as Charles Willeford and David Goodis, explored seamier locales that made the worlds traveled by Spade and Marlowe seem like clean well-lighted places. Meanwhile, the schizophrenia, seediness, and skepticism of the crime fiction of the decade come together in their most spectacular form in the work of the notorious Jim Thompson, who may thus be the most representative crime writer of the long 1950s. According to Tony Hilfer, for example, "no one has yet taken the possibilities of the crime novel farther than Jim Thompson" (137). Indeed, Thompson was not only the darkest and most outrageous of the pulp fiction writers of the 1950s but also a writer who consistently transcended the genre, introducing literary elements more reminiscent of the works of modernist and avant-garde writers.

Thompson was, in his own marginal way, a prominent figure in the American culture of the second half of the twentieth century. He was the author of 29 published novels, several of which were made into films, including such highly commercial efforts as the two film versions of *The Getaway* (in 1972 and 1993) and the film version of *The Grifters* (1990). He was instrumental in the writing of the screenplays of *The Killing* (1956) and *Paths of Glory* (1957), two important films that helped launch the directorial career of Kubrick. He would even become, years after his death, the protagonist of a novel by the award-winning crime novelist Domenic Stansberry.

Thompson was also the subject of a literary revival in the 1980s and 1990s, a revival partly spurred by the crucial role given Thompson in Geoffrey O'Brien's rousing survey of pulp crime fiction, *Hardboiled America: Lurid Paperbacks and the Masters of Noir* (first published in 1981). This revival saw the majority of his novels come back into print and that led to the publication of two book-length biographies, Michael McCauley's *Jim Thompson: Sleep with the Devil* (1991) and Robert Polito's award-winning *Savage Art: A Biography of Jim Thompson* (1995). During that revival, Thompson's work also received considerable critical attention, including the publication of a book-length critical study, Gay Brewer's *Laughing Like Hell* (1996). Thompson was even a central figure in Timothy Arthur Dayton's 1990 Duke University doctoral dissertation on "U.S. literary modernism."

Yet Thompson remains one of those odd figures who are famous for being unknown. A mere footnote to the narrative of modern American literature, he is a writer whose work remains noncanonical, excluded from the university reading lists and classrooms, except perhaps in specialized classes on crime fiction. Thompson's curious double status as excluded pariah and legendary icon in itself suggests a great deal about the cultural climate of America in the second half of the twentieth century and could no doubt provide material for a fascinating case study in the politics of canonization. For my purposes, however, what is most interesting is the stark contrast between the resolutely anti-utopian nature of Thompson's fiction, written mostly in the long 1950s, and nostalgic visions of that era as a halcyon time before the pastoral tranquility of American life was disrupted by the upheavals of the 1960s.

Thompson served a considerable literary apprenticeship, mostly in pulp crime magazines, prior to the publication of his first novel, *Now and on Earth*, in 1942. Described by Polito as "a thinly veiled proletarian memoir in the style of the 1930s," *Now and on Earth* quite clearly grew out of the proletarian culture of the 1930s (5). The book chronicles several weeks in the life of a working-class family, including substantial descriptions of the experiences of its narrator/protagonist, Jim Dillon, as he works in a San Diego aircraft factory. To this extent, Thompson here carries out the call of leftist cultural leaders, such as Mike Gold, for workers to document their experience through writing fiction. Moreover, *Now and on Earth* does have a potentially powerful anticapitalist message: in its description of the radical alienation of its protagonist, it can be taken, as can essentially all of Thompson's novels, as a critique of the maiming of the individual psyche within the context of modern capitalism. Beyond this, however, *Now and on Earth* has very little in common with the proletarian literature of the 1930s. It does not, for example, suggest that socialism might provide a preferable alternative to capitalism. In fact, the book contains no collective utopian dimension whatsoever. For Jim Dillon, hell is other people: he is so alienated from his family and coworkers that his dream of an ideal life involves a vision, not of community but of solitude, where he can pursue his dream of being a writer in peace, without quarreling children and nagging women swirling about his head like shrapnel. Like Greta Garbo, he wants to be alone.

Thompson's second novel, *Heed the Thunder* (1947) is, in many ways, less dark than *Now and on Earth*, but it is still very much indicative of the almost total lack of any genuine utopian imagination in Thompson's work. *Heed the Thunder* is a historical novel, based on Thompson's own family background, that details the trials and tribulations of the Fargo clan of Verdon, Nebraska, roughly during the period 1907–1914.[1] As a historical novel, *Heed the Thunder* seems to have considerable utopian potential, if only because it is set during the time of the most rapid change in American history. One recalls here Georg Lukács's belief that socialist writers in the twentieth century should look for inspiration to the great bourgeois realist novelists of the early nineteenth century. In particular, Lukács suggests in *The Historical Novel* that realist historical novels of the early nineteenth century were particularly powerful because they captured the sense of sweeping historical change that accompanied the rise to power of the European bourgeoisie. These novels thus contained a powerful utopian component, because they showed a strong faith in the possibility — even the inevitability — of revolutionary historical change.

*Heed the Thunder* often shows a strong sense of the incredibly rapid changes that took place in American society with the rise of consumer capitalism in the early years of the twentieth century. Indeed, the "thunder" that is being heeded apparently consists of the signs of capitalist modernization that are beginning to be felt even on the rural prairie of Nebraska. Most of these signs, however, are presented as negative, pointing not to a utopian future but to the darkness of Thompson's later fiction. To make the point clear, Thompson ends his agrarian historical novel with a paean to the land, in what seems to promise to be a utopian moment. But it is a moment that points to a traditional past that the book has depicted as already in the throes of destruction by capitalist modernization. To drive the point home, Thompson ends his song to the land on the darkest possible note, describing the land of America as a land "that was slipping so surely, so swiftly, into the black abyss of the night" (297). In short, the revolutionary changes underway in early twentieth-century America simply serve to make the rich richer and the poor poorer, solidifying, rather than destroying, the power of the bourgeois ruling class, a power that would be further consolidated in the coming century, not just by advertising and consumerization but also by world wars in Europe and imperial military actions around the world.

Given this dark beginning, perhaps it is no surprise that Thompson turned to crime fiction with his next novel, *Nothing More Than Murder* (1949). This early effort is, by Thompson's later standards, a relatively conventional crime novel, described by Polito as being, at least on the surface, "a classic doomed love triangle/insurance scam shocker from the tradition of James M. Cain" (314). Still, *Nothing More Than Murder* already contains many of the elements that would come to distinguish Thompson's later and better-known crime novels. The novel is narrated by protagonist Joe Wilmot, thus providing a first-person account of its central crime from the perspective of the criminal. Moreover, Wilmot, like many of Thompson's murderers, is an oddly sympathetic figure, himself a victim of an impoverished childhood and an unfair social system. Having spent most of his childhood in an orphanage and his adolescence in a gruesome reform school (where he was sent for what was essentially an innocent mistake, not a real crime), Joe is determined to do whatever is necessary to advance in the world and escape his tortured background. But this advancement is continually thwarted by Joe's background, which marks him as a delinquent in the manner described by Michel Foucault in *Discipline and Punish* (1978, translated from *Surveiller et punir*, 1975).

In short, Joe is an essentially decent man, a man with considerable talents and abilities and a man who, because of the larger circumstances in the carceral society that surrounds him, is doomed to a life of failure and despair. Joe's story also anticipates Thompson's later novels in its detailed presentation of Joe's work as the manager of the movie house that Elizabeth has inherited from her father. Indeed, beginning with *Now and on Earth*, Thompson's novels, as a whole, show his characters actually at work and on the job far more than is typical of American fiction. One can perhaps see this focus most clearly in *Bad Boy* (1953) and *Roughneck* (1954), the two highly fictionalized volumes of Thompson's autobiography. These volumes (which together detail his life from early childhood to the publication of his first novel) are truly striking in the intensity of their focus on the economic dimension of Thompson's life, particularly on the various jobs at which he worked in the years prior to his eventual success as a writer. Both *Bad Boy* and *Roughneck* are essentially narratives of work, and the typical movement from chapter to chapter simply follows Thompson from one job to another. Meanwhile, many of Thompson's novels, especially the later ones, include detailed descriptions of work at various jobs Thompson himself once performed, including oil-field narratives such as *Wild Town* (1957), *Texas by the Tail* (1965) and *South of Heaven* (1967) and hotel narratives such as *A Swell-Looking Babe* (1954) and, again, *Wild Town* (1957). Even Thompson's crime novels often present their characters as simply doing their jobs, which may be extralegal but which do not differ in any real way from the more respectable activities of capitalist businessmen. Here, *The Grifters* (1963), which focuses on con man Roy Dillon, and *Texas by the Tail*, which focuses on professional gambler Mitch Corley, are particularly important.

In every case, the economic details presented by Thompson not only enrich our understanding of the texture of the characters' lives but also provide some trenchant criticisms of the American capitalist system in which the characters must operate. In *Nothing More Than Murder*, Joe remains trapped not just within miserable private personal relations but within the dog-eat-dog public world of modern capitalism. In this world, he has some initial success as the operator of a movie house by driving his only competitor, Bower, out of business. But, in this system, what goes around comes around, and Joe's success at the expense of his competitors turns to failure when movie house mogul Sol Panzer decides to move into town and to drive Joe out of business, much as Joe had done to Bower. Unlike Bower, Joe is clever enough to see it coming, but there is little he can do in the face of Panzer's superior resources — not to mention the fact that Joe is not functioning at full strength due to the distractions surrounding the seemingly fake, but ultimately actual, death of Elizabeth. Joe is perfectly aware that Panzer will win their confrontation and that he will lose, just as the basic design of capitalism ensures that one man's gain must come at the expense of another man's loss, because "the money had to come from somewhere" (188). As Joe puts it, trying for stoicism in the midst of his mounting hysteria, "That's business" (119).

Joe remains disgusted by the fact that he is forced to exploit others to get anywhere in life, but he concludes that, under the current system, he has little choice: "But when everyone else is the same what choice have you got?" (66). At one point, however, he does come close to proposing a radical political solution. Looking around him, he concludes that the only people he knows of who are "dependable and hard working" are capitalism's losers, the winners being nothing but glorifying con men. Then he envisions a possible collective action of these losers to seize power from the unscrupulous winners: "I wondered why, when there was so damned many of 'em, they didn't get together and run things themselves. And I made up my mind if they ever did get an organization — a going organization, that is — they could count me in!" (68).

This evocation of a collective takeover by capitalism's underclass has clear socialist overtones, though Joe's proviso that he would join only a "going organization" would seem to exclude the then-dysfunctional American Communist Party, of which Thompson had been a member in the 1930s. On the other hand, one could also argue that, in the cultural climate of 1949 America, this seeming exclusion of the Communist Party was absolutely necessary in order for Thompson to be able to make such a statement at all. Indeed, one finds a number of vague references to socialist ideas in Thompson's later novels as well, but always in a disguised form, suggesting the sense of Thompson (and his publishers) that any criticism of capitalism that included the proposal of a socialist alternative to capitalism could be couched only in a sort of Aesopian language that would leave room for more innocuous interpretations.

Nevertheless, the stridency of Thompson's denunciations of American capitalism remains striking, especially within the repressive climate of the 1950s, when even more overtly leftist writers tended to retreat from the radical class-warfare stances that marked the proletarian culture of the 1930s. Thus, McCauley argues that Thompson's crime novels are really "subversive, sociopolitical novels" that draw their principal power from the fact that "his criminals and their actions are only the most extreme examples of a whole world gone wrong" (242). Polito, meanwhile, is more specific, noting that reading the works of Marx was one of the crucial formative experiences of Thompson's life as a writer. Polito quotes Thompson as having told a colleague at the Writers' Project, Gordon Friesen, that reading Marx was "the turning point in his life ... his first real education." Marx, Thompson apparently proclaimed, had "given him the words to understand his life" (128). Importantly, Polito concludes that much of this basic Marxist outlook survived the 1930s and Thompson's membership in the party during that decade. He quotes the testimony of another Thompson friend, Pierre Rissient, that Thompson continued to see all of literature—and the world—through a fundamentally Marxist lens as late as the 1960s (128–29).

Marxism does indeed provide a crucial framework within which to read Thompson's critique of American capitalism, even if socialism does not appear to provide, for Thompson, a strong utopian alternative to capitalism. For example, much of the criticism of capitalism in Thompson's crime fiction predictably arises from Brechtian suggestions of close parallels between the activities of capitalists and those of criminals. Thus, the narrator of *Savage Night* (1953), diminutive hit man Charlie Bigger (aka Carl Bigelow), is not a psychotic killer who murders out of sickness, though his psyche does unravel by the end of the text. He is a professional who kills for money. At the same time, in keeping with his five-foot height, he is a small-time criminal, a small fish in a capitalist pond where the smaller fish like him tend to be eaten by bigger ones. Like most of Thompson's killers, he is thus as much a victim as a villain. And his primary victimizer is The Man, a big-time crime boss, who forces Bigger out of retirement, assigning him to eliminate a former bookie slated to testify against The Man's criminal operations. And, while Bigger is a downtrodden and marginal figure, The Man is a solid citizen indeed, famous nationwide not for his criminal activities but for his "legitimate" business operations. In addition to his crime syndicate, he controls "shipping companies and distilleries, race tracks and jobbing houses, wire services and loan companies." He is, in fact, a walking deconstruction of the opposition between the legitimate and the illegitimate. He is a well-known supporter of major labor unions, and his credentials include letters from top labor leaders thanking him for his support; yet his own businesses are not unionized, thus allowing him to exploit his employees more thoroughly. Despite his control of race tracks and loan companies, he is a prominent supporter of legislation banning race tracks and loan sharking. And no one is likely to call him to account for these inconsistencies or for any of his other questionable activities, because "he's too big, too powerful" (56). In Thompson's modern America, anyone who is rich enough and powerful enough can literally get away with murder — and is likely to take advantage of the opportunity.

In *The Killer Inside Me* (1952), Thompson's best-known novel, narrator-protagonist Lou Ford makes similar comments about the collapse of boundaries between the respectable and the disreputable in modern America, telling young Johnnie Pappas (shortly before he murders him) that, in the modern world, the police are often crooks and that it is often the crooks who must do police duty. Moreover, in a seeming anticipation of the later rise of the religious Right as a political force (and the subsequent scramble of politicians to claim a greater moral stature than their opponents), he tells Johnnie that, today, the "politicians are preachers, and the preachers are politicians" (78). On the other hand, they, of course, have no objection to any comforts that the rich and powerful might seek. The rich and powerful, in fact, can do anything they want. Later, when Ford himself is arrested and stashed in the "cooler," where he had earlier murdered Johnnie Pappas, he explains that the authorities can do this to him because "they can do anything they're big enough to do and you're little enough to take" (138). In Thompson's world, the rich and powerful, who flout the presumed rules, are likely to be protected, even heroicized by the system; when the marginal little men whom the rich and powerful prey upon commit smaller crimes in an effort to survive, they are likely to be caught and punished.

The motif of the invincibility of the rich and powerful culminates, as do numerous Thompson themes, in *Pop. 1280* (1964), arguably Thompson's single finest book. Here, narrator/protagonist Nick Corey, a seemingly oafish small-town Southern sheriff, goes on a killing spree, announcing that, as the second coming of Christ, he is obligated to mete out suffering and punishment. There is in this motif a great deal of religious satire, of course, as Corey points up the absurdity of the vengeful God of the Judaeo-Christian tradition, noting that it is his job, as Christ, to make sure that people suffer just for being people (206). But there is also a typical Thompson commentary on class in this motif. Corey acknowledges that the rich and powerful are the most sinful of all but sadly explains that he is not allowed to take his vengeance upon them. After all, religion being an opiate of the masses, the very concept of God is part of an ideological superstructure that works to the advantage of the rich and powerful. Therefore, Corey compensates by meting out double punishment on "white trash and Negroes," working hard at his job because the Lord (whose job it is to see that workers stay in their place and create surplus value for the bourgeoisie by doing more work than they are paid for) "liketh to see a man bustin' his ass during workin' hours" (206).

On the other hand, while the rich and powerful as a group remain invincible, there is no guarantee that a given rich and powerful individual will remain so. Thompson's central characters are especially insecure, being marginal from the beginning. But no one in Thompson's fiction is immune to the exigencies of capitalist insecurity. This theme appears repeatedly in Thompson's work, perhaps most strikingly in *Roughneck* (1954), the second of Thompson's two volumes of "autobiography." Despite the obvious suppression of any discussion of Thompson's involvement in the Communist Party during the 1930s, *Roughneck* includes a number of telling commentaries about capitalism. For one thing, Thompson the protagonist continually slides back and forth between the "legitimate" economy of capitalism and the underworld economy of crime and in ways that suggest that the line between these two worlds is not so distinct as one might think. In *Roughneck*, capitalism *is* crime, and businessmen work to bilk their customers just as surely as con men work to dupe their marks. *Roughneck* also again includes several capsule summaries of capitalism, as when Durkin, Thompson's supervisor on his job as a bill collector, tries to explain to him the competitive nature of the system: "'It's him or us,'" Durkin explains, "'Them or us. What's a guy going to do?'" (54).

This same job (which forms the basis of the 1954 crime novel *A Hell of a Woman*) also provides another extremely telling commentary on capitalism. Durkin and Thompson work for a store that is part of a large chain and thus has considerable economic power behind it. Yet, in the climate of the Depression, even this large chain eventually fails, leaving Durkin and Thompson unemployed. Durkin is probably unaware of the warnings of Marx and Engels, in *The Communist Manifesto*, that, in the frenetic environment of capitalism, there can be no security, that, under capitalism, nothing lasts, and "all that is solid melts into air" (Marx and Engels 476). He is, therefore, staggered by the collapse of the economic colossus for which he had worked, stunned that such resources could suddenly dissolve into nothingness:

"All the people'n the buildings'n the factories'n the b-banks'n the warehouses'n the ... the everything. Didn't let 'em jus' tell me. Saw it m'self. Know it's there — g-gotta be. Somethin's there it's *there*. 'S'there an' thass all there is to it. Where — w-where the hell's it gonna be if it ain't there? What ... where'n hell is anything gonna be?" (68–69)

Such insecurity forms one-half of the double whammy of modern capitalism, the other half of which is the conformism and regimentation of American life in the 1950s. Thompson's critique of American capitalism often focuses on this second motif in ways that recall Foucault's descriptions of modern carceral societies. Indeed, the potential relevance of Foucault's delineation of the carceral to crime fiction in general — and Thompson's fiction in particular — should be obvious. Thompson's criminal characters, for example, are quite often the kind of delinquents that Foucault discusses. They become criminals not in opposition to, or defiance of, the system but are, in fact, forced into crime by a legal system that labels them early on (many of them are reform-school graduates) as marginal and suspect members of a society that subsequently follows them with suspicion through the rest of their lives. In addition to Joe Wilmot, numerous other Thompson protagonists have been labeled as delinquents by official institutions of carceral power. In *Recoil* (1953), for example, narrator-protagonist Pat "Airplane Red" Cosgrove is paroled from prison precisely because, as a former convict, he has been labeled as a delinquent and is thus presumably ideal for exploitation in a scheme being engineered by Dr. Roland Luther, a corrupt political lobbyist, who plans to fake his own death and frame Cosgrove for the murder. Luther himself explains Cosgrove's experience with the legal system, which has labeled him as a criminal for what was essentially a youthful mistake in judgment: "'Pat served fifteen years for a robbery in which nothing was lost and no one was hurt. He served it not because he was a criminal, but because he wasn't'" (33). Kid Collins, the narrator-protagonist of *After Dark, My Sweet*, has similarly been classified as a delinquent because of the time he has spent in various mental institutions, all of which have diagnosed and labeled him in similar ways. These institutions identify him as a dangerous psychotic, so that, even when he escapes into the outside world, he still finds carceral restraints everywhere in a society terrified of the mentally ill. *After Dark, My Sweet*, then, recalls Foucault's work not merely in *Discipline and Punish* but in *Madness and Civilization*, where Foucault argues that our modern, "enlightened" view of madness as mental illness is really just a more subtle form of criminalization.

In addition to such overt meditations on the production of delinquents in carceral institutions, Thompson goes further than perhaps any other American crime writer to indicate the way in which carceral power penetrates every aspect of modern life, going well beyond the world of prisons and mental asylums. Very much in accord with Foucault's description of modern carceral society, Thompson's delinquents remain imprisoned, even when they are outside specific carceral institutions. In Thompson, families, schools, and workplaces can be as suffocatingly carceral as actual prisons. Many of Thompson's delinquents (including such notable examples as Lou Ford in *The Killer Inside Me* and Nick Corey in *Pop. 1280*) are produced not by prisons but by dysfunctional families. Further, the carceral system depicted by Thompson exerts a rigid control over the behavior not just of delinquents but of the entire population. In fact, what is most powerful and chilling about Thompson's fiction is not its direct portrayal of a dark, criminal underworld but its implied portrayal of the everyday world of mainstream modern America.

In a similar fashion, what is powerful in Thompson's fictional world is not, ultimately, the prevalence of graphic and spectacular violence but the thorough saturation of this world by paralyzing, stifling regimentation and routine. Certainly, Thompson's fictions do contain memorable moments of graphic violence, such as Lou Ford's detached, but gut-wrenching (in more ways than one), description in *The Killer Inside Me* of his calmly brutal murder of Amy Stanton, his longtime lover. However, reading Thompson through Foucault, we can see that such moments in Thompson may be so striking partly because they are relatively rare, despite Thompson's reputation. Such moments of graphic violence represent shocking breakdowns in the carceral order that is the texture not only of our own real world but of Thompson's own fictional world, in which hellish violence is not, as some critics would have it, the norm but an explosive disruption of the mind-numbing carceral routine. This is one reason the moments of violence in Thompson often seem so strange. What, after all, could be stranger than the abject weirdness of the end of *Savage Night*, in which the one-legged assassin Ruthie Dorne hacks protagonist Charlie Bigger into bits with an ax, while they hide out together on a darkly Rabelaisian Vermont farm where female genitalia are grown in rows, fertilized by the manure of goats driven mad by the odor emanating from the crops?

Of course, one could argue that such moments of the eruption of violence might potentially offer an almost utopian consolation in their suggestion that the seemingly total grip of carceral power might, in fact, be breakable. Yet Thompson is careful to make these moments so horrifying that only the most superficial reader could conclude that he offers such violence as a positive alternative. Instead, he offers it as a doleful commentary on the almost total lack of such alternatives within the carceral climate of modern capitalist America. Indeed, Dayton notes that, as a whole, "Thompson's novels articulate in an expressionistic fashion and within (at least some of) the generic conventions of crime fiction the (temporary) withering away of any visible alternative to the dominant culture" (242).

All of Thompson's novels are, in one way or another, narratives of attempted escape from carceral control, generally leading to dire consequences for the attempted escapees. So it may not be surprising that his most overt escape narrative, *The Getaway* (1958), also contains, in the description of the Mexican criminal kingdom of El Rey, his most powerful reminder of just what can happen to those who seek utopian asylum from carceral control. This chapter reads something like a coda or epilogue, outside the flow of the plot, but it is, in fact, the telos of the entire book, the point to which the getaway of the title is aimed. By reaching the kingdom of El Rey, Doc and Carol McCoy do ostensibly succeed in escaping pursuit by the legal authorities. But this criminal "utopia" offers anything but an escape from carceral control. Indeed, conditions in the kingdom (typically figured by critics as a version of hell) are so dystopian that, at first glance, the United States looks virtually utopian in comparison. This first glance would, however, be deceiving, simply repeating the movement through which, according to Foucault, the modern prison functions as a striking image of the loss of freedom, encouraging individuals in the society at large to believe, wrongly, that they are, in comparison, virtually free of carceral control.

Structurally, the kingdom of El Rey is, in fact, merely the logical conclusion of the series of carceral images that appears throughout *The Getaway*. Thematically, as one of El Rey's own armed guards explains, conditions in the kingdom are nothing more than the literal equivalent of the figurative conditions that the inhabitants experienced during their lives in North America before their flight south of the border (175). The kingdom of El Rey is, in fact, an allegorical repetition of the American capitalist system, with many of the ideological disguises removed. In this "egalitarian" kingdom, everyone is welcome, regardless of his or her background—as long as he or she has sufficient funds to pay for the various amenities offered, all of which are strictly first-class. In fact, relations in the kingdom are reduced to an almost entirely economic dimension. The dominant institution in the kingdom is El Rey's own official bank, the only place where the inhabitants can deposit their money with assurances that it will be safe. This bank, in return for the offer of complete security, charges, rather than pays, interest at rates that increase as the account balance decreases. As a result, the depositors' funds gradually waste away, especially since they generally come to the kingdom with a fixed stake and no sources of additional income.

Eventually, then, the inhabitants run out of resources altogether, at which point they are moved to a special village on the outskirts of the kingdom. There, in Thompson's most horrific image of capitalist competition and of the commodification of individuals under capitalism, the debased inhabitants quite literally feed on one another. Wandering out to the village, Doc notices that the air is filled with the "odor of peppery, roasting flesh" (175). He realizes, with horror, that this flesh is the flesh of human beings. Driven to the last extreme of economic competition, the stronger inhabitants of the village feed on the weaker, until they are, in turn, overcome by stronger newcomers, and so on.

Meanwhile, this final village is merely the logical extension of the conditions that obtain throughout El Rey's kingdom—just as the conditions in that kingdom are a direct extension of the carceral conditions of capitalism. In a clear parody of the bourgeois institution of marriage, most of the inhabitants of the kingdom live as couples, not out of any genuine emotional attachment but so they can pool their resources in joint bank accounts in an effort to keep their balances up. As these balances begin to fall, the two partners begin to compete against one another for the dwindling resources, leading to a battle in which only the shrewder and more ruthless of the two survives. And this competition between even the most intimate of associates is typical of the antagonistic social relations that obtain in the kingdom as whole, where everyone suspects everyone else of plotting against them—to the point that there is virtually no social life and individuals tend to avoid one another altogether.

The inhabitants of the kingdom are, in short, alienated individuals, forced by the system to regard one another as competitors, rather than comrades. It should come as no surprise, then, that the mistrust and tension that have brewed between Doc and Carol throughout the book continue unabated in El Rey's kingdom. Indeed, both partners attempt to have the other murdered, though the mutual plot collapses. When each learns of the other's plot, they simply shrug it off as exactly what one would expect. Then, they reaffirm their vows of love but conclude that this love makes absolutely no difference given the circumstances in which they are forced to live, which will force them to compete more and more bitterly as their resources dwindle. They end the text ironically toasting their "successful" getaway, simultaneously indicating the irony embedded in the title of the book.

Given such scenes, it is interesting and perhaps surprising that *The Getaway* contains some of the most positive scenes of interpersonal solidarity that appear in all of Thompson's fiction. At the same time, this solidarity is experienced only within marginal groups that do not really participate in the capitalist system. As Doc and Carol begin their cross-country flight to Mexico, the narrator—in one of the few acknowledgments of the value of collective action in Thompson's fiction—announces that such flights are a difficult undertaking that cannot be accomplished unaided. One is not likely, of course, to find this aid among society's solid citizens, unless, of course, the aid is obtained by force, as when Clinton is forced to help Torrento. The charming Doc, however, has an entire network of criminal friends spread throughout the country, and these friends help out by planting red herrings that throw the police off the trail of the fugitives.

Doc and Carol receive more direct help as well, from a family of migratory farm-workers. This group, consisting of a husband, a wife, and nine children, is itself moving across the country struggling to survive without most of the benefits that supposedly come to those who work hard in the promised land of America. In this sense, they are very much in the same situation as Doc and Carol, even though their only crime is to be poor. And they are able to survive only by banding together against the powerful forces that oppose them:

In a sense they were an autonomous body, functioning within a society which was organized to grind them down. The law did not protect them; for them it was merely an instrument of harassment, a means of moving them on when it was against their interest to move, or detaining them where it was to their disadvantage to stay. (123)

Carol, a former librarian from an essentially middle-class background, is extremely uncomfortable with this family. Doc, however, seems well able to communicate with all sorts of people, and he strikes up an immediate rapport with the father of this migratory family. Asking no questions, the family takes Carol and Doc in, hiding them in their truck and taking them across country with them. In return, Doc provides money to help the family fix up its old truck and buy food, but the text makes it clear that these funds were not construed as a bribe. They were merely a part of an exchange in which each party provided what resources it had in order to help out the other. From each according to his ability, to each according to his need. Eventually, Doc and Carol make it all the way to California inside the cramped truck, itself a sort of carceral image. Then, they part company with the family and go their own way.

This family (reminiscent of Steinbeck's Joads) is, not surprisingly, absent from both film versions of *The Getaway*, replaced in both cases by a single, cantankerous old geezer who provides help to Doc and Carol without the potentially radical political message provided in Thompson's version of this motif.[2] The other image of solidarity provided in Thompson's novel is less openly socialist in its orientation but still decidedly out of the mainstream of American cultural imagery and certainly outside the bounds of realism—and thus absent from both film versions altogether. As with the migratory farm-workers, this second image involves solidarity within a family group, itself a highly unusual notion in Thompson's fiction, where family members tend to be each other's worst enemies. This second family is the outlaw Santis clan, or at least what is left of it, two sons having been shot down by police and two other sons having been, like their father, executed in the electric chair. Another son is currently in prison, leaving only Ma Santis and her son, Earl, at large.

The Santis clan, we are told, are not criminals as the word is normally understood but rebels and outlaws, perhaps in the vein of the privateers or soldiers of fortune from earlier eras (141). They are also, unlike the typical Thompson criminal, honorable and trustworthy. As a result, they never betray a true friend or forget a favor that has been done for them. At the same time, they never forget an injury, either, and their enemies are likely to suffer severe retribution. They are also completely unable to function in modern American society, being radical individualists who are simply unable to conform. As a result, they are outcasts in a carceral society "which insisted upon conformity and pardoned no breakage of its laws, regardless of one's needs or motives" (141). That the clan has been so decimated is, of course, a sign of the high price of rebellion against this powerful carceral system.

Thompson's description of the Santis clan and their battle against conformism represents one of the most overt criticisms of American society in all of Thompson's fiction. At the same time, Thompson's description of the encounter between the McCoys and the Santises represents one of those numerous moments when Thompson's fiction engages in its own battle against conformity and convention by slipping off the tracks of genre crime fiction and careening off into the depths of surreal allegory. Ma Santis first appears in the text, literally out of nowhere, taking Doc and Carol to safety just as they seem on the verge of being ensnared by a police roadblock. "Safety," however, is a relative word. Ma Santis takes them in and hides them from the police until they can finally be smuggled into Mexico by boat. But the hiding places that she provides for them are anything but comfortable sanctuaries. They are, in fact, hells on earth, except that the literal descriptions of these hells go so far beyond what one might expect from a realistic narrative that the reader is clearly invited to interpret them allegorically.

First, Ma lowers both Doc and an extremely reluctant Carol by rope into cramped underground caves, which are essentially nothing more than holes in the ground, partly filled with water. This metaphorical descent into the womb of the earth through these vagina-like caves cries out for a Freudian interpretation—so much so that such an interpretation would be pointless. Meanwhile, this literal descent into the underworld (anticipating the moment in *Texas by the Tail* when the sinister rich woman Gidge Lord has her minions lower Mitch Corley into an abandoned oil drilling shaft) is sheer physical torture, especially for Carol, for whom the claustrophobic conditions are exacerbated by a suspicion that Doc and Ma Santis may actually be plotting to get rid of her by burying her alive. Carol specifically compares her cave to a coffin, then begins to grow more and more panicky until she almost injures herself severely by thrashing about in the grave-like confines of the cave, saving herself only by taking the sleeping pills given her by Ma Santis, which are powerful enough to render her unconscious for most of her stay in the cave, until Ma Santis finally hauls her out (146–53).

Aside from the very real terror offered by the entrapment within this cramped, watery tomb, this scene also offers a number of allegorical resonances. As Tony Hilfer notes, as Doc and Carol wait in the caves, they are "in the same predicament but isolated from each other, an exact structural analogue to the relationship between two committed egoists." Indeed, Hilfer notes that the various hiding places occupied by Doc and Carol tend to "accumulate allegorical implications" as they go along, though for Hilfer the allegorical referent is essentially metaphysical, making their journey a descent into hell (138). There are, however, far more social and political implications of these allegorical hiding places. Suspended in the caves, sharing the same predicament but unable to communicate or share the experience, Doc and Carol occupy very much the position of any two bourgeois subjects, suspended in an individualist ideology of competition designed to ensure that they will not band together to make common cause against a carceral system that is, in its own way, just as confining as these caves.

Eventually Ma's remaining son, Earl, hauls the McCoys up to the surface, then takes them to his remote farm, where they can presumably hide out under somewhat better conditions. They have a hearty meal of country "vittles" and are somewhat restored, though Carol remains suspicious that the Santises may not be quite as trustworthy as they seem. Indeed, the meal itself has an almost sinister aspect. The main course is a large beef roast, which Ma slaps directly onto the table without a platter and which Earl essentially attacks with a sort of machete, whacking it into "great bleeding chunks" (154). Little wonder, then, that Carol, fresh from her ordeal in the caves, experiences a bout of nausea when she first sees the food, even though she is unaware that the image of this bleeding meat anticipates the cannibalism practiced in the kingdom of El Rey.

After the meal, Doc and Carol are taken to a second hiding place, this one also hellish, but in an almost comic way. Indeed, the text at this point moves away from Dante and toward Rabelais, as the couple are stashed inside a haystack-sized mound of manure, which has been hollowed out on the inside to provide a hiding place. Doc and Carol themselves appreciate the humor of this situation, laughing as they disrobe in an attempt to deal with the growing heat inside the mound as the day progresses. In fact, stripped nude and alone inside the mound, they even become amorous, attempting at last to try to resume their once-torrid sexual relationship, interrupted by Doc's years in prison and their subsequent weeks on the run. Carol takes Doc's face in her hands and moves to kiss him, when suddenly a soggy mass of manure breaks free from overhead and strikes her square in the face (156).[3]

The mood broken, Carol settles back into her own thoughts, as manure continues to drop around them, joined by swarming flies and crawling grub worms. Disgusted, Carol grimly thinks to herself how different their situation is from the romantic scenes that one might expect from the typical images of outlaw life in "the movies" (158). Here, Thompson is almost prescient in his anticipation of the way Hollywood would treat his novel when it was adapted to the screen. Both screen versions gain considerable energy from the sexual chemistry between their costars, Steve McQueen and Ali MacGraw or Alec Baldwin and Kim Basinger, as the case may be. In the novel, however, Doc and Carol have considerable difficulty getting together at all, experiencing, as Brewer puts it, "an insuperable, sometimes comic, *coitus interruptus*" as the text proceeds (89). McQueen and MacGraw have some difficulties and interruptions but do get together, while Baldwin and Basinger have few difficulties at all.[4] More importantly, both film couples end up riding off into the Mexican sunset, seemingly to live happily ever after, while the Doc and Carol of the book descend even further into hell as they settle into El Rey's kingdom.

In this kingdom, virtually all aspects of human life and human relationships are reduced to a matter of economics, to the point that human beings literally become consumable commodities, even though they have come to Mexico seeking escape from the capitalist routine. A similar phenomenon is central to the relatively late (and little known) *Texas by the Tail*, which strives for a kind of utopian escape by seeming to propose rural Texas as a superior alternative to the corrupt world of urban capitalism. Here Thompson includes some of his most overt criticism of early-1950s American society, in terms that still sound remarkably familiar at the beginning of the twenty-first century. Thompson's third-person narrator does not hesitate to point out the racism of Houston (20) or the conformism and corruption of Dallas (151), but these are big cities. Texas as a whole is a different story. Despite great variations in conditions around the huge state, the narrator tells us, "there was one generalization you could make about Texas. You could say flatly and positively that the wanton and open flouting of every principle of decency and fair play which was becoming commonplace in other states was wholly foreign to Texas." In addition to preserving traditional values lost in the rest of the nation, we are told, Texas entirely avoids the conditions found in "some cities of America," where

the streets were roamed by gangs of rowdies: overgrown louts who had been slobbered over far too long by professional do-gooders and who needed nothing quite so much as a goddamned good beating. ... And this scum, these outrageous brutes, prowled the streets of those American cities, knocking down wholly inoffensive citizens, publicly committing robbery, mayhem and murder. Doing it because they knew they could get away with it, that a hundred people might look on but not a one would interfere. (196)

Thompson comes as close here as he does anywhere in his work to a criticism of American society from a perspective that sounds rather right-wing, though one should also recall that this statement comes from an unidentified narrator, whose perspective does not necessarily match that of Thompson himself. In any case, *Texas by the Tail* contains relatively little philosophizing, but strives for a high-suspense plot, with lots of twists and turns. Polito notes that *Texas by the Tail* "aims for the light, high notes of the professional thriller, and frequently hits them" (459). Nevertheless, while *Texas by the Tail* focuses on the activities of Mitch Corley, a high-stakes gambler, rather than ordinary working people, its focus on the economic is among the sharpest in Thompson's oeuvre. Indeed, the real plot of the book, despite being spiced with the typical pulp elements of sex and violence, is almost entirely economic. Most of the action of the book shows Corley doing his job, which involves as pure a quest for money as can be conceived. Indeed, as befits the ups and downs of the life of a professional gambler, the principal plot device of the book is simply the level of Corley's bankroll, which we follow through various ups and downs in the course of his wins and losses in the game of dice and the game of life.

Of course, given Thompson's continual insistence on the precarious nature of financial life under American capitalism, the triumphs and tribulations of a professional gambler provide a perfect metaphor for the American economic system as a whole. Moreover, Corley's world repeatedly overlaps the more conventional world of business, virtually effacing the boundary between the underground economy of dice games and the banks and businesses. We are told, for example, that gamblers routinely require the cooperation of a willing banker, who, while perhaps doing nothing technically illegal, seriously stretches the rules of banking to help con men and gamblers perform the financial high jinks that are sometimes required by their occupations. Corley himself is in cahoots with Agate, a shady Houston banker who, for exorbitant fees, helps Corley with his various banking needs. Agate is a completely sleazy figure, a man of no morals and just as little talent who has gotten his position as a bank executive by sheer luck and who holds it primarily through virtue of his seniority in the company.

Among other things, Agate helps Corley conceal from his girlfriend, Red (the tail of the book's double entendre title and a virtual walking male fantasy of female sexuality), that they are seriously short of cash because he has used most of their money to make blackmail payments to his long-estranged wife, Teddy, whose existence Corley is hiding from Red. Corley also seeks Agate's help in acquiring an under-the-table loan that will allow him to take advantage of a once-in-a-lifetime stock-option deal offered him by big-time oil magnate Jake Zearsdale. Zearsdale is a self-made millionaire who has risen from poverty to a position of immense wealth through his successes in the oil business. But, if Zearsdale's rise seems, for once in Thompson's work, to put a positive spin on the possibilities offered by the American dream, it is also the case that, in

*Texas by the Tail*, the idealized world of wildcat oil drilling, described so nostalgically in the earlier *Wild Town*, has been replaced by the routinized (and brutal) world of big business. If the earlier book presented the search for oil as a battle of man against nature, with no need to defeat competitors in order to succeed, *Texas by the Tail* presents its more contemporary oil business as a cutthroat Darwinian world where only the fittest survive and where fitness is defined by ruthlessness and willingness to do anything to destroy one's competitors. To survive in this business, Thompson's narrator concludes, you had to have "an instinct for the jugular. A conviction that the destruction of an enemy was as necessary as defecation. A social outlook that was as intestinal as it was amoral; seeing one's neighbors as something to be gobbled up, and a knife in the back as the best way to a man's heart" (67).

Zearsdale is presented in a relatively positive light, characterized as strong, honorable, and unpretentious, thus becoming a paragon of the rural Texas values that Thompson frequently sets against big-city decadence and corruption in his later work. On the other hand, given Thompson's description of the oil business, it is not surprising that he can also be coldly ruthless, especially with those over whom he has economic power. In one of the book's most telling scenes, he confronts Albert, a loyal African American employee of 23 years, after the man makes a simple (and harmless, as it turns out) mistake. Zearsdale declares that Albert is worthless, pointing out, in high racist fashion: "'Treat you like a white man, don't I, instead of a jig?'" Albert, in turn expresses his appreciation for this treatment and his devotion to Zearsdale, explaining that his two children are named after Zearsdale and Zearsdale's mother. Zearsdale announces his pleasure at this news, then fires Albert for his obsequiousness, because "a man without pride is no good" (143–44).

Zearsdale ultimately befriends Corley precisely because Corley does have pride, though the resolution of the book (in which Zearsdale accuses Corley of cheating him at dice, then reverses his judgment simply because of Corley's defiant and impassioned response to this charge) is contrived. In a similar fashion, the fiery Red, who learns of the existence of Teddy, seems about ready to murder Corley for his deception, then forgives him and declares her undying loyalty. In the meantime, Corley will now be able to participate in the stock-option deal with Zearsdale, on top of which he has recovered the blackmail money he has paid to Teddy and managed (with Zearsdale's support) to collect on a large gambling debt from the sinister Lords (one of Texas's oldest—and most dangerous—families).

In short, Corley's ultimate triumph is financial. Even the restoration of his relationship with Red has an economic tone to it, because she is overtly presented throughout the book as a sexual commodity. She is, among other things, a great asset to Corley in his work, so sexy and beautiful that she helps him get a foot in the door in various games, while at the same time distracting his opponents and giving him a competitive advantage. Even her value as a sexual partner is described in economic terms, as when Thompson's narrator describes her small, but opulent, body as "the well-stocked commissary of her flesh" (10). In addition, Red is a sort of modern-day Galatea, whom Corley discovered as an unsophisticated rural waif, then molded into a glamorous companion and useful business partner, much as Doc McCoy had done with Carol.

If Thompson often recalls Balzac in his portrayal of an all-out struggle for success that leaves even the most successful with no assurance of maintaining their past gains, he also recalls Flaubert in his portrayal of a society driven by the commodification of everything. Along with the 1950s example of Nabokov's Lolita, Red's most direct literary precedent may be Flaubert's Emma Bovary, who has a similar rural background and who similarly entertains fantasies of escape from that background, fantasies reinforced in Emma's case by her reading of romantic novels and in Red's case by her schoolgirl reading of "the adventures of Mary Jane and her Magic Pony" (147). "Magic," in fact, is a key word here. Like Emma, Red finds that her fantasies are unfulfillable in the thoroughly commodified and routinized atmosphere of the modern bourgeois world. Granted, Red, unlike Emma, does enter the exciting world of high-stakes gambling, traveling widely and visiting a variety of gleaming cities. But these adventures are ultimately empty. In a modern capitalist world completely stripped of its magic by the mind-numbing effects of bourgeois routinization, the romance that Red seeks is simply not available.

Particularly telling here are Red's periodic dime-store shopping sprees (mirroring Emma's trips to the shop of the sinister Lheureux, but in a debased form), during which she seeks to recover her childhood sense of wonder by purchasing cheap objects that have value only as commodity fetishes (and that can also be read as stand-ins for pulp novels), fulfilling fantasies from her impoverished early years. But the magic of the commodity fetish is a bogus one, and the joy Red experiences on these outings is tempered with a sorrow that Corley understands well, even if he lacks a Marxist vocabulary, diagnosing it as arising from "the loss of innocence before it had ever endured. The cruel shearing away of all but the utterly practical, as pastoral man was caught up in an industrial society" (147).

Here Thompson echoes Weber on routinization almost exactly, also recalling Jameson's suggestion, drawing on Weber's account, that the persistence of forms of romance in Western culture even into the twentieth century arises from a utopian longing for the absent magic that no longer exists in the modern world. Jameson himself makes this connection even more clear when he goes on to indicate the relevance of his comments to contemporary American popular culture: "On this view, the oral tales of tribal society, the fairy tales that are the irrepressible voice and expression of the underclasses of the great systems of domination, adventure stories and melodrama, and the popular or mass culture of our own time are all syllables and broken fragments of some single immense story" (*Political* 105). This story, of course, involves last-ditch, rear-guard actions of cultural resistance against the historical onslaught of what Jameson has in several places described as the "bourgeois cultural revolution," the ultimate triumph of which is marked, in the field of culture, by the hegemony of postmodernism.

In his subsequent work, Jameson adds postcolonial literature and modernist literature to his list of cultural forms that resist the inexorable advance of the global dominance of late capitalism. In particular, he emphasizes that all of the marginal cultural forms he identifies maintain a strong utopian dimension, an ability to image a better alternative world that has been largely lost in postmodernism. On this score, however, Thompson's work, with its extremely weak utopianism, appears less as a cry of protest against postmodernism than as an example of postmodernism in its own right. Thus, Corley, while realizing that there is an emptiness at the heart of the modern capitalist world, is unable to envision any sort of historical movement toward a better alternative. As Red retreats into tears after the momentary high of one of her dime-store shopping trips, Corley himself begins to weep, "not for an idealized dream of things past, but for the immutable realities of the present. Not for what had been lost but for what had never been. Not for what might have been but for what could never be" (147).

In the course of the first half or so of the twentieth century, American culture comes from Carrie Meeber's longing for the fancy clothing that she sees in turn-of-the-century Chicago's new department stores, to Red's tawdry dime-store shopping sprees in *Texas by the Tail*. What is at stake, here, is a debasement of desire itself, part of the phenomenon Jameson describes as the "waning of affect," which he sees as a crucial symptom of the postmodern condition. This waning of affect (a symptom frequently observed in schizophrenic patients) arises, for Jameson, from the fragmentation of the postmodern subject, which thereby becomes too scattered and tenuous to be able to support any truly strong and sustained desire. Thus, if for Jameson the modern psychologization of desire is a crucial source of the intensity of Dreiser's fiction, then the dissolution of this desire is central to the lack of emotional intensity in most postmodern works.

Even when Thompson's characters do experience what passes for desire, they do so in ways that are transparently inauthentic. Crucial here are *A Swell-Looking Babe* and *A Hell of a Woman*, two 1954 novels in which the very titles call attention to the central roles played by individual women as objects of desire. In the former, however, the desire of young bellboy Dusty Rhodes for the mysterious Marcia Bascom is so preposterously oedipal that the book has to be read either as a parody of

Freud or as such an ostentatiously bad novel that it parodies itself, even if inadvertently. Meanwhile, in *A Hell of a Woman*, Dolly Dillon's desire for Mona Farrell begins when her "aunt" offers her to him as payment for a set of silverware, making particularly obvious her role as a sexual commodity. Predictably, Dillon soon finds Mona at least as threatening as she is desirable, then conveniently gets rid of her when she falls (or is perhaps pushed by Dillon) in front of a truck. Dillon then escapes from desire in his own way, possibly castrating himself or at least fantasizing about being castrated.

Of course, if Thompson's characters are too fragmented to sustain desire, Thompson's texts have little chance of building an effective utopian alternative to the present, given that they tend to be so fragmented and self-parodic that they collapse beneath their own weight. In fact, the textual fragmentation of Thompson's novels is often accompanied by the psychic fragmentation of his characters and narrators. By the end of *Savage Night*, for example, not only is Charlie Bigger physically fragmented as Ruthie Dorne (apparently) hacks him to pieces, but his narrative begins to break apart as well. The chapters become shorter and shorter, the narrative voice begins to fragment (indicated by intermixed roman and italic type), and the imagery becomes increasingly surreal and incoherent.

*The Criminal* (1953) is formally fragmented through the use of multiple narrators, while the various narrations never combine to do what crime fiction conventionally does: identify the criminal. This particular book centers on 15-year-old Bob Talbert, who, as the book begins, has been charged with the brutal rape and murder of 14-year-old Josie Eddleman, a girl from his neighborhood. The title of the book seems to declare Bob guilty from the beginning, as does the initial chapter, narrated by Bob's father, Allen, and detailing the way in which Bob, since entering adolescence, seems to have grown increasingly bitter and withdrawn. As the narration proceeds, subsequent chapters are narrated by Bob's mother, Martha; by Bob himself; and by a variety of local notables, including newspaper editor Donald Skysmith; newspaper reporter William Willis; and Bob's lawyer, I. Kossmeyer. As these narrations proceed, it begins to appear less and less likely that Bob is really the killer, though it remains entirely possible that he will be convicted, despite Kossmeyer's able efforts on his behalf. Indeed, readers who have jumped early on to the conclusion that Bob is guilty are likely to find themselves face-to-face with the realization that they have followed the course of many in the community, who assume that Bob is guilty without any real evidence.

Bob, in fact, may be the most innocent individual in the book, though it should also be said that the text never presents incontrovertible evidence of his innocence. Even Josie, the victim, seems to have had a questionable character and may have been killed by an older man she was blackmailing because of his sexual relationship with her. Thus, one is tempted to conclude that the book's title must refer to someone other than Bob, with the most likely candidate (among several) probably being the Captain, publisher of a local newspaper, the *Star*. Just as the police and district attorney have concluded that Bob is innocent and are about to release him, the Captain, whose sadistic sense of humor in some ways resembles that of the notorious Lou Ford, calls Skysmith, his managing editor, and demands that he play up the story of the rape-murder in an effort to increase the circulation of the paper. Skysmith reluctantly agrees, assigning the even more reluctant Willis to the job. Willis himself finds Bob's less than articulate explanation of his whereabouts at the time of the crime unconvincing, though he is also leery of the stories he hears from Bob's teachers and neighbors, who seem eager to claim credit for having seen Bob's turn to murder coming. Indeed, the ultimate "criminal" of the book may not be any individual character, but the collective community, which seems so anxious to convict Bob without any real evidence.

In any case, this community pressure, spurred by the *Star*'s sensationalization of the story, leads the police not only to keep Bob in custody but to step up their interrogation, eventually eliciting a questionable confession. At this point, Kossmeyer comes on the scene to work on Bob's behalf, but the text ends before Bob comes to trial, with the district attorney still mulling over a variety of tips he has received identifying several potential killers, including Bob. Meanwhile, the Captain changes course, concluding that the paper can now get more mileage from coming to Bob's defense. He and Skysmith have words and, as the text ends, the heartless Captain fires Skysmith on the spot, simultaneously expressing his condolences for the death of Skysmith's wife the night before.

In short, *The Criminal* is not so much the story of a crime and its consequences as a profile of a fragmented community steeped in greed, hypocrisy, pettiness, and spite. Meanwhile, its structure, with nine different narrators, each speaking in a distinctively individual style, is, as Polito notes, reminiscent of William Faulkner's technique in *As I Lay Dying*, though it has precedents in crime fiction as well (373). In fact, the most obvious precedent for the technique might be Akira Kurosawa's classic film *Rashomon* (released two years before the publication of *The Criminal* and widely known after its Best Foreign Language Film Oscar for 1951), which also deals with an attempt to unravel the truth of a rape-murder through the testimony of multiple narrators.

However, the multiple-narrator technique functions far differently in the texts of Faulkner and Kurosawa, both of which are fundamentally modernist, than in Thompson's text, which introduces, via the technique, a far more radical epistemological uncertainty. The varying accounts of Kurosawa's four different narrators amount to a meditation on human nature and on the way in which the same events can be perceived differently by different people. *Rashomon* thus suggests that human perception of truth is variable and relative, though it leaves intact the notion of truth itself. In a similarly centripetal way, the different narrators of *As I Lay Dying* present details that, despite their differences in point of view, gradually accumulate, allowing readers to assemble a relatively coherent story. Faulkner's use of the multiple-narrator technique in the book thus becomes simply a variant on the narrative structures of all of his best novels, which typically invite readers to assemble clues in an attempt to figure out what "really" happened, much in the mode of a detective. Indeed, it should be remembered that *The Sound and the Fury* and *Absalom, Absalom!* are also multiple-narrator novels, again requiring such detective work on the part of readers, who may never be able to answer all of the questions raised by these complex novels, but who are tempted to try, on the basis of the assumption that these answers do exist, however hard they may be to find.

In contrast, the different bits of testimony presented by the different narrators in *The Criminal* are not complementary and do not even invite readers to piece them together to determine the truth. Instead, the varying narrative points of view simply act to deprive the text of any dependable epistemological center, combining in centrifugal ways that radiate outward from the central mystery and deflect attention from it. Despite the institutional location of Thompson's book within the genre of crime fiction, it is far less of a detective story than *Rashomon, As I Lay Dying*, or *Absalom, Absalom!* In the far more skeptical and cynical world of Thompson, there is no real point to seeking the truth. Social prejudices and systemic corruption form an insurmountable barrier to any attempt to find truth, while rendering that truth irrelevant in any case. Thus, the stance taken by the *Star* has nothing to do with Bob's guilt or innocence but is determined entirely by marketing concerns, by the quest to report the story in such a way as to maximize circulation and profit. Similarly, Kossmeyer, competent advocate that he is, will do all he can to exonerate Bob, regardless of Bob's guilt or innocence.

At first glance, *The Kill-Off*, Thompson's other multiple-narrator novel, seems less radical in its deconstruction of reality and truth, because Pete Pavlov, the twelfth and last narrator, ends the book by confessing to the killing of Luane DeVore. In addition, *The Kill-Off* resembles the fictions of Faulkner in that the overlapping narrations do eventually combine to produce a relatively coherent narrative. At the same time, *The Kill-Off* is far less plot-driven than most works of crime fiction or even the modernist novels of Faulkner. The main effect of the different narrations (there are 12 chapters, each with a different narrator) is to produce a cross-sectional view of the small Long Island seaside town of Manduwoc. In keeping with Thompson's consistent focus on the difficulty of intersubjective contact and understanding in modern America, this cross-section depicts anything but a community. Virtually all of the narrators are outsiders and outcasts, including Kossmeyer, who again appears and is again marginalized by his Jewishness, in addition to the fact that he does not actually live in Manduwoc but merely vacations there.

Another of the narrators, singer Danny Lee (real name Agnes Tuttle), is also not from the town but is merely there to perform with the band led by Rags McGuire, another narrator, who is from Manduwoc but spends relatively little time there. Once fairly successful, McGuire's professional career is in decline, while his personal life is in a state of collapse after an auto accident kills his two sons and disfigures his wife, who had formerly sung with the band. Now, he and his failing band are performing in a dance pavilion owned by Pavlov, a local businessman who may be the most unpopular man in town. Pavlov's unattractive teenage daughter, Myra, a pregnant narcotics addict, also narrates a chapter, as does Luane DeVore, the much-despised town gossip, and Luane's much abused (and much younger) husband, Ralph DeVore. Two professional men, Dr. James Aston and county attorney Henry Clay Williams, also narrate chapters, but neither is as successful as his professional title might indicate, and both are miserable. The remaining narrators are the most marginalized of all, including Dr. Ashton's sociopathic teenage son, Bobbie, Ashton's black housekeeper, Hattie, and Marmaduke "Goofy" Gannder, the mentally defective town beggar.

Given this gallery of marginal and dysfunctional narrators, it should come as no surprise that no vision of community arises from their collective narrations. As a matter of fact, even the confessional solution to the mystery is unstable. After all, innocent people confess all the time to crimes they didn't commit, as the example of Bob Talbert has already reminded us. Indeed, Bobbie Ashton (*The Kill-Off*'s version of Bob Talbert), in addition to Pavlov, also confesses to the killing of Luane. There is no reason to believe that Pavlov's private confession is untrue, since he is under no particular duress. However, he himself declares that Luane's death was actually an accident, he having inadvertently knocked her down the stairs when, desperate for cash, he went to her home to collect money that her father cheated him out of years earlier, with Luane's help. Moreover, he is not even certain that the fall killed her. Perhaps, he concludes, she was just knocked out, and someone else came along and killed her later. After all, she was so despised by so many people in the town that it seemed only a matter of time until someone killed her. The question was simply who would win the contest to kill her first, thus the title of the novel.

What is clear is that, soon after Luane's death, Pavlov kills his daughter, Myra, along with Bobbie Ashton, as the two teenagers lie together necking on the beach. However, Bobbie's death is essentially a suicide, he having carefully engineered events so that Pavlov would be virtually certain to kill him. It is thus not clear whether Pavlov can be considered entirely culpable for the death of Bobbie. And, the fact that Bobbie used Myra to induce Pavlov to kill him (both getting her pregnant and hooking her on narcotics stolen from his doctor father) raises the question of whether it is not really Bobbie who is guilty of the death of Myra as well.

Via such questions, *The Kill-Off* is one of Thompson's most compelling meditations on the nature of guilt and innocence and on the fine line between them, the fragmentation of the multiple-narrator text acting to undermine any sense that there is a stable point of view from which this distinction can be unequivocally drawn. Virtually everyone in the book is guilty of wanting to kill Luane, and Luane herself is such a nasty person that their desires seem understandable. In fact, Pavlov, the multiple murderer, seems through most of the book the town's most admirable character, despite the cranky disposition that makes him despised by most of the locals. Bobbie, on the other hand, is set up as one of Thompson's famous psychotic killers, meditating throughout his narration on various murders he might commit and generally terrorizing his parents. At the same time, like most of Thompson's pathological characters, Bobbie is not so much a villain as a victim. His bitterness arises from specific social causes, in this case his awareness that, as the product of an illicit union between his father and the father's black housekeeper, Hattie, he occupies a highly stigmatized position in the racist society of modern America. In fact, James Ashton originally moved to Manduwoc with Hattie and Bobbie to escape that stigma, concocting a story that Mrs. Ashton, Bobbie's mother, had died. Unfortunately, Luane DeVore, inveterate gossip that she was, somehow got word of Bobbie's true background and immediately spread the word all over town, leading Bobbie to drop out of school and descend into bitterness and hatred not only of Luane but of his parents and everyone else.

*A Hell of a Woman* is the classic example of textual fragmentation among Thompson's novels. For the one thing, this text is rather unstable throughout, with the main narrative being interrupted at two points by rival (and often contradictory) versions of the same events, as presented by "Knarf Nollid," the anagrammatic alter ego of protagonist/narrator Frank "Dolly" Dillon. Nollid's narrative is a pure specimen of debased pulp fiction that lacks the usual embellishments of Thompson's fictions, thus enacting another of Thompson's attacks on the genre by showing what the genre is like in its most reduced form. Of course, these continual assaults on popular fiction have larger social implications as well: if such works are popular in America, then that must tell us something about American taste and the American mind. As Polito puts it, Nollid seems like an "inmate" who has "escaped from the collective popular unconscious" (364). On the other hand, the Nollid chapters add a paradoxical richness to *A Hell of a Woman* through their dialogic interaction with the main chapters of the text. In this sense, the Nollid chapters as a whole would seem to have somewhat the same effect as the "Nausicaa" chapter of Joyce's *Ulysses*, which places the language of popular women's magazines in the midst of a modernist masterpiece. Thompson, however, places pulp fiction in the midst of, well, pulp fiction, and thus achieves less contrast than does Joyce, making the Nollid chapters less effectively parodic than "Nausicaa," leaning toward pastiche, rather than parody, in good postmodernist fashion.

One might also describe the interaction between the Nollid chapters and the rest of *A Hell of a Woman* as a dialogic confrontation between different styles, much in the manner of Dreiser (as discussed by Petrey) or in the manner of the novel in general (as discussed by Bakhtin). Of course, the "baseline" style of *A Hell of a Woman* is, in a sense, more Dillon's than Thompson's. In fact, so many of Thompson's most important novels feature first-person narrators that it becomes difficult to talk about "his" style in this way, because the narrative styles of his texts are specifically figured as the styles of narrators, such as Lou Ford and Nick Corey. In fact, the closest thing to Dreiser's conflict of styles that occurs in Thompson resides within the speech patterns of Ford and Corey, Thompson's two most notorious narrator protagonists. Both Ford and Corey speak a stream of down-home, folksy platitudes and clichés, only occasionally, at key moments, resorting to a much more sophisticated, formal style that clearly identifies their usual folksiness as a fake. But this fake style lacks the utopian resonances (whether one sees them as positive or negative) that reside in the sentimental style of *Sister Carrie*, again indicating the weakness of utopian energies in Thompson. In general, however, it is difficult to make any general observations about Thompson's style, except that it tends to be a bit sloppy and to show the hastiness with which his novels were typically composed. In fact, the lack of a consistent and distinctive style is one of the aspects of Thompson's work that make it so hard to characterize: just as his narration seems to be proceeding in a reasonably typical version of hard-boiled noir style, it suddenly veers off into modernist stream-of-consciousness or surrealist fantasy.

Thompson, then, again becomes an excellent example of postmodernism, as diagnosed by Jameson. For Jameson, a key characteristic of postmodern writers is the lack of any identifiable personal style, a logical consequence of the general dissolution of distinctive personal identities under late capitalism. Lacking such an identity of his or her own, the postmodern writer has little choice but to cannibalize preexisting style, ranging freely over the menu of available styles but never really endorsing or challenging any of them. For Jameson, then, the postmodern stylistic tool par excellence is pastiche, which he distinguishes from parody in that it is entirely neutral, "without any of parody's ulterior motives, amputated of the satiric impulse, devoid of any laughter and of any conviction that alongside the abnormal tongue you have momentarily borrowed, some healthy linguistic normality still exists" (*Postmodernism* 17).

By this characterization, the contrast between the baseline objective realist language and overblown romantic language in Dreiser is a quintessential example of parody. But this resource is unavailable to Thompson, who lacks any "normal" stylistic base from which to sally forth in parodic attacks on other styles. If all styles are inauthentic in Thompson, then that still leaves a sort of kamikaze approach, in which he attacks all styles at once, which may explain those distinctive moments in which Thompson's texts seem to blow up in the reader's face, fragmenting into multiple styles emanating from multiple sources, none of which can be identified as the principal source, thus the weirdness of the endings of texts such as *A Hell of a Woman* and *Savage Night*, in which not only the narrators, but the texts themselves seem to go insane. And, even in texts, such as *The Getaway*, that maintain a relatively consistent style to the end, the content tends to become weird at the end, going well beyond the bounds of normal crime fiction.

On this more obvious, thematic level, Thompson's kamikaze approach, which might be identified as a form of self-parody, can also be detected in his continual assault on the pulp fiction genre in which he works. As Dayton puts it, comparing Thompson's fiction to Peter Bürger's influential characterization of the avant-garde as an assault on the institution of art, "Thompson's work within mass culture is at the same time a refusal of and an attempt to destroy mass culture as such" (237). Virtually all of Thompson's crime novels can be read as parodies of crime novels, but he also frequently includes explicit commentary on the genre. The most spectacular example of this commentary occurs in *Savage Night* in the weird scene in which Charlie Bigger recalls having once been picked up while hitchhiking by a writer who seems suspiciously similar to Thompson. The writer claims to live on a farm in Vermont, where the only viable crop these days is female genitalia. This motif can clearly be read as the most overt of Thompson's many commentaries on the commodification of the female body.[5] However, it is also clear from the context that the scene is meant more as a comment on the commodification of pulp literature. "I used to grow other things," explains the writer to a bemused Bigger: "Bodies. Faces. Eyes. Expressions. Brains. I grew them in a three-dollar-a-week room down on Fourteenth Street and I ate aspirin when I couldn't raise enough dough for a hamburger. And every now and then some lordly book publisher would come down and reap my crop and package it at two-fifty a copy" (70).

In short, the writer once produced more substantial material, but market pressures have forced him to reduce his work to the least common denominator level, leaving out all but the most rudimentary elements that are required to satisfy the desires of readers. "Even butts and breasts are becoming a drug on the market," he adds, making clear the purely economic forces that have forced him to reduce his product to its current debased level.

In *Savage Night*, however, the metaphorical motif collapses when the Vermont genital farm, which seems to be purely metaphorical, suddenly appears as a "real" place in the end of Thompson's narrative, when Bigger and Ruthie Dorne take refuge there in their flight from The Man, a New York crime kingpin. By this time, of course, the text has completely escaped the bounds of realist crime fiction, mixing ontological levels (in good postmodern fashion)[6] and making it impossible to tell what is "actually" happening and what is merely a mad fantasy in the rapidly disintegrating mind of the narrator/protagonist. This moment in the text, of course, goes well beyond the bare-minimum approach described by the writer who had occupied the farm, illustrating the way in which Thompson, market pressures notwithstanding, consistently managed to add more than the mere rudiments of formulaic crime fiction to his books, attacking the pulp matrices of his own texts with subversive assaults on the genre (and institution) of pulp fiction. Among other things, this aspect of Thompson's work helps to explain why the most interesting motifs in his books tend to be eliminated when those books are adapted to film. Unfortunately, the weakness of utopian vision in Thompson's work is such that he is not able to offer any real alternative to the debased commercial fiction he criticizes. Instead, his texts seem to self-destruct at the end, leaving nothing in their wake but confused fragments — and confused readers.

This kamikaze approach is central to Thompson's particular style of satire, which seems to undercut everything it touches, including itself, while leaving nothing standing as a preferred alternative. Of course, depending on one's point of view, one might describe this form of satire as particularly cynical or as particularly democratic and dialogic, perhaps in the mode described by Bakhtin.[7] Indeed, the actual nature of Thompson's satire has long proved problematic to critics, who tend to characterize Thompson as a satirist but to say little beyond that. Brewer, for example, highlights the motif of satire in the subtitle of his book on Thompson, then says relatively little about satire in the book itself.

In any case, *A Hell of a Woman*, like so many Thompson texts, virtually self-destructs at the end. Dillon's earlier forays into the role of Nollid turn out to anticipate his more radical psychic fragmentation as his narration unravels at the end of the text. The final chapter is another insert, this time by "Derf Senoj," Dillon apparently now having assumed a new identity as Fred Jones. But this new identity is highly unstable. After Mona's death (accidental or not), Dillon/Jones continues his life on the run, eventually hooking up with still another dangerous woman, Helene, though Helene is probably a figment of his imagination. Thompson had originally conceived the ending of this text as being printed in parallel columns to indicate the narrator's fragmentation, but his editors felt that this technique would be too confusing, so the book again employs the strategy of mixing Roman and italic type. This mixture is even more radical than in *Savage Night*, narrating the final dissolution of Dillon's identity and ending as he castrates himself (or is castrated by Helene) and throws himself out the window.

Thompson also uses the castration motif in *The Nothing Man*, though here the castration of the protagonist, Clint Brown, seems to function as a somewhat more straightforward marker of alienation, perhaps in the mode of Hemingway's Jake Barnes.[8] Indeed, alienation would, at first glance, seem to be the master trope of all of Thompson's fiction. His characters, even when they are not psychotic, tend to have a radical sense that they somehow do not fit in with the world around. Of course, the same might be said for many of the protagonists not only in pulp crime fiction but in the most respected canonical works of the twentieth century. As Lukács notes, many of the canonical works of modernist fiction feature psychotic or at least mentally ill characters, such as the psychopathic killer Christian Moosbrugger in Robert Musil's *The Man Without Qualities*, the suicidal, shell-shocked, World War I vet Septimus Smith in Virginia Woolf's *Mrs. Dalloway*, or William Faulkner's Joe Christmas, ostracized by an oppressive, racist, society, then driven to murder and finally himself murdered (and castrated) by the right-wing sociopath (and proto-Nazi) Percy Grimm. Christmas thus becomes the forerunner of such characters as Richard Wright's Bigger Thomas, the quintessential example of the alienated victim of society who eventually turns to murder as an expression of inarticulate pain and rage.

Thompson's alienated characters are often similarly marginalized. For example, Charlie Bigger in *Savage Night* experiences a sense of alienation that is marked not merely by his emotional estrangement from all of those around him but even by his physical appearance. Barely five feet tall, he is a tiny man, despite his name and occupation. He also suffers from tuberculosis, bad eyes, and bad teeth. He is, in fact, literally falling part, thus experiencing a sense of dissolution that is more postmodernist than modernist, recalling, for example, Thomas Pynchon's *V.* or the crippled and decaying characters of Samuel Beckett. Bigger's unusual physical appearance is central to his alienation: he is convinced that everyone he meets looks at him with aversion and contempt. Thus, when he goes to enroll in a local teachers' college in order to keep up his cover, he never feels that he fits in with the other students: "I was always by myself, with the others in back or ahead of me, nudging each other when they thought I wasn't looking; laughing and whispering and talking. About my clothes, about the way I looked, about—everything. Because nothing about me was right" (116).

Clint Brown has a similar sense of not being "right," due to the fact that he was emasculated by stepping on a land mine in World War II. Brown's bitter sense of separation from the mainstream of American life becomes immediately clear, even in the first paragraph of his narration, as he sits alone in the offices of the newspaper where he works as a rewrite man:

Well, they are all gone now, all but me: all those clear-eyed, clear-thinking people—people with their heads in the clouds and their feet firmly planted on the
ground—who comprise the editorial staff of the Pacific City *Courier*. Warmed
with the knowledge of a day's work well done, they have retired to their homes.
They have fled to the sweet refuge of their families, to the welcoming arms of
brave little women and the joyous embrace of laughing kiddies. (3)

The nature of Brown's wound gradually becomes clear, as does the
fact that his current boss, *Courier* editor Dave Randall, was also Brown's
commander in the war; it was Randall who gave the order that led to
Brown's wound, leaving a physical lack that mirrors the spiritual void at
the center of his being. This emptiness leads to a bitterness against Randall and all those "normal" people living their ordinary, routine, bourgeois lives in the bosoms of their typical American families. This bitterness is directed especially toward women. Unable to have normal sexual
relations, Brown substitutes violence, launching a series of would-be
murders of women, starting with his own wife, whom he seems to kill
largely to avoid having to tell her about his injury. Indeed, he tells no
one, feeling a sense of shame over his condition that sets him apart from
those around him. But Brown's condition also sets him apart from himself, leading to a fragmentation of his very identity. Thus, he sometimes
looks into the mirror and converses with the "strange guy" there, debat-
ing his next action with the man in the reflection (129). At other times, he
contemplates suicide but concludes that there is nothing there to kill,
leaving him in the situation of living on forever "in a world of snickers
and whisperings and amused pity" (36).

Within the context of the 1950s, Brown's alienation, combined with his
missing phallus, seems to beg for a Freudian explanation. In fact,
Thompson often seems to invite such explanations, most obviously in the
highly oedipal *A Swell-Looking Babe*, where 11-year-old Dusty Rhodes
sexually fondles his adoptive mother, then later destroys his adoptive father by signing his name on a petition, causing him to become a target of
anticommunist hysteria. One could, of course, read *A Swell-Looking Babe*
as a clumsy attempt to apply fashionable Freudian explanations in fiction. There are, however, good reasons to believe that Thompson intends
to undermine Freudian explanations in the book. For one thing, Thompson's treatment of the theme, especially in the scene in which the young
Dusty badgers his doting adoptive mother into allowing him to fondle
and suckle her breasts as if he were a baby, is simply too overt. One need
only compare Lawrence's much more nuanced treatment of the oedipal
theme in *Sons and Lovers* to conclude that Thompson is up to something
very different from the modernist attempt to employ Freud's ideas to
develop new insights into the human psyche. Moreover, Thompson is
careful to have Dusty adopted by his new parents at age 5, well beyond

the typical age at which the oedipal drama is acted out. Finally, the particular method through which Dusty enacts vengeance against his adoptive father subtly suggests the insane and criminal nature of the anticommunist crusades that swept America in the late 1940s and early 1950s. Unable, in this context, openly to speak out, Thompson conducts whatever subversive critique he can get away with, employing oblique, Aesopian techniques that allow his occasional and seemingly offhand passing mentions of American anticommunism to take on potentially powerful critical dimensions.[9]

In general, Thompson's characters are so fragmented that there is almost nothing left for psychoanalysis to analyze. Lou Ford, in *The Killer Inside Me*, is perhaps the central example of a Thompson protagonist whose psychic condition goes beyond the modernist experience of alienation into the postmodernist experience of schizophrenic psychic fragmentation. Whether or not Ford's surname is taken to link his predicament with Henry Ford, that ultimate icon of American capitalism, it is certainly the case that Lou Ford is a quintessential example of the postmodern fractured psyche. The very title of Thompson's book indicates the fragmented nature of Ford's identity, as if the person who commits the murders in the book is a sinister alien presence residing inside the seemingly placid deputy sheriff. Similarly, Ford's speech patterns, which can suddenly shift from good-old-boy colloquialisms, to sophisticated intellectual pronouncements, indicate the multiplicity of his identity.

The multiple and contradictory nature of Ford's character has been noted by numerous critics. McCauley suggests that the mystery of Ford's actual nature is unsolvable because "there's not enough left inside him to render him guilty or innocent" (172). In addition, McCauley describes Ford as a "trapped intellectual forced to play a dumb, sardonic clown" and suggests that he thereby resembles Thompson (175). Further, he notes that "Ford is the prototypical Thompson murderer-priest, simultaneously disengaged from the inexplicable ferocity of his acts yet naturally sympathetic to his victims" (19). Brewer, meanwhile, is impressed by Ford's dual role as a crazed killer and a sort of Christ figure. He describes Ford as a common killer "transmogrified into a laughing Christ, a scapegoat murderer who enigmatically both relishes and resents his fated role, ideal to administer last rites over a floundering American dream" (22). Finally, Polito notes that Ford has lived a "double life" since adolescence, that his vision is "clear, if double and loathsome," that he consistently follows a "forked path," and that the apocalyptic end of the novel "consummates the terrifying logic of his split" (346, 348, 350).

Ford's complex and contradictory nature is evident from the very beginning of the text, when he appears in a Central City diner and explains to a woman customer that he doesn't need a gun despite his profession because, in his experience, if you are good to people, they will respond in kind. The owner of the diner then extols Ford for his kindness and generosity to the owner's son, to which Ford reacts with a weird nastiness, mocking the man with a barrage of intentionally corny clichés. Ford then steps out into the night and brutally grinds his lit cigar into the palm of a bum who approaches him, explaining his cruelty from the fact that his recent involvement with local prostitute Joyce Lakeland has reactivated the mental "sickness" that has plagued him since childhood.

In fact, one of the most striking aspects of Ford's character is the extent to which he is conscious of this sickness, which he himself attributes, in good Freudian fashion, to certain childhood sexual experiences. The autodidact Ford, self-educated by reading in his physician father's extensive library, has a strong sense of his own fragmentation, which he at one point appears to diagnose as "schizophrenia, paranoid type" (144). At the same time, Ford identifies this diagnosis as the kind that might be arrived at by a psychiatrist, then goes on to suggest that psychiatrists are not really capable of dealing with his condition. Psychiatrists, after all, are trained to probe the human psyche, which, according to the Freudian model, is a fairly stable object of epistemological inquiry. Ford's fragmented psyche gives psychiatrists very little to get a handle on: "Plenty of pretty smart psychiatrists have been fooled by guys like me, and you can't really fault 'em for it. There's just not much they can put their hands on, know what I mean?" (146).

Much of Ford's background as related in the book involves aberrant childhood sexual experience, seeming to invite a Freudian explanation. At the same time, Ford also offers an alternative social explanation for his crisis. Talking with young Johnnie Pappas just before he strangles him in his jail cell, Thompson launches into a speech on the corruption and hypocrisy of modern American society, in which values seem turned upside-down. In this "bitched up" environment, Ford says, "the Bad People want us to have more dough, and the Good People are fighting to keep it from us. ... If we all had all we wanted to eat, we'd crap too much. We'd have inflation in the toilet paper industry" (78).

Ford's analysis here can be read in a number of ways, and it should certainly be kept in mind that Ford is (apparently) a psychopath. But this statement can be taken as another Aesopian evasion of censorship, as a coded critique of capitalism that, in the repressive environment of McCarthyite America, could not be delivered directly if Thompson wanted to have any hope of survival as a commercial novelist. From this point of view, the "Bad People" mentioned by Ford can be none other than communists, or at least socialists, who hope, through the redistribution of wealth, to provide "more dough" to poor workers like Johnnie Pappas. The "Good People" (who cannot stand to see little people like Johnnie have any comforts) would then be the proponents of capitalism, who believe this redistribution would be a bad thing because it would disrupt the growth and productivity of the capitalist system. That Ford uses such specifically capitalist language to represent the arguments of these supposedly Good People would seem to support this interpretation of his statement.

Ford also explains that this system can continue to function in this way because most people are simply unable to recognize what is going on. Ford, however, identifies himself as an individual with the superior insight that is required to see through the system but also suggests that he himself is so implicated in the system that he is unable fully to extricate himself from it, despite his understanding of its pernicious nature. He thus finds himself both opposed to, and aligned with, the system, leading to his own psychic fragmentation: "I guess I kind of got a foot on both fences, Johnnie. I planted 'em there early and now they've taken root, and I can't move either way and I can't jump. All I can do is wait until I split. Right down the middle" (78).

Ultimately, after a series of brutal murders, Ford does not simply split down the middle but essentially explodes in all directions, accompanied, in fact, by a literal explosion that brings the book to an apocalyptic close by destroying Ford, his house, Joyce Lakeland, and the police who have come to arrest Ford for his crimes. Ford, however, was such a compelling character that even this ending did not prevent Thompson from (apparently) resurrecting him in *Wild Town* (1957), presumably a prequel to *The Killer Inside Me*. However, the relationship between these two texts (and the two Lou Fords) is quite complex and highly unstable. *Wild Town* seems to be a relatively ordinary detective story that focuses on the attempts of a detective-protagonist to solve a murder that occurs early in the novel.

But *Wild Town* is anything but a conventional detective novel. The book, in fact, borders on the surreal, deviating from the standard, hard-boiled detective story in a number of ways. The protagonist, Bugs McKenna, has a great deal in common with predecessors such as Philip Marlowe, Sam Spade, and Lew Archer. For example, he is a tough former cop who finds it difficult to conform to the routine of modern bourgeois society, thereby living on the edge of that society. But McKenna is far more marginalized than his predecessors, who tend to seem far more capable and self-sufficient than is he. Where they typically operate as independent, self-employed private detectives, he occupies a lowly position as the hotel detective in the Hanlon Hotel in Ragtown, a shabby Texas oil town. McKenna's personal baggage is also considerably heavier than that of the typical fictional detective, as can be seen from the fact that his police career ended not through a classic case of insubordination but through his shooting of a fellow officer and subsequent imprisonment. McKenna also has some of the same hostility toward women that is typical of male protagonists in American noir fiction, but he takes that hostility to a pathological extreme, continuing to harbor the bitterness that earlier caused him to beat his wife so savagely that he went to prison for that as well.

In general, McKenna lives in somewhat the same world as do the protagonists of mainstream American detective fiction, but that world is pushed to an extreme, making it far darker, shabbier, and weirder. Indeed, *Wild Town*, like much of Thompson's fiction, operates consistently in a mode of exaggeration, making it properly a work of satire, rather than straightforward detective fiction—though it is certainly the case that the works of masters such as Hammett and Chandler often have a strong satirical component as well. In particular, *Wild Town* takes the everyday world of American capitalism to a defamiliarizing extreme that forces readers to come to grips with dark aspects of American life, battling against the process of reification that makes it possible for individuals to ignore those dark aspects under normal conditions.

Shabby Ragtown is itself an allegorical setting that once again emphasizes the temporary and unstable nature of success in the frantic world of modern capitalism. It is a ramshackle collection of rickety and temporary buildings that has sprung up almost overnight in the midst of the Texas oil fields, always with the recognition that all that seems solid about it can melt into air as rapidly as it appeared. The apparent exception is the Hanlon Hotel, a fine, fourteen-story structure constructed by oilman Mike Hanlon, whose earlier wildcat oil strikes were principally responsible for the sudden growth of the town. Hanlon is anything but a typical figure of the powerful, tophatted, capitalist magnate. For one thing, he remains a rough-hewn Texan, without the refinements that one might expect to go with his wealth. He is also himself contemptuous of the competitive world of capitalism, where one person's success almost invariably arises from the failure of others. Late in the book, for example, he explains to McKenna that he was originally attracted to the world of wildcat oil drilling because "'you could help yourself in it—get rich maybe—without hurting other people. You didn't have to squeeze 'em. You didn't have to push them down to push yourself up. All you had to do was find the oil, and everyone was better off, and no one was hurt'" (148).

This idealized world, if it ever existed, has been lost amid the growing power of cutthroat capitalism. Indeed, in a swirl of corruption and subterfuge, no one in *Wild Town* is who he or she appears to be, and everyone seems determined to undo everyone else. Thompson, meanwhile, seems determined to undo his readers. One of the central figures in *Wild Town* is Lou Ford, the deputy sheriff of Ragtown. Readers of *The Killer Inside Me* naturally approach *Wild Town* with expectations that Ford is the same man who serves as the psychotic killer-narrator of the earlier novel. Indeed, Thompson supplies enough biographical details to encourage this identification, making *Wild Town* appear to be a prequel to *The Killer Inside Me*. Readers thus think they know Ford, verifying, in an apparent case of dramatic irony, McKenna's suspicions that Ford is corrupt and perhaps murderous. Thompson supplies a number of hints to reinforce this conclusion, having Ford behave in apparently sinister ways throughout the book. Then, at the end of the book, Thompson turns these expectations on their heads by having Ford emerge as a virtuous, even heroic figure; he solves the crime and saves Hanlon from the machinations of the evil women, Joyce and Rosalie.

As Polito puts it, *Wild Town* transpires in a sort of parallel universe to the world of *The Killer Inside Me*, and its play with the expectations of readers can be taken as a "wink" at the "cult" of Thompson's earlier fiction (411, 413). In a sense, however, this playful wink can be taken as a betrayal of Thompson's own readers that reinforces the underlying theme of *Wild Town* that no one can be trusted. Thompson even plays subtle games with the identity of Amy Standish, Ford's virtuous schoolteacher girlfriend. Amy seems to be the one completely honest and trustworthy figure in the book, and her apparent virtue is given a special poignancy by the fact that readers of *The Killer Inside Me* know that she will eventually be murdered by Ford. Or so they think. But the parallel universe metaphor again holds. If the Ford of *Wild Town* is not quite the same person as the Ford of *The Killer Inside Me*, then the same holds for Amy. In fact, Ford's girlfriend in *The Killer Inside Me* is named Amy *Stanton*, not Standish. The similarity of the two names entices readers who are less than fully alert to believe that the two women are one and the same, but more alert readers are again warned not to take anything for granted.

Ford (almost) reappears once again in *The Transgressors* (1961), which continues the parallel universe motif of *Wild Town*, introducing a protagonist, Tom Lord, who is another version of Lou Ford.[10] The chief deputy sheriff in the West Texas oil town of Big Sands, Lord is a man of precarious sanity, and his psychic instabilities sometimes lead to violent behavior. He is so alienated that he is estranged even from himself; his psyche is informed by a constant internal debate that Lord himself continually refers to as "Lord vs. Lord." Other aspects of the plot of *The Transgressors* recall *The Killer Inside Me* as well. For example, Lord is involved with a local prostitute, Joyce Lakewood, who is another version of the earlier Joyce Lakeland, just as Amy Standish of *Wild Town* mirrors Amy Stanton from *The Killer Inside Me*. Joyce Lakewood, like Joyce Lakeland, is brutally murdered, and various other parallels with *The Killer Inside Me* again seem designed to create the expectation that Lord is the killer. Lord, however, resembles the virtuous Ford of *Wild Town* far more than the psychotic Ford of *The Killer Inside Me*. He does not turn out to be the killer. In fact, for once, he even gets the girl, settling, as the book closes, into what will apparently be a rewarding personal relationship with Donna McBride, the widow of a man Lord may (or may not) have earlier killed.

Despite this unusual (for Thompson) happy ending, *The Transgressors* is, in many ways, essentially an amalgam of familiar Thompson themes and motifs. If, as Jameson suggests, postmodernist texts are constructed largely by cannibalizing pervious texts in a mode of pastiche, then Thompson takes the technique one step further in his later work, cannibalizing his own earlier texts, which had already themselves been cobbled together from a collection of literary flotsam and jetsam. In addition to the parallel characters (such as Lou Ford/Tom Lord and Joyce Lakeland/Joyce Lakewood), the book abounds in familiar Thompson devices. There are at least two different plans to stage an apparent double murder in the book, as Ford does in *The Killer Inside Me* and as Thompson characters do in any number of other books. Lord's uncertainty about whether he actually killed McBride recalls the uncertain murders committed by Clint Brown in *The Nothing Man*. Donna McBride closely resembles Lord's mother, just as Roy Dillon notes a striking resemblance between his mother and Moira Langtry in *The Grifters*, and Dusty Rhodes is drawn to Marcia Bascom because of her resemblance to his adoptive mother in *A Swell-Looking Babe*. Big Springs (which also appears in *Texas by the Tail*) bears many direct similarities to Ragtown, including the fact that it boasts a 14-floor hotel. And so on.

*The Transgressors* is certainly one of Thompson's weakest novels, though, at the same time, this recycling of materials from earlier books can, itself, be an interesting literary phenomenon, rather than simply a sign of the author's haste, laziness, or lack of imagination. Repeating characters, settings and motifs often occur in fiction, as when the recurring characters and settings in Balzac help him to flesh out and solidify the realism of his sweeping depiction of nineteenth-century French society in the ninety-plus volumes of his *Comédie humaine*. On the other hand, Thompson's particular use of recurring characters tends to destabilize, rather than stabilize and solidify, his texts. Relevant here is Brian McHale's argument that the device of *retour de personages* in Balzac seems aimed at creating an air of versimilitude, while the use of similar devices in many postmodernist works has the opposite effect, creating an air of ontological instability that undermines any stable recuperation of the text (57–58).

Meanwhile, crime fiction, especially detective fiction, often features series of works with the same setting and protagonist. But, where the continuation of Philip Marlowe or Lew Archer from one novel to the next provides a steadying anchor that helps readers keep their moorings amid the corrupt worlds of noir detective fiction, the not-quite-recurring towns and characters of Thompson only add more confusion and instability, enhancing the consistent theme that, in contemporary capitalist America, identity is unstable, no one can be trusted, and nothing can be counted on. If Balzac, Hammett, Chandler, and Ross Macdonald often make the same points about their own societies, one could argue that the repetition with a difference that informs Thompson's *Comédie diabolique* represents a technical advance, the invention of a new device for conveying the insecure situation of the individual subject in the tumultuous, shifting, changing world of modern capitalism, where nothing, after all, is ever quite the same as it used to be.[11]

In fact, the only character who reappears with seeming consistency in Thompson's fiction is the diminutive Jewish lawyer, I. Kossmeyer. Yet Kossmeyer himself turns out to be a figure of problematic postmodern identity, or, alternatively, of the tenuousness of individual identity in the difficult climate of the 1950s. Indeed, his major talent seems to be his uncanny ability to change his appearance to match that of those around him. For example, Kossmeyer first appears in *Cropper's Cabin* (1952), in which he plays a relatively small role as the defense attorney for 19-year-old narrator, Tommy Carver. Here, Kossmeyer's clowning theatrics in the courtroom are mirrored, by his theatrical behavior outside the courtroom. When he first meets the sullen Tommy in the latter's jail cell, he breaks the ice by entertaining his new client with his talent for mimicry. Tommy explains:

He didn't actually look like me at all, but he was looking like me now; in a way, say, that a cartoon will look like a man. He had his lips pushed way out, and his mouth pulled way down until the corners almost met under his chin. His eyes were rolled down and in, looking at the wisp of hair he'd pulled down over his forehead. (*Cropper's Cabin* 102)

This talent for mimicry remains central to Thompson's characterization of Kossmeyer throughout his subsequent appearances. Ultimately, Kossmeyer begins to function as a sort of cipher, who, having no substantial identity of his own, simply reflects the identities of those around him. Kossmeyer's most prominent role in Thompson's fiction occurs in *A Swell-Looking Babe*, where he functions as a sort of avenging angel, trying to ensure that Dusty Rhodes is punished for his crimes. Central to this role, however, is his talent for mimicry, as he first makes himself a "hideous caricature" of Dusty (41), then enacts the dying agony of Dusty's father, driven to death by Dusty's own actions (144), then enacts the hanging that he believes Dusty deserves in retribution (145). In *The Kill-Off*, Kossmeyer is a minor character. His narration opens the book and shows him mimicking his own wife, while at the same time explaining that he has developed his talent for mimicry because, as a five-foot-tall lawyer with no actual formal legal education, he must develop and use any talent he can (4–5).

Kossmeyer's seeming ability to change his appearance at will marks his unstable identity as postmodern role-playing. In this, he resembles any number of figures from the long 1950s. The most obvious analogue from crime fiction would be Highsmith's Tom Ripley, but figures such as Nabokov's Humbert Humbert (whose very name is, we are assured, a pseudonym) also constantly play roles. Not surprisingly, this motif of subjectivity-as-acting was often played out on movie screens of the period as well. In film noir, for example, characters are constantly in disguise, assuming so many fake identities that the concept of a real identity comes to have virtually no meaning. Moreover, American film in the long 1950s was dominated by major stars, whose performances were overtly marked as artificial, if only because audiences were so intensely aware of their "real" identities. The quintessential case might be Marilyn Monroe, who, in one film after another, simply played a caricature of herself—leading to Frank Tashlin's *Will Success Spoil Rock Hunter?* (1957), in which Jayne Mansfield played a cartoonish caricature of the caricature. Of course, cartoonish films of the long 1950s were dominated by, well, cartoons, especially the productions of Walt Disney company, which, along with the films of Alfred Hitchcock, provided some of the best illustrations of the postmodern, anti-utopian orientation of the period in numerous other ways as well. I discuss the films of Hitchcock and Disney in the next chapter.

# ━ Chapter 4 ━

## American Film in the Long 1950s:
## From Hitchcock to Disney

In the 1951 Disney short *Plutopia* Mickey and Pluto vacation in the presumably idyllic setting of Camp Utopia. Mickey, being "human," likes it fine, but one cartoon character's dream is another one's nightmare, and Pluto soon discovers that the camp is anything but an ideal world for dogs. Not only is he not allowed inside the cabin, but he is required to be muzzled and leashed at all times, making it possible for the camp cat (cats are almost invariably evil in Disney films of the period) to taunt him from just outside his reach. Finally, Pluto escapes the carceral environment of the camp by falling asleep, where he can experience a dream world in which the cat is his slave and even begs to be bitten.

The ideology of *Plutopia* is typical not only of Disney films from the long 1950s but also of American culture as a whole during the period. For one thing, Pluto's definition of the ideal life as one in which he defeats the threatening cat suggests the extent to which American utopian thought depends upon violent conquest of the Other. For another, the film shows a strong skepticism toward the achievability of utopia in the material world, even through such violent victory, suggesting that the ideal life can be achieved only in the unreal world of fantasy and dream.

Indeed, the utopian images produced in the Disney films and theme parks tend to be consistently problematic. Thus, Henry Giroux gives the subtitle "Disney's troubled utopia" to the introduction to his book-length study of Disney's role in shaping American popular culture. For Giroux, "Disney's power lies, in part, in its ability to tap into the lost hopes, abortive dreams, and utopian potential of popular culture" (5). But Giroux notes that the utopian energies of Disney products are complex and contradictory, sometimes offering genuine elements of pleasure and wish fulfillment, but also tending to "turn children's desires and dreams into fodder for the Disney Stores and power-lunch brokers" (12).

Disney's theme parks are particularly ostentatious displays of consumer capitalism, and Disneyland, opened in 1955, is an extremely representative phenomenon of the 1950s. Perhaps the ultimate examples of
the commodification of utopia in American popular culture, Disneyland
and the later, larger Disney World (opened near Orlando, Florida, in
1971) have attracted a tremendous amount of attention from cultural critics who have seen significant problems in the packaging of utopia in the
parks.[1] For example, Disneyland functions for Jean Baudrillard much as
the prison functions for Michel Foucault, to encourage the general population placidly to accept the status quo. In particular, Baudrillard argues
that Disneyland functions to encourage the general population to accept
the reality of a consumer capitalist social world that is, in fact, "hyperreal," saturated with images and simulations:

Disneyland is there to conceal the fact that it is the "real" country, all of "real"
America, which *is* Disneyland (just as prisons are there to conceal the fact that it
is the social in its entirety, in its banal omnipresence, which is carceral). Disneyland is presented as imaginary in order to make us all believe that the rest is real,
when in fact all of Los Angeles and the America surrounding it are no longer
real, but of the order of the hyperreal and of simulation. (172)

Among other things, Disneyland and Disney World are saturated
with utopian images of "better living," but the very placement of these
images within the ostentatiously artificial environments of the parks
tends to suggest the fictionality of utopia, discouraging park-goers from
seeking utopia in the real world. But even the fictional utopias portrayed
in the parks have a definite dystopian side, as anyone who has ever been
bothered by the efficiency with which the parks are able to control and
manipulate the vast populations who visit them has noticed. This side of
Disneyland is well captured in Doctorow's *The Book of Daniel* (1971),
when the park is visited by protagonist Daniel Isaacson, the son of fictional parents based on Julius and Ethel Rosenberg. Doctorow's description of Disneyland (presented in an objective, reportorial style) provides
the reader with a great deal of information about contemporary America.
Not only is the park's simulation of reality presented in great detail, but
the sinister aspects of this simulation are made quite clear. The park's
real achievement, we are told, is the "handling of crowds," who are
taught complete obedience to the corporate ideology with which the park
is saturated: "The ideal Disneyland patron may be said to be one who
responds to a process of symbolic manipulation that offers him his culminating and quintessential sentiment at the moment of a purchase"
(289). In short, Disneyland embodies the ultimate triumph of precisely
the forces against which Daniel's leftist father had warned him in his
childhood, signaling the complete historical failure of the old Left to
counter the growth of consumer capitalism in America.

Disney's films of the long 1950s presented similarly packaged and commodified versions of utopia. They are, in this and other senses, among the central products of American culture in the decade, when the Disney company produced an impressive string of animated classics. In fact, American film production as a whole was particularly rich in this period, even though it was in many ways a very troubled time for the American film industry. In addition to the anticommunist purges that focused on Hollywood as a convenient scapegoat, the major studios were besieged by antitrust actions such as the Paramount case, which brought to an end the vertical integration that had been crucial to studio profits. The increasing independence of directors and stars further helped to shatter the hegemony of the big studios. The rise of television introduced a competitive threat that was only the most obvious of several reasons that movie attendance plummeted during the decade. To address this threat, studios introduced a number of technological innovations, many of which are now regarded as diametrically opposed to the production of genuine film art, if not downright laughable. The greatly remembered image of movie crowds wearing identical 3-D glasses now seems comical, even if, at the time, it was an uncomfortably apt image of the decade's pressures toward (and concomitant fear of) conformity.

Nevertheless, the list of films released during the long 1950s is impressive. The American Film Institute's (AFI) recent (1998) list of the 100 greatest American films of the twentieth century includes 31 films from the long 1950s and 20 from the 1950s proper, more than any other decade. In comparison, twenty-seven of the top 100 films were released in the two "golden" decades of the 1930s and 1940s combined. Meanwhile, fully half of the top twenty films on the AFI list were released in the long 1950s.[2]

American film in the long 1950s reflects many of the same concerns as the American novel from the same period. For one thing, a quick look at the top box-office films of the decade shows an almost total domination by escapist fantasies. Disney was central to this phenomenon, continuing a long record of commercial success. Mickey Mouse had been born in 1928, and the Disney animated feature film format had been perfected as early as 1937, with the release of *Snow White and the Seven Dwarfs*. Meanwhile, by 1940, with the release of *Fantasia*, Walt Disney had made clear his ambition to participate in (or perhaps appropriate for his own artistic, ideological, and commercial purposes) the Western high-cultural tradition. In the 1930s, *Snow White* was surpassed at the box office only by *Gone with the Wind*, and the Disney company remained dominant at the box office through the 1940s and long 1950s, in which animated classics such as *Song of the South* (1946), *Cinderella* (1950), *Peter Pan* (1953), *Lady and the Tramp* (1955), *Sleeping Beauty* (1959), and *101 Dalmatians* (1961) were major box-office successes, even if the high costs of making the

the films meant that they were not always as profitable for the company as the box-office receipts might seem to indicate.

Quasi-religious historical romances, such as *The Ten Commandments* (1956) and *The Robe* (1953), were also huge hits in the long 1950s, indicating a widespread desire on the part of moviegoers to recover through film spectacle the sense of the magical that they had lost in their everyday lives. Finally, the success of *Around the World in Eighty Days* (1956) and *South Pacific* (1958) also bespoke the longing of American audiences for the kind of exotic experience that could not be obtained in suburbia, though the film version of *Peyton Place* (1957), which titillated audiences with the domesticated exoticism of small-town sexual adventurism, was only slightly less popular.

*Peyton Place* was not the only escapist film of the long 1950s to have a potentially dark core. The classic case here is Frank Capra's *It's a Wonderful Life* (1946), which would eventually become one of the most beloved and respected (it ranked 11th on the AFI Top 100 list) films of the long 1950s. Capra's film also did a good job of capturing much of the spirit of the coming years. It should be remembered, of course, that Capra's film was neither a commercial nor a critical success on its initial release and that it rose to its current prominence only as a result of its emergence as a holiday favorite in the 1970s. That particular history is partly responsible for the fact that the film is now widely regarded as feel-good Christmas fare. However, as Robert Ray notes, *It's a Wonderful Life* "was almost frighteningly bleak for most of its 129 minutes" (183). In fact, it is in many ways an extremely dark and cynical film, which may account for its initial lack of popularity with a moviegoing public anxious for relief from the tensions of the war years—and from the subsequent tensions and doubts that were already lurking in the margins of postwar American triumphalism. After all, the most striking image from *It's a Wonderful Life* is not the contrived happy ending but the scenes in which pastoral Bedford Falls has been transformed into the raucous consumer capitalist dystopia of Pottersville, thanks to the unchecked dominance of the evil capitalist, Mr. Potter.

The 1950s was also a particularly rich time for the production of Westerns, as filmmakers such as John Ford attempted to parlay the wide-open spaces of the American West into widescreen spectaculars that could offer a viewing experience unavailable on the small screen of television. Again, however, films such as *High Noon* (1952), *Shane* 1953), and *The Searchers* (1956) were not merely escapist adventures that offered compensation for the routinized world of American life in the 1950s. Instead, they tended to have apprehensive edges and dark undertones that suggested the anxieties of life in modern America. Indeed, the long 1950s is probably best remembered for the dark turn taken by so many films of the decade, most especially film noir and the related thrillers of Alfred Hitchcock.

Many of the most important noir classics, including John Huston's *The Maltese Falcon* (1941), Billy Wilder's *Double Indemnity* (1944) and *The Lost Weekend* (1945), Otto Preminger's *Laura* (1944), and Edward Dmytryk's *Murder, My Sweet* (1944), were actually released during World War II. But the noir phenomenon continued well into the long 1950s, with the production of such noir films as Robert Rossen's *Body and Soul* (1947), Abraham Polonsky's *Force of Evil* (1948), Orson Welles's *The Lady from Shanghai* (1948), Huston's *The Asphalt Jungle* (1950), Rudolph Maté's *D.O.A.* (1950), Cy Endfield's *Try and Get Me* (1951), Mark Robson's *The Harder They Fall* (1956), and Alexander Mackendrick's *Sweet Smell of Success* (1957). Meanwhile, film noir, always cynical, even became skeptical of its own premises, beginning to take a self-conscious, campy turn as early as 1950, with the release of Wilder's *Sunset Boulevard*. Welles's *Touch of Evil* (1958) then virtually finished off the noir cycle with a self-parodic, postmodernist masterpiece, while Samuel Fuller's *Shock Corridor* (1963) took the form as far as it could go with one last over-the-top finale.

This skepticism toward film noir suggested not that noir darkness was out of style but that American skepticism and cynicism were beginning to go beyond even the scope of film noir. Hitchcock's films are exemplary of this phenomenon. Lesley Brill, among others, has attempted to argue for a kinder, gentler Hitchcock, whose films are really about romance and redemption. But, in order to do so, Brill is forced to declare such classics from the long 1950s as *Vertigo* and *Psycho* to be aberrations, while placing great emphasis on films, such as *Young and Innocent* (1937) and *Mr. and Mrs. Smith* (1941), that were made prior to the long 1950s. In point of fact, though slicker, brighter, and more expensive than most noir films (and often in brilliant color), most of Hitchcock's films of the long 1950s are in many ways thematically darker than most true noir films, suggesting as they do a darkness that resides not in back alleys, but on Main Street—or even in posh suburbs. Thus, Engelhardt sees the prominence of Hitchcock during this period as a key marker of a disorienting blurring of boundaries associated with the collapse of American "victory culture" (88).

Hitchcock was, in fact, the perfect director for the anxiety-ridden long 1950s. In his ability to create an atmosphere of anxiety and dread within the framework of commercially successful genre pictures, he was also the perfect director for a consumer capitalist culture that was increasingly worried about the ability of commodities to bring happiness. As Robert Ray puts it, Hitchcock's greatest asset, in fact, was his "ability to mix his personal sense of Cold War realities with entertainment movies" (158). Hitchcock's films of the long 1950s, up until *Psycho*, which was a sort of intentional throwback, tend to become progressively slicker and glossier, leaving their film noir roots behind while retaining the thematic darkness of film noir.

At first glance, Hitchcock and Disney together would seem to mark the opposite extremes of American culture in the long 1950s, with Disney suggesting the optimism of an increasingly affluent postwar American society and Hitchcock suggesting the anxieties that threatened to undermine that affluence. Meanwhile, Hitchcock's films are known for their (especially psychological) maturity and complexity, while, in Disney, flicks are for kids. Even the material circumstances of production seem to be polar opposites in these two cases. The name "Hitchcock" is the signifier of an individual auteur, with a distinct style presumably emanating from the director's unique talents and psychology; the name "Disney" is the signifier of a corporation, with Walt Disney himself providing a basic vision and management skills but with the films themselves being produced by a well-coordinated corporate team of virtually anonymous professional employees.

Given these differences, what is truly striking about the Hitchcock and Disney films of the long 1950s is their basic similarity. Of course, Hitchcock himself had acknowledged the relevance of Disney to his own work as early as 1936 in *Sabotage* (an adaptation of Joseph Conrad's *The Secret Agent*), in which characters watch the comic murderous violence of Disney's *Who Killed Cock Robin?* as a commentary on the content of the Hitchcock film and the Conrad novel. By the long 1950s, the similarities between Hitchcock and Disney continued to grow, showing the power of Cold War paradigms during the period. For example, the films of both Hitchcock and Disney during this period are built on the basic Cold War premise that American domestic bliss is threatened by a number of sinister outside forces. Moreover, in both cases this sense of threat translates into a number of incipient postmodernist characteristics, the most important of which (at least for my purposes here) is a basic skepticism, on the part of both Hitchcock and Disney, toward utopian thought.

Disney's films of the long 1950s function rather transparently as propaganda intended to brainwash American children into conformist orthodoxy. Their involvement within the rhetoric of the Cold War thus seems particularly obvious. But Hitchcock's inscription within the basic parameters of Cold War thought has been a particular object of inquiry for film scholars in recent years as well. For example, Hitchcock's films gain a great deal of their power from the tension between opposed inclinations in the films, perhaps most notably Hitchcock's own simultaneous (and seemingly contradictory) horror of routinization and disorder.[3] This contradiction, however, was typical of American thought in the long 1950s, which may be one reason that Hitchcock's films were so successful during the period. Indeed, several critics (most notably Robert Corber) have noted Hitchcock's firm inscription within the ideology of the Cold War, an inscription that, among other things, makes him a typical director of the period and seriously challenges the once-hegemonic view of Hitchcock as a modernist auteur with a unique and individual style.

Thomas M. Leitch thus notes that virtually all critics, by the late 1990s, acknowledged that much of Hitchcock's genius lay in his ability to displace the spectator's desire and bring it "into alignment with the nation's security interests." For Leitch, "everybody knows that Hitchcock's films from *Strangers on a Train* to *Psycho* use the discourses of national security—in particular systematically valorizing the nuclear family dominated by a professional male and stigmatizing the homosexual villain—to organize the character's desires and the audiences' fantasies" (4). But Leitch also finds that this reading tells us very little about Hitchcock himself, since much the same can be said for virtually all American films of the Cold War period.

Leitch's discussion builds, among other things, on the crucial work of Corber, who has vigorously argued the notion that Hitchcock's notorious homophobia is, in fact, crucially involved with the anticommunist rhetoric of the Cold War, homosexuals joining communists as depraved others against whom we must defend the American way of life, even if that defense requires the establishment of an extensive security state and extensive curtailment of civil liberties. In particular, Hitchcock's films participate in a crucial way in the postwar liberal consensus (epitomized by the New York Intellectuals), which, for Corber, mobilized anticommunist and homophobic rhetoric to enforce an ideological orthodoxy that severely limited "the fund of interpretive possibilities" available to women and minorities, thus containing any threat that such groups might pose to the mainstream status quo (*Name* 3).

Hitchcock began the long 1950s with the 1946 release of *Notorious*, which would have made a perfect Cold War spy thriller, except that it is a pre–Cold War piece that still figures the German Nazis as America's principal enemies in the world. A Grant-Bergman vehicle, *Notorious* was one of several important anti-Nazi thrillers—others included Dmytryk's *Cornered* (1945) and Welles's *The Stranger* (1946)—that together suggested the ongoing threat of Nazism even in the wake of the allied victory in World War II. *The Stranger*, with its vision of an important Nazi hiding out in tranquil small-town America,[4] is perhaps the most sinister of all of these films, but *Notorious*, with its vision of Nazis working to develop atomic weapons in South America, is particularly suggestive of the anxieties of the long 1950s, with its combination of the Nazi threat with the notion of dark forces lurking in the Third World.[5] Thus, the film draws upon the popular sense that, however affluent, postwar America was surrounded by dangerous enemies and thus could ill afford to rest in utopian bliss.

In *Notorious*, American agent T. R. Devlin (Grant) helps to recruit Alicia Huberman (Bergman), daughter of a convicted Nazi spy, to work with the Americans in an effort to root out a ring of Nazi agents known to be operating in Brazil. Devlin succeeds in recruiting Alicia, and the two of them go together to Rio de Janeiro to begin the mission. They also begin a torrid love affair, only to learn after their arrival in Brazil that it will be Alicia's mission to seduce Alexander Sebastian (Claude Rains), a key member of the Nazi ring, who also happens to be an old friend of Alicia's father and to have formerly been Alicia's lover.

Alicia agrees to take the assignment, though the nature of it breeds considerable tension between her and Devlin, who is furiously jealous of Sebastian and highly suspicious of Alicia's quick subsequent success in winning the Nazi's confidence—and hand in marriage. Using that confidence, she is able to help the American agents of the film track down an entire uranium smuggling operation being run by the Nazis, presumably toward the eventual development of nuclear weapons for use in a Nazi comeback. In the meantime, Sebastian realizes that Alicia is an American agent. He and his sinister mother (Mme. Leopoldine Constantine) then concoct a plot slowly to poison Alicia, making her death seem due to natural causes and thus making it unnecessary to reveal to the other Nazis Sebastian's gullibility in allowing himself to be seduced by the American. Devlin, however, manages to rescue Alicia in such a way that assures that the other Nazis will put two and two together and take a quick vengeance on Sebastian for allowing himself to be duped by Alicia. Devlin thus ensures that Sebastian will get his just deserts for his Nazi activity, though it is clear that Devlin's real motive is to take revenge on Sebastian for his marriage to Alicia.

The Nazis of *Notorious* are suitably ruthless and dangerous, though there is little to indicate that the Americans of the film are any less so. Indeed, the dark atmosphere of the film has as much to do with the characterization of Devlin as with that of the Nazis. Obsessed with Alicia's checkered past, Devlin is consistently cruel in reminding her of it—and often violent in his treatment of her. Meanwhile, the film's moral ambiguity is intensified not only in the blurring of the boundary between the Americans and the Nazis but in the contrast between the behavior of respectable American women and the notorious Alicia, who turns out to be trustworthy and even heroic, at least from an American point of view. Thus, Devlin angrily responds to one of his American handlers, who worries about their reliance on a woman of Alicia's "sort." "Miss Huberman is first, last, and always not a lady," Devlin bitterly remarks. "She may be risking her life, but when it comes to being a lady, she doesn't hold a candle to your wife, sir, sitting in Washington playing bridge with three other ladies of great honor and virtue."

In the meantime, Devlin's rescue of Alicia is partial at best. For one thing, it is not made entirely clear that she will even recover from her poisoning. For another, given the events of the film, the likelihood that Devlin and Alicia will go on to have a happy life together is quite small, especially as the powerful sexual current that runs between them seems to contain a strong element of sadism, at least on Devlin's part. After all, until the discovery of her treachery, Sebastian had treated Alicia far better and more tenderly than Devlin ever had, and jumping from a life with Sebastian to one with Devlin seems a little bit like going from the frying pan into the fire. As Thomas Schatz puts it, the film's supposedly happy ending is "blatantly arbitrary and unsettling," leaving audiences with "a lingering concern, if not a sense of downright dread, about a destabilized personality and relationships that can never again be fixed, whole, or in balance" (382).

If the respectable Americans of *Notorious* are less than saintly figures, the central characters of *Rope* (1948) are downright sinister. Based on the similarly titled 1929 play by the British Marxist writer Patrick Hamilton, the story (loosely based on the Leopold-Loeb case) is clearly intended as a commentary on bourgeois decadence. Shifting the play's Oxford setting to New York City (and muting the play's politics), the film focuses on Brandon Shaw (John Dall) and Phillip Morgan (Farley Granger), two wealthy young (vaguely homosexual) men so bored with life that they murder David Kentley, an acquaintance, just "for the sake of danger and the sake of killing." Shaw, the true instigator, likens murder to art, suggesting to Morgan that, by committing the perfect murder and getting away with it, they will have created an artistic masterpiece. Then, for a further thrill (or perhaps a further artistic flourish), they invite a group of acquaintances (including the dead man's father and girlfriend) to a dinner party in their well-appointed apartment, which features a huge window with a panoramic view of the New York skyline, as if to emphasize the film's setting in the capital city of capitalism. In a further macabre touch, they serve dinner buffet-style off a chest containing the still-fresh body.

This motif speaks volumes concerning the emptiness of life under capitalism. It also suggests the poverty of the bourgeois imagination in seeking utopian alternatives to the banal routine of everyday life. Indeed, the film virtually lampoons the very notion of social reform when Rupert Cadell (James Stewart) entertains the attendees at the party with a lengthy discourse on the benefits of murder as a solution to various social ills and annoyances of modern life. Shaw pitches in, agreeing with Cadell that murder is perfectly justified as long as it is committed by men of superior intellect on victims who are their inferiors. Horrified at this Nietzschean suggestion, Mr. Kentley (Cedric Hardwicke) opines that it smacks of Hitler, once again linking fascism and the American upper classes, but Shaw rejects the comparison so angrily that Cadell, who had only been jesting, begins to get suspicious.

Cadell's suspicions grow as Morgan begins to unravel under the pressure, behaving more and more erratically as the party proceeds. Eventually, a horrified Cadell uncovers the murder and summons help, waiting in the apartment with the two killers as sirens signal the approach of the police. Thus, murder (predictably) does not turn out to be the path to artistic perfection, anticipating Humbert Humbert's later failure to achieve artistic bliss through the statutory rape of Lolita and later murder of Clare Quilty. On the other hand, the film does not offer any alternative suggestions for ways to escape bourgeois routinization, leaving audiences with the assurance that the murderers will be apprehended but with no reason to believe that the social conditions that produced the murderers can be improved. The strongest utopian energies of *Rope* probably inhere in the film's experimental technique: Hitchcock boldly filmed the entire piece in roughly 10-minute takes (the maximum length of film that would fit in the camera at one time), thus minimizing the number of cuts, which are themselves then made as inconspicuous as possible, creating the illusion that the entire film is a single continuous take. On the other hand, this bit of bravura editing (or nonediting) is undercut by the premise of the film, in which the attempt to make murder into an aesthetic masterpiece calls into question the ability of pure form ever to be truly utopian, without some sort of corresponding hopeful content.

Hitchcock continued his interrogation of polite American society in *Strangers on a Train* (1951), loosely based on the novel of that title by Patricia Highsmith. Here, the villain is Bruno Anthony (Robert Walker), the Oedipally deranged (and obviously homosexual) scion of a wealthy and respectable upper-class family. The plot of the film revolves around the conversion of murder into an economic transaction. In particular, Anthony offers to kill the despicable wife of Guy Haines (Granger again), a professional tennis player who plans soon to begin a respectable career in government. In return, Haines is to murder Anthony's father on the premise that it will be much easier to get away with the murders because Haines has no motive for killing the elder Anthony, and Anthony has no motive for killing Miriam Haines. Haines does not agree to the exchange and, in fact, regards it as a sick joke. After all, Haines is (apparently) the text's marker of normality and decency.

Many aspects of the film undermine this straightforward reading of Haines. Not only is he obviously attracted to the idea of Miriam's murder, but his relationship with Anthony clearly suggests a latent homosexuality on his own part. Given that homosexuality is, in Hitchcock, a standard emblem of the threat posed to a normal, orderly life by the forces of chaos, Haines's status as a marker of social stability is thus seriously threatened. In Corber's terms, this threat is closely associated with the politics of the Cold War, an association that he sees as emphasized by Hitchcock's decision to locate much of the film's action in the nation's capital (*Name* 70). For Corber, then, *Strangers on a Train* "invokes the homophobic categories of cold-war political discourse to secure its representation of Bruno as the emotionally unstable homosexual who threatens national security" (72).

Of course, the attraction felt by Haines for Anthony emphasizes the dangerous allure of homoeroticism (and, by extension, communism), but it also threatens to undermine the Cold War polarities of Us versus Them by making Haines almost a double, rather than a polar opposite of Anthony. As the plot proceeds, Anthony does, in fact, kill Miriam, after which he expects Haines to kill the elder Anthony. Haines balks, but is meanwhile suspected of killing Miriam, triggering a typical Hitchcockian chain of suspense that finally ends when Anthony is weirdly killed in an amusement park carousel crash, then revealed to be the killer. The ornate carousel, of course, is a perfect emblem of the commodification and routinization of romance in the long 1950s: apparently offering images of adventure and escape from the routine, it, in fact, does nothing but go in circles, taking its passengers nowhere—until police inadvertently shoot the operator, who (in a preposterous scene that veers in the direction of self-parodic camp) falls on the speed control and sends the apparatus into overdrive.

Anthony's high social and economic positions suggest dark leanings among the rich and powerful, especially when they become weak and decadent, rather than ever-vigilant. Meanwhile, Hitchcock's placement of all of the film's scenes of actual violence in the presumably idyllic space of a small-town amusement park (in addition to Anthony's death on the carousel, Miriam is murdered in the park's lover's lane) indicates that danger and violence lie just beneath the surface of even the most placid of American settings. Indeed, these scenes link the amusement park to the longer tradition of the carnival, which, as Michael André Bernstein has pointed out in response to the evocation of the carnival by Mikhail Bakhtin, has always contained a dark and violent side.[6] Meanwhile, the park itself is tawdry, suggesting the vulgarity of consumer capitalism, with its confinement of utopian spaces to such commodified settings.

Like *Notorious* (and, for that matter, most Hitchcock films of the period), *Strangers on a Train* appears to have a conventional happy ending. Anthony is killed, Haines is cleared of Miriam's murder, and Haines and Ann are free to be married. Much of the film, however, seems to suggest that this marriage may be a troubled one, a suggestion that is reinforced by the seemingly comic scene in which the Haines frantically shies away from still another stranger he and Ann meet on a train. That this stranger is a clergyman supposedly implies that Haines is comically overreacting to his previous misadventure. However, as Spoto points out, the flight of this newly formed couple from a minister—an occupation traditionally associated with the cementing of wedding bonds—"carries an ominous omen beneath the humor," so that Haines's sought-after "life of order and quiet dignity ... is in grave doubt indeed" (196, 197).

From this point of view, it is interesting to note that *Dial M for Murder* (1954) functions as a sort of sequel to *Strangers on a Train*, suggesting dire directions for the Haines–Ann relationship. Here, Grace Kelly plays the unfaithful wife of an ex-professional tennis player (Ray Milland), who, in turn, attempts to have her murdered. But Hitchcock's major effort of

1954, also featuring Kelly, was *Rear Window*, described by Robin Wood as the filmmaker's first true "masterpiece" (100). Though a suspenseful thriller, *Rear Window* also includes numerous elements of romantic comedy, announcing the mixture of genres and modes that would come to mark most of Hitchcock's best-known films of the long 1950s. The premise of the film is simple: professional photographer L. B. Jefferies (Stewart) has been confined to his two-room New York apartment for six weeks due to a broken leg sustained while photographing an auto race while standing in the middle of the track. Accustomed to a life of action and adventure, Jefferies does not take well to this confinement; he experiences considerable boredom and restlessness, which he attempts to alleviate by observing his neighbors in the apartment building across a courtyard. In the process, he believes he finds evidence that one of the neighbors, Lars Thorwald (Raymond Burr), may have murdered his wife. Jefferies relays his suspicions to his friend, police Lieutenant Tom Doyle (Wendell Corey), but Doyle's initial checks convince him that the suspicions are unfounded. Jefferies remains convinced, however, and eventually manages to acquire incriminating evidence, aided by his girlfriend, the ultraperfect Lisa Fremont (Grace Kelly), who makes a daring foray into Thorwald's apartment and is nearly killed in the process. Jefferies is nearly killed as well, as Thorwald comes to his apartment and pushes him out the window. In the end, however, the police apprehend Thorwald, and Jefferies survives the fall, which leaves him with *two* broken legs. Lisa, meanwhile, sits with him and seems to have proved her fitness for the life of action she would have as his wife. However, in typical Hitchcock fashion, their relationship remains unresolved, and it is not at all clear that they will be wed.

Within this simple scenario, the film manages to address a number of important issues. For one thing, the film serves as a commentary on the alienation of the inhabitants of the buildings surrounding the courtyard. In a strong anti-utopian gesture, this group of people is presented as anything but a community; they are merely a collection of individuals, most of whom do not even know each other's names. They seemed trapped within their apartments and within their lives, appearing, according to Wood, like "semi-live puppets enclosed in little boxes" (107). The alienation of the neighbors is brought home most clearly when Thorwald kills a small dog to keep it from digging up evidence he has buried in his flower bed in the courtyard. The dog's owner, finding it dead, immediately (and correctly) assumes that it has been intentionally killed by one of her neighbors. She then addresses the entire neighborhood from her balcony: "None of you know the meaning of the word neighbor! Neighbors like each other. Speak to each other. Care if anybody lives or dies. But none of you do!"

Many of the inhabitants, especially the women, observed by Jefferies live alone. The women seem particularly lonely, as in the case of the

spinster whom Jefferies dubs "Miss Lonelyhearts," or even the voluptuous dancer, "Miss Torso," who entertains numerous potential suitors but
connects with none of them because she is waiting (we learn at the end of
the film) for the return of her true love from the army. Meanwhile, married couples who share apartments and lives tend not to get along. The
dog's owners are a married couple but seem more devoted to the dog
than to each other; Thorwald murders his wife; even two passionate
newlyweds who move into the building are at odds by the time the film
ends. Jefferies, meanwhile, not only lives alone but is determined to keep
it that way, evading Lisa's desire for marriage. The relationship between
Lisa and Jefferies thus seems to enact the typical 1950s scenario of the
wandering male, seeking an escape from routine through adventure but
pursued by the domesticating female, who hopes to tame him and divert
his energies into family life.

At the same time, Jefferies's spying is a violation of the private domestic spaces of his neighbors' homes, suggesting that, in the paranoid
political climate of the 1950s, the sanctity of the home was in jeopardy.
Spoto, among others, notes the ways in which Jefferies becomes a sort of
stand-in for Hitchcock, making *Rear Window* "nothing so much as a
movie about moviemaking" (219). Meanwhile, Corber links the emphasis
on voyeuristic surveillance in the film to the atmosphere of the Cold War
security state, in which surveillance of potential subversives was consistently portrayed as necessary for national security. However, for Corber,
Hitchcock seeks, in *Rear Window*, to "recuperate the cinematic apparatus
from its contamination by the emergence of the national security state"
("Resisting" 127). Thus, while the film seems to "confess" the complicity
of film and film technology in the rise of the surveillance state, this
confession serves as a critique of the misuse of technology in the
McCarthyite purges, its portrayal of surveillance as a form of voyeurism
"indirectly attacking the government surveillance of suspected Communists, homosexuals, and lesbians as a form of psychopathology" (128).
McCarthyism thus becomes a form of "corruption" of the kind of
spectatorial pleasure that is central to cinema and that Hitchcock wants
to reclaim for cinema (139). At the same time, this very suggestion that
such pleasure *can* be recuperated indicates, for Corber, the film's basic
support for the liberal postwar consensus (143). In particular, *Rear
Window* "tries to resolve the postwar crisis by extending the liberal
consensus beyond the political to the cultural realm. Its representation of
Jeff and Lisa's relationship insists that liberal democratic principles can
provide the most effective structures for everyday life" (146).

This complicity with the liberal consensus of the 1950s is itself a postmodern gesture that suggests the impossibility of thinking beyond the
current liberal status quo. In short, it is related to a thoroughgoing rejection of utopianism, a rejection that can be seen in all of Hitchcock's films
of the 1950s, even the relatively "light" ones, such as *To Catch a Thief* and

*The Trouble with Harry* (both 1955). The first is a glossy and glamorous production that involves a certain amount of Hitchcockian suspense but is probably most notable for its lovely scenery (the French Riviéra) and even lovelier stars (Grant and Kelly). All of this loveliness contributes to a film that might be described as Hitchcock light, lacking the tension and underlying darkness of Hitchcock's more important productions. Indeed, though it has a rudimentary suspense-story plot (and a couple of suspenseful moments), *To Catch a Thief* is really a romantic comedy that uses this plot to bring ex-jewel thief John Robie (Grant) together with beautiful heiress Frances Stevens (Kelly), the problems that brought them together having been essentially solved—except for the fact that, as with most of Hitchcock's romance endings, it is not at all clear that the couple is a good match that will actually last. Meanwhile, with its depiction of Robie as a onetime thief who is now a paragon of virtue, combined with its suggestions that the Stevens family may have gained its wealth at least partly from the illegal shenanigans of Frances's con-man father, Jeremiah, *To Catch a Thief* effaces the line between criminality and respectability, indicating that thievery of one form or another is the norm in modern capitalist society.

Like *To Catch a Thief*, *The Trouble with Harry* is largely memorable for its fine cinematography, in this case of splendid New England autumn landscapes. Here, however, the beautiful scenery reinforces the comic mode of the film, while both the scenery and the comedy contrast in almost Brechtian fashion with the fundamentally dark subject matter. Again suggesting a possible darkness at the heart of the idyllic small American town, *The Trouble with Harry* presents a community of locals who band together to dispose of the corpse of one Harry Worp before it can be discovered by the local deputy sheriff (played by Royal Dano). Brill sees the film as a central instance of Hitchcockian utopian romance, with the deputy being the only one of the locals who has been contaminated by modernity, the others remaining in an Edenic state of innocence. For Brill, this is a world marked by the "total exclusion of destruction. No event or person in *The Trouble with Harry* is allowed to cause or suffer real pain" (290).

One problem with this reading, of course, is the trouble with Harry: he's dead and remains so, even if his death does trigger a comic chain of events. The central actors in this comedy of errors are local artist Sam Marlowe (John Forsythe), ostensibly single mom Jennifer Rogers (Shirley MacLaine, in her first film role), crusty ex-sea captain (or so he claims) Albert Wales (Edmund Gwenn), and old maid Miss Ivy Gravely (Mildred Natwick). All work together to conceal the corpse (Captain Wales and Miss Gravely separately go through most of the film believing that they have inadvertently killed Harry), with much of the comedy residing in the repeated burials and exhumations to which the corpse is subjected due to twists in the plot.

The collective actions of these individuals clearly contain utopian elements, as does Marlowe's rejection of the possibility of great wealth when a millionaire becomes enamored of his paintings, a movement that resembles the contempt for material wealth expressed by Jessie Stevens in *To Catch a Thief*. However, a number of problems lurk beneath the comic surface of the film. True, the main trouble with Harry's death seems over in the end, as Harry turns out to have died of a heart attack, clearing the way for Jennifer (who happens to have secretly been Harry's estranged wife) to marry Marlowe, while the senior citizens Captain Wales and Miss Gravely, cleared of the killing, appear headed for nuptials as well. What is peculiar, however, is the lack of concern of any of the locals (including Jennifer, who found Harry a nuisance, though admitting that he was practically a saint) for the deceased. After all, he is an outsider and not a member of their community. Also telling is the conservative nature of the film's collective action: far from working to transform society, the characters work to keep things just as they are, hoping to prevent Harry's death from disrupting the peaceful atmosphere of their idyllic town. Meanwhile, lurking just beneath the surface is the suggestion that the citizens of rural America may be willing to countenance the murder of anyone who threatens such a disruption, a suggestion of small-town murderousness that is subtly reinforced by the scenes in which Jennifer's small son, Arnie (a pre-*Leave It to Beaver* Jerry Mathers), skips gleefully about the town carrying either toy guns or the stiffened corpse of a rabbit shot by the captain. The film's comedy, which is often extremely funny, may not be typical Hitchcock, but even the romance ending of the film cannot allay a certain Hitchcockian uneasiness that all is not quite well.

*The Man Who Knew Too Much* (1956) is another happy-ending film that leaves disturbing questions unanswered. Critics have been divided on whether this remake was superior to Hitchcock's own similarly titled film of 1934, though almost all critics who have compared the films have tended to discuss the difference between the two versions in terms of Hitchcock's own personal intentions. The remake thus becomes a linchpin of auteur theory, which Corber identifies as complicit with Cold War ideology in its emphasis on individualism and its focus on the private psychological intentions of directors, rather than public, historically situated circumstances. In contrast, Corber locates the difference between the two films in changes in Hitchcock's historical context. He thus emphasizes "the remake's participation in the network of discourses that helped to underwrite and legitimate the postwar settlement" (*Name* 148).

It is certainly the case that the 1956 version invests the film with typical American concerns of the 1950s. For one thing, the protagonists are now American, rather than British, not only signaling Hitchcock's new status as a director of American films but also suggesting America's growing international role during the period. In the film, an American surgeon, Ben McKenna (James Stewart), travels with his wife, Jo (Doris Day), and son, Hank (Christopher Olsen), to French Morocco on a family vacation. In the exotic Third World setting of Marrakesh, the McKennas predictably encounter sinister forces. In particular, a murdered British agent whispers his last words to Dr. McKenna, warning him of an upcoming assassination plot in London but dying before he can give full details. Realizing that McKenna may have this information, agents of the group (they appear to be European, but their nationality is never specified) involved in the plot kidnap and hold Hank in an attempt to ensure McKenna's silence.

Sinister forces in the world at large thus disrupt the utopian structure of the McKenna family, families always tending, in the context of the Cold War, to serve as besieged and imperiled bastions of private tranquility, surrounded by dangerous public threats. This kidnapping leads to a number of suspenseful situations, though the film as a whole is slow-moving by Hitchcock's standards and lacks the powerful atmosphere of anxiety that is typical of Hitchcock's finest films. In fact, the film may be best remembered for introducing Day's rendition of the song "Que Sera, Sera," a profoundly conservative imprecation to quietism that urges audiences to accept whatever comes without making any attempt to make their own history. In the end, the plot is foiled, Hank is saved, and the McKennas return to their apparently idyllic family existence. Nevertheless, the film's suggestion that there are dark forces in the world that threaten American domestic tranquility bespoke a perception that was central to the American national consciousness in the mid-1950s. In addition, the film is remarkable for the peculiar constitution of its ideal American family, which addresses a number of the era's anxieties concerning gender roles. Or, rather, it calls attention to these anxieties by *not* really addressing them. McKenna is a successful professional, but hardly a glamorous figure, and Hitchcock's situation of McKenna's medical practice in Indianapolis helps to identify him as a relatively ordinary American. Yet Jo McKenna is a former international star of the musical stage who has now given up her successful career in order to live in domestic bliss with her husband and son. The film does not question this unlikely match (though it does suggest certain tensions by indicating that Jo would prefer to resume her career) or explain how it came about, presenting it as perfectly normal and unsurprising that Jo would sacrifice her career, however successful, for marriage. As Corber puts it, the film "participated in a set of discursive practices that tried to discourage women from pursuing careers outside the home" (*Name* 137).

The year 1956 also saw the release of *The Wrong Man*, another film not usually considered among the major works of Hitchcock's career. Yet, for me, *The Wrong Man* is rivaled in its power to disturb only by *Vertigo* and *Psycho*. Based on a true story (a fact greatly emphasized in the marketing of the film), *The Wrong Man* is shot in black and white in a quasi-documentary style that, at least on the surface, lacks the elegance of Hitchcock's more elaborate films. Both the subject matter and the visual style make the film the closest of all of Hitchcock's films to being straight film noir, as David Sterritt correctly notes (77). Sterritt is also correct, I think, in his suggestion that "of all the films Hitchcock made during the 1950s, *The Wrong Man* captures most vividly and chillingly the American spirit of its time" (65).

And this spirit is a dark one indeed. For most of its 105 minutes, *The Wrong Man* is unremittingly bleak, depicting its protagonist, Manny Balestrero (Henry Fonda), in the clutches of powerful and mysterious institutional forces beyond his control or understanding. Despite working as a jazz musician (one of the decade's central countercultural occupations), Balestrero is a solid citizen who works hard, loves his family, and does exactly what the gray-flanneled orthodoxy of the period demands of him. This orthodoxy helps to explain the almost weirdly passive way that he submits to the forces of authority when he is falsely accused of a series of holdups, then arrested and processed through a grimly carceral criminal justice system, seeming to be heading, through most of the film, for certain conviction and long-term imprisonment.

But the criminal justice system, the impersonal workings of which are shown in great detail in the film, is only the most overt of a number of carceral images in the film. Together, these images depict American society as grimly dystopian. In fact, the film systematically considers, then rejects a whole range of potential utopian alternatives. The first of these is Balestrero's job as a club musician, a job that seems to promise access to certain utopian compensations but that serves merely as another source of confinement. Balestrero plays his bass fiddle not for the joy of the music but to make money to pay his interminable bills. In fact, when shown playing in the film, he seems almost numb, going through the motions of just another dead-end job that he must do to try to meet the domestic obligations of his family life.

The Balestrero family is, in fact, the most subtly (and chillingly) carceral of the various institutions depicted in the film. A seemingly perfect middle-class group, the Balestreros consist of Manny, his loving wife, Rose (Vera Miles), and their two clean-cut and well-behaved children, aged five and eight. The family seemingly lives a relatively comfortable middle-class existence, but we soon learn that this existence is precarious at best, paid for on the installment plan, forcing Manny to run as fast as he can on the treadmill of his life just to try to stay where he is. Thus, when Rose needs $300 worth of dental work, this seemingly minor difficulty triggers a major crisis in the family finances. Manny shows a momentary grimace of pain when he first gets the news but regains his composure and accepts the situation with his usual passivity. He'll simply find a way to borrow the money. Rose, always less willing to accept their situation in life without resistance (perhaps because her life as a housewife involves considerably more drudgery than his life as a musician), complains that "every time we get up, something comes along and knocks us back down again."

As if this depiction of American life were not harsh enough, Manny then goes to an insurance office to try to borrow money on his wife's policy, only to be misrecognized by the clerks there as the man who earlier robbed them. This misidentification triggers the series of events that leads to Manny's incarceration. The scenes of his arrest, interrogation, and confinement are among the most painful and chilling in American cinema, made all the more so by Manny's seemingly passive acceptance of it all, as if he had been so thoroughly interpellated by the ethos of conformism that he is unable to mount any sort of protest against official authority. Indeed, the word "interpellation" literally means being called before a judge, and Althusser clearly intends the term to suggest acquiescence to the legal system as a metaphor for general obedience to the expectations of official ideology. Indeed, one feels that Manny accepts his role as husband and father in the same passive way that he submits to the judges and police, going through the motions simply because he thinks that is what is expected of him. In some ways, the true power of the film comes from the fact that, once Manny finally gets out on bail, he finds that life outside jail remains stifling and oppressive. After all, the family's money troubles are now worse than ever, and Rose, on the edge from the very beginning, is soon pushed into a mental breakdown and institutionalized. Even after Manny is (seemingly miraculously) cleared of the robbery charges, Rose remains distracted and numb; she even suggests when Manny gives her the good news that it doesn't make much difference whether she is in a sanitarium or Manny is in jail: their life is carceral and confined, within these institutions or without.

James Naremore notes that *The Wrong Man* is "one of the bleakest movies ever produced in Hollywood," made even more bleak by the fact that it is "less about crime and punishment than about the breakdown of a fragile, lower middle-class marriage under the pressure of debt and patriarchy, and the slow descent of one of its members into an unglamorous, psychological darkness" (268). This darkness is particularly powerful—and anti-utopian—for the very reason that the family functioned so consistently in the discourse of the 1950s as a utopian oasis in which individuals could be sheltered from the vicissitudes of public life within their own private, protected worlds. But in *The Wrong Man* the family is not just inadequate as a haven from trouble; it is really the main source of the troubles of both Rose and Manny, leaving no source of relief from the gloom of the film.

Neither is this darkness relieved by the nominally happy ending, which is even more unstable than most of Hitchcock's happy endings. The film, in fact, is unstable throughout, with the misrecognition of Manny by the various witnesses serving as a sort of analog to potential misreadings of the film by unsophisticated viewers. As Paula Marantz Cohen notes, *The Wrong Man* is filled with examples of misinterpretation that, along with the absorption and effacement of Manny's identity by larger forces, seem to move the film "in the direction of a postmodern American esthetic" (155).

This is particularly the case with the happy endings, the first of which occurs when the "right" man is apprehended, seemingly by divine intervention, clearing Manny of the robbery charges. However, this ending is problematic in a number of ways. For one thing, that it occurs apparently in answer to Manny's prayers combines with the figuration throughout the film of Manny as a sort of Christ image to suggest a powerful religious message. This divine intervention radically denies the Marxist notion that men make their own history, suggesting that good things come to those who suffer the slings and arrows of outrageous fortune, not to those who take arms against a sea of troubles. But even this form of bad utopianism is undermined by any close look at the film, which makes it clear that the evidence against the "right" man is exactly the same as the evidence that had been presented against Manny, which means that this second suspect might also be misidentified. In any case, this new suspect also identifies himself as a family man, which means that his arrest leads to the destruction of still another American family.

Brill sees this miraculous intervention as a basic instance of the "underlying dominance of a romantic, religious optimism" in Hitchcock's films (124), though the man who is apprehended in Manny's place might see it differently. Indeed, in order to produce this optimistic reading, Brill is forced to see Manny's original arrest as a case of pure bad luck, while his eventual exoneration is due to divine intervention. Slavoj Zizek, on the other hand, suggests that, if the film suggests the intervention of the divine in human affairs, then Manny's overall troubles must be attributed to the machinations of a "cruel, arbitrary and impenetrable God who can bring down catastrophe at any moment" (130).

In the second happy ending, we are told, at the end of the film, that Rose, whom we last saw distracted and wan in the asylum, has (again, perhaps miraculously) recovered and is now living happily with Manny and their children in Florida. But this tacked-on happy ending (so reminiscent of the "and they lived happily ever after" endings of numerous Disney films of the period) is so blatantly artificial as to call attention to its own unbelievability. The ending is, among other things, typical of the bad utopianism of the 1950s, though it is so extreme as to function as a potential parody of such utopianism. Indeed, Sterritt notes that this artificial "reality-denying" ending is one of the "most 1950s-ish components" of the film (76). Though he notes that Hitchcock may simply have been trying to pacify his audiences in the 1950s by tossing them a bone to mitigate the grimness of the film, Sterritt suggests that this device is more likely intended as "profoundly ironic" commentary on the "shallow" optimism of the mid-1950s (77).

Indeed, the happy ending of *The Wrong Man* undermines the entire logic of the preceding narrative (much like the notorious, tacked-on happy ending of Welles's *The Magnificent Ambersons*), thus calling into question the validity of narrative (and, by extension, history) in general as an organizing principle and as a path to the resolution of difficulties. Narrative is similarly challenged in Hitchcock's next major film, *Vertigo* (1958). If *The Wrong Man* is stylistically the plainest of Hitchcock's films from the 1950s, then *Vertigo* is the fanciest, a true virtuoso performance in filmmaking. But these two films are, in many ways, companion pieces, especially in the way *Vertigo* continues the remorseless destruction of romance that lies at the heart of the endings of *The Wrong Man*.

A recognized classic of the American cinema, *Vertigo* is perhaps the Hitchcock film most admired by critics, at least in recent years. Spoto, for example, calls it Hitchcock's "great masterpiece" (265), while lauding the "astonishing purity and formal perfection in every element" (299). Similarly, Robin Wood sees the film as "the nearest to perfection" of all of Hitchcock's films (129), a great work of art that "can as well as any film be taken to represent the cinema's claims to be treated with the respect accorded to the longer established art forms" (130) — and this despite Wood's own acknowledgment that the plot of the film is "quite fantastic" and totally unbelievable (109). Indeed, *Vertigo*, of all of Hitchcock's films, relies the least on plot and on that most Hitchcockian of all plot devices, suspense. Hitchcock, in fact, systematically dismantles conventional elements of narrative in the course of the film, breaking the rules in ways that are interestingly effective but that also suggest the demise of narrative that Engelhardt sees as a crucial element of the loss of utopian vision in the 1950s and that Jameson sees as a crucial aspect of the postmodernist loss of historical sense.

As Spoto notes, the "overarching theme of *Vertigo* is that a romantic fantasy is a dangerous hoax, potentially fatal for all involved" (298). In this, the film resembles nothing more than Nabokov's *Lolita*, which also explores the destructive consequences of an attempt to escape 1950s routinization through the pursuit of a sexual obsession. *Vertigo*, however, lacks the linguistic shenanigans of *Lolita*, making it an altogether darker work, so much so that even Brill is forced to admit that *Vertigo*, along with *Psycho*, thoroughly subverts the conventions of romance, which these films "raise only to disappoint or reverse" (201).

*Lolita* also subverts the conventions of romance, of course, but the subversion of *Vertigo* is made all the more radical through its replacement of the weirdo intellectual foreigner Humbert Humbert by that paragon of postwar American manhood, the much beloved and terribly likable James Stewart, in the central role of John "Scottie" Ferguson.[7] This casting tends to increase audience identification with Ferguson, implicating us all in his dark fantasies, while Stewart's iconic status suggests that Ferguson's inclinations are not mere personal eccentricities but symptoms of something larger in the society as a whole.

From the beginning, Ferguson is not, if one looks carefully and objectively at the film, an especially attractive figure, and it is a marker of Hitchcock's famous ability to manipulate audiences that almost no one seems to have noticed this. Hitchcock is also able to hook audiences with his preposterous plot, the ludicrousness of which no one seems to mind. *Vertigo* thus undermines both audience identification with the hero and believable plot, probably the two major devices through which Hollywood cinema does its work. It is, thus, a sort of antifilm, much in the way that the fragmented structure and intrusive camera movements of *Citizen Kane* (which also features an unpleasant protagonist) make Welles's masterpiece an antifilm, or at least an anti-Hollywood film.

*Vertigo*, however, is much more radical than *Citizen Kane* in its subversion of convention, tending to flaunt its artificiality as an element of postmodernist skepticism about the nature of reality and truth, as opposed to the modernist sense, in *Kane*, that reality and truth are complex and hard to determine but ultimately knowable.[8] *Vertigo* begins with a prologue in which Ferguson, a police detective, pursues a man (presumably a criminal) across San Francisco rooftops. Ferguson slips and nearly falls (Stewart always seems to be in danger of falling in Hitchcock films), hanging precariously from a gutter while experiencing an attack of acrophobia and consequent vertigo. A uniformed policeman attempts to save Ferguson but falls to his death, leaving Ferguson hanging from the gutter. Hitchcock then cuts to the comfortable apartment of Midge Wood (Barbara Bel Geddes), Ferguson's longtime friend and onetime fiancée—with absolutely no explanation of the seemingly miraculous rescue of Ferguson, who seemed certain to fall to his death in the previous scene.

Midge serves structurally in the film as a paragon of solidity and routine, thus fulfilling the Widow Douglas role, long established in American literature, of the woman who threatens to tame and domesticate the male protagonist, ending his pursuit of adventure once and for all. Midge is, in fact, an almost allegorical figure. But this role, of course, had a special resonance in the 1950s. Though a relatively sympathetic character, Midge marks a number of negative aspects of American life in the 1950s, particularly commodification and routinization. A talented artist, she squanders (according to Ferguson) her talents sketching advertisements for brassieres, an occupation that also marks her modern, matter-of-fact attitude toward sexuality, an attitude that, as Robin Wood notes, is "entirely devoid of mystery or reserve" (111). Indeed, the potentially sexy garments that she sketches turn out to be entirely practical devices, objects not of romance but of modern engineering—as in the high-tech bra "based on the principle of the cantilever bridge" that she shows to Ferguson.

Midge's structural opposite in the film is the putative Madeleine El-ster (Kim Novak), who clearly fascinates Ferguson, at least partly be-cause of the contrast with Midge. Where Midge is safe and certain, Madeleine is dangerous and mysterious; where Midge is practical and modern, Madeleine is romantic and vaguely anachronistic. Indeed, Madeleine's aura of mystery arises largely from the fact that she seems a figure from the nineteenth century (she has supposedly been possessed by the ghost of her own great-grandmother, Carlotta Valdes), displaced into modern San Francisco. Perhaps it is little wonder, then, that Fergu-son, apparently desperate for a romantic escape from the routine, falls for her so quickly and so thoroughly, despite the fact that a romance with her is both personally and professionally unethical on his part, as he has been hired to keep tabs on her by her apparent husband, Gavin Elster (Tom Helmore), an old college acquaintance of Ferguson's. Nor is Fergu-son dissuaded (he seems, in fact, attracted) by the fact that Madeleine is half his age and appears to be nuts, possessed by a ghost, or both.

But, with Hitchcock at the controls, no one seems to mind that the ro-mance between Ferguson and the dreamy Madeleine is both unlikely and inappropriate, even though Hitchcock tosses a number of monkey wrenches into the gears of his own narrative machinery. As a result, the film tends to challenge the notion of coherent narrative altogether, a mo-tif that can be taken, per Jameson, to suggest a schizophrenic inability to maintain a sense of subjective coherence over time or, per Linda Hutch-eon, a potential challenge to received notions of history. Indeed, the film clearly hints at the suppression of certain elements of the American past (as in the story of Carlotta Valdes, the Mexican woman seduced, aban-doned, and driven to suicide by a rich Anglo man). Thus, Corber notes that the film attempts to "construct a counternarrative of the nation's his-tory and culture in which the exploitation of Mexicans figures promi-nently," while also stressing "the consequences of the nation's refusal to acknowledge its history of miscegenation" ("'Thumbprints'" 306). How-ever important this critical reexamination of the past may be, the film proposes little in the way of a utopian alternative to the official history it undermines, leaving us with a suggestion of past abuses but no indica-tion of potential future rectification. Indeed, the film suggests the un-changeability of history when it merely repeats the fate of Carlotta Val-des, with the part-Mexican Madeleine Elster being killed by her powerful Anglo husband when he tires of her. Judy Barton then meets a similar fate, though she is disempowered relative to Ferguson, not by ethnicity but by class, suggesting a confusion of class and race that is typical of American culture throughout its history.[9]

The film's challenge to narrative coherence is part and parcel of its skeptical treatment of romance as a whole. Thus, the film's climactic romantic moments are consistently self-undermining. The most striking of these (other than the sheer unlikelihood of the whole scenario) occurs in the scene of the first kiss between Ferguson and Madeleine, which Hitchcock artfully places precisely at the midpoint of the film. In this scene, Madeleine repeatedly calls Ferguson "Scottie," the appellation preferred, we have already been told, by acquaintances who are not close friends. Indeed, we have learned that Madeline herself prefers the name "John," which is what friends use, except for Midge, who tends to call him "Johnny-O," presumably a sign that she is closer to Ferguson that anyone else is. Madeleine and Scottie then kiss passionately, as waves break on the shore behind them, and the romantic score in the background increases in volume.

This scene, of course, is completely over-the-top, recalling the self-conscious romanticism of the fireworks display that is intercut with the famous kiss between John Robie and Francie Stevens in *To Catch a Thief* (a scene itself reminiscent of the "Nausicaa" chapter in *Ulysses*, during which fireworks explode as Leopold Bloom masturbates while leering at a teenage girl on the beach). We will learn only later, of course, that the excessive staginess of the kissing scene is meant to indicate that the scene has, in fact, been staged and that both Madeleine (knowingly) and Ferguson (unknowingly) are merely acting out parts scripted and directed by Gavin Elster, thus making Elster (the most villainous figure in the film) an emblem of directorial power and even of Hitchcock himself, who in this sense, makes even more than his usual cameo appearance in the film.[10]

Of course, the roles will soon shift as Ferguson, traumatized by the apparent suicide death of Madeleine, starts to seek a replacement obscure object of his desire, finding a good prospect in the lowly shopgirl Judy Barton, who resembles Madeleine, but in a vulgar and unsophisticated way. Ferguson then becomes the scriptwriter and director as he sets about transforming Judy into a carbon copy of Madeleine. In this action, of course, Ferguson resembles not only the mythical Pygmalion but also Nabokov's Humbert, who similarly sees the world through the optic of fantasy, attempting to remake Dolly Haze into the image of his lost Annabell Lee. Here, though, Hitchcock again jettisons the usual conventions of narrative, revealing to the audience (but not to Ferguson) very early on that Judy really *is* Madeleine, or at least the woman Ferguson thought was Madeleine, and that she had merely been playing the role of Madeleine in order to entice Ferguson into witnessing her suicide, which thus served as the perfect cover for Elster's murder of the real Madeleine.

The intricacy of this plot, of course, requires that Ferguson's every move in response to the fake Madeleine has been anticipated to an entirely implausible degree in Elster's diabolical plan. Judy, though, knows exactly what Ferguson has in mind in his makeover, so that her adherence to his script is at least more plausible in that regard. The sense of loss with which she gives up her identity as Judy in order to become the embodiment of Ferguson's fantasies is thereby made all the more poignant, as Judy, desperate for love, wishes he could love her for herself. But, as Marantz Cohen points out, there's no there there, and the "real" Judy is just as constructed as the "fake" Madeleine (169). Ferguson, as suggested by his multiple names, has no real identity either, and the film as a whole tends to depict identity as mere role-playing, not existential reality.

The makeover is then capped off by a second preposterously overblown kissing scene, in which the two lovers embrace while the camera moves 360 degrees around them, the background shifting midway through from Judy's hotel room to the carriage room at the San Juan Bautista Mission, at which point Ferguson becomes momentarily distracted, stepping out of the frame to notice the change in background and losing his concentration on the staged kiss.[11] This change of scenery emphasizes both the extent to which this is a moment of fantasy realization for Ferguson and the extent to which this is still another scripted moment, complete with artificial (and thus changeable) stage settings in the background.

Within two minutes after this kiss, Ferguson spots the fateful necklace, which suddenly makes clear to him that Judy really is the woman he had thought to be Madeleine, though the interpretive leap that leads him to this conclusion is again rather farfetched. Then he drives her back to the scene of the crime, where he brutally drags her up the stairs to the top of the mission bell tower (this time miraculously overcoming his vertigo), from which she again falls to her death, at which point the film ends. We are not told what happens to the already-unhinged Ferguson, just as we never learn whether Elster is ever implicated in the murder of his wife. Such details are not important in this work, which is concerned not with the construction of narrative but with the deconstruction of narrative and the demolition of the notion that utopian bliss can be achieved through romance.

As if in compensation, Hitchcock followed the darkness of *Vertigo* with the relatively light-hearted *North by Northwest* (1959), a film that can be read as a sort of parody of *Vertigo*—and of virtually all of Hitchcock's earlier films of the long 1950s. Thematically, in fact, *North by Northwest* serves as a sort of summation of all of Hitchcock's films of the period, leading Brill to argue that "the whole of Hitchcock's career ... can be understood in terms of the themes, underlying assumptions, and techniques that shape the central meaning of *North by Northwest*" (4). For example, like *Notorious*, the film involves the use, by the American intelligence establishment, of a blond woman as a sexual lure in their espionage work, though this time the enemies are updated from Nazis to communists. Like *Strangers on a Train*, *North by Northwest* involves a son's excessive oedipal attachment to his mother and features a murderous homosexual.

Like *Rear Window, North by Northwest* depends in crucial ways on the motif of surveillance, and, like *The Wrong Man*, it pivots on a case of mistaken identity. Finally, like *Vertigo, North by Northwest* involves assumed identities and the danger of falls from great heights. Most importantly, *North by Northwest* (appropriately, given its comic mode) seems to want to suggest a solution to all of the problems posed by these other films, though that solution is a banal and conventional one indeed: mature heterosexual marriage.

Of course, there is nothing unusual in all of this, and each Hitchcock film of the latter half of his career tends to refer to the earlier films. Thus, if *North by Northwest*, for Brill, sums up Hitchcock's career, Jameson finds that the subsequent *Psycho* (1960) is a "summa and testament" to Hitchcock's earlier work (*Signatures* 122). Such instances of self-reference, like Hitchcock's famed cameo appearances in his own films, help to create the sense of Hitchcock's films as the oeuvre of a modernist auteur, an impression that Hitchcock himself sought to create and that subsequent Hitchcock critics have diligently worked to reinforce. But these self-referential moments in Hitchcock can also be seen as postmodernist boundary-crossings; Hitchcock's cameos collapse the ontological separation between real-life author and fictional work, while the migration of motifs from one film to another threatens to burst the illusion of self-contained fictional worlds and reveals the films as artificial (and somewhat arbitrary) constructs built from a sort of filmmaker's erector set. In Benjamin's terms, these motifs shatter the aura of the Hitchcock film as a self-contained masterpiece, a phenomenon that Benjamin sees as positive in the way it encourages critical thinking and challenges the status quo. But, in this context, it also encourages skepticism toward any sort of totalizing vision, of which utopian projections would constitute a central instance.

The plot of *North by Northwest* is rudimentary and vaguely ridiculous (Hitchcock himself called it "absurd"), which is perfectly fitting given that the film is a mere romp, even if it deals with a number of serious issues. But it is also a sort of road movie, one of the main characters of which is really the American landscape. The plot begins as advertising man Roger Thornhill (Cary Grant) is mistaken by enemy agents for American operative George Kaplan, triggering a series of adventures and misadventures in which Thornhill is repeatedly threatened with death at the hands of evil communists, while the American intelligence establishment (the agents represent the FBI, the CIA, or some other component of "the same alphabet soup," we are told) looks on and decides to do nothing to help, as the misidentification of Thornhill by the communists serves as an effective decoy for the real American spies.

Along the way, Thornhill is wrongly implicated in a murder that takes place in the New York headquarters of the United Nations, after which he hops a train for Chicago, seeking the real Kaplan (whom he does not realize is a fictional decoy invented by the American agents). On the train, Thornhill is seduced by Eve Kendall (Eve Marie Saint), whom we later learn to be the mistress of communist agent Phillip Vandamm (James Mason), who thus becomes this film's Gavin Elster. But Eve, like Judy Barton before her, really falls in love with the man she has been hired to pretend to love, a situation in this case complicated by the fact that she has actually been working as a double agent for the Americans all along, helping them to gather information on Vandamm's nefarious activities.

Nevertheless, the suggestively named Eve (apparently on the instructions of her American handlers, who turn out to be just as ruthless and unscrupulous as the communists, just as the Americans of *Notorious* were every bit as dangerous as their Nazi foes) nearly sends Thornhill to his death. To be precise, she sends him out into a good old American cornfield where, in one of the most famous sequences in all of Hitchcock (or, for that matter, all of American film), he is attacked by a crop duster, which first tries to run him over, then tries to machine-gun him. This being a comedy, he escapes, of course, just as Vandamm is ultimately apprehended, while both Thornhill and Eve are saved from attempted murder at the hands (or, actually, foot) of Mr. Leonard (Martin Landau), Vandamm's homosexual accomplice. The final scene, in which they are nearly killed by Leonard, is the culmination not only of the insane logic of the rest of the film but of all of Hitchcock's career to this point, functioning as it does as a send-up of the notorious Hitchcockian moment of suspense. Pursued by Leonard across the giant faces on Mount Rushmore, Thornhill ends up hanging from the sheer rock face by one hand, while his other hand tenuously grips that of Eve, who dangles helplessly below. To make matters worse, Leonard grinds his foot into Thornhill's hand on the rock, seeming sure to send both Thornhill and Eve to their deaths.

But never fear. The American agents arrive with a uniformed officer (apparently a park ranger) who shoots Leonard and sends him plunging into the abyss below. But the new arrivals are still too far away to help Thornhill and Eve, who, realistically, still seem to stand little chance of surviving their current predicament. Then, in a sudden cut that seems to parody Ferguson's unexplained rescue at the beginning of *Vertigo*, the couple, now happily married, is magically transplanted into their honeymoon bedroom, again on a train, which at this point symbolically plunges its throbbing length into the eager darkness of a waiting tunnel.

Such silliness aside, *North by Northwest* addresses a number of serious issues. For one thing, it is Hitchcock's most direct take on the politics of the Cold War, which it addresses in a particularly telling and fascinating way. By depicting both sides as equally ruthless and nefarious and by even having Thornhill declare at one point that it would be better to lose the Cold War than to resort to such extremes to win it, the film ostensibly declares its own courageous neutrality. But only ostensibly. In fact, what the film does is reject all political and governmental action in favor of individual action, which places it squarely and precisely in the mainstream of American Cold War rhetoric, which tended to tar all government and all politics with the same brush, thus simultaneously sweeping aside Stalinism and the progressive politics of the New Deal period, with its suspect legacy of Popular Front fellow traveling. It was, after all, Dwight Eisenhower, not some lefty pinko radical intellectual, who, in the midst of the long 1950s, warned us against the looming threat of the military-industrial complex. Thus, in the terms of Cold War rhetoric, Stalinism was equated with big government in general, and Americanism was equated with individualist distaste for government, thus drawing upon, but also radically strengthening, a long American tradition that would ultimately help to create a cynical nation of nonvoters, punctuated by fanatical antigovernment right-wing militias.

Most commentators, meanwhile, have found *North by Northwest* most fascinating for its exploration of the fluid and unstable nature of personal identity in the late 1950s, a characteristic that clearly identifies the film as a work of postmodernism. Indeed, numerous aspects of the film are clearly postmodern, from the confusing urban hubbub of the opening sequence (which evokes Jameson's notion, via Kevin Lynch's work on urban environments, of the difficulty of cognitive mapping in the postmodern era), to the clear way in which the plot has been arranged spatially more than temporally. But the film's treatment of identity is particularly striking, especially in its initial portrayal of Thornhill as a hollow man with no real identity at all, thus making it perfectly natural to mistake him for the nonexistent Kaplan. As Thornhill himself explains, his initials are "R-O-T, rot," but the "O" is really a zero, signifying an emptiness at the heart of his identity.

Within the film's complex of psychoanalytic imagery, of course, Thornhill's lack of identity signifies his failure to make the proper oedipal break with his mother, to whom he remains unnaturally attached even into middle age and after two (failed, of course) marriages. Within this logic, the film simply tells the story of Thornhill's maturation as he eventually cuts his oedipal umbilical cord and prepares at last to pursue a mature marriage with Eve, who has similarly been matured and tempered by the fire of their recent harrowing experiences together. But this same story can be told in a more social way as well. For one thing, as Corber repeatedly emphasizes, Hitchcock's general psychologization of human behavior directly reinforces the antipolitical aims of the American Cold War effort. In this particular case, Corber argues that "in following the example of contemporary psychiatric discourse and tracing Thornhill's lack of a sutured identity to his continuing dependence on his mother, *North by Northwest* participated in the network of diverse but congruent discourses that in the 1950s linked communism and homosexuality in the nation's political imaginary" (*Name* 196). Indeed, though Hitchcock's negative depiction of maternal influence here and elsewhere would seem to run counter to the official family-oriented rhetoric of the long 1950s, Corber points out that mothers were often seen in the period as threatening figures who might sap the strength of young males by excessive mothering.[12]

In addition, Thornhill begins the film as the ideal postmodern subject, living entirely on the surface in a world of fakery and simulation—the world, in short, of advertising, where "there is no such thing as a lie. There is only the expedient exaggeration," as he tells his harried secretary in the film's opening scene. Then he goes through the film shifting rather easily from one role to another, though Vandamm does complain at one point that Thornhill seems to be shifting a bit too easily, "overplaying" his roles. But then Thornhill's stagy behavior is perfectly suited to the postmodern shifts in his identity—as is Grant's theatrical acting style. After all, Grant was always more of a movie star than an actor, and audiences of the film were very well aware that they were watching not Roger Thornhill but Cary Grant playing Thornhill.[13]

Of course, if Thornhill can shift this easily from one identity to another, then the final resolution of the film, in which he has supposedly matured to the point that he can assume his "real," stable identity at last, is strongly called into question. This is, after all, his third marriage, the third time he has supposedly escaped his libidinal orbit around his mother and veered off in a new, more mature direction. Indeed, the jokey and artificial way that the film shifts from peril on the face of Mount Rushmore to newly wedded bliss on a train tends to undermine the notion that his experiences in the course of the film have worked profound changes in his character.

In *Psycho* (1960), Hitchcock veered away from the lavish color productions of *Vertigo* and *North by Northwest*, returning to black-and-white in a film shot, not by his usual cinematic crew but by the more modest crew that was used to shoot his television series. But the result is an acknowledged classic, Hitchcock's best-known film and one that rivals even *Vertigo* in critical reception. In addition to its near-universal reputation as a great work of cinematic art, *Psycho* is widely regarded as one of the most frightening films of the American cinema, its famed shower scene perhaps the most shocking sequence put on film to that date. In this sense, the gritty black-and-white photography becomes a definite asset, helping to produce a mood of dread and gloom. At the same time, by 1960, for Hitchcock to shoot a film in this style becomes a postmodernist gesture, nostalgically looking back to the cinematic past, even as it breaks shocking new ground. Indeed, critics have begun in recent years to discuss *Psycho* as a postmodernist work, as when Linda Williams sees the film as a crucial marker of the end of "classic" Hollywood cinema and the beginning of the postmodernist era in film. Meanwhile, despite its intentionally retrograde look, the film moves radically forward in its extension of Hitchcock's postmodernist deconstruction of the logic of narrative, and particularly of the logic of romantic narrative.

The film begins as Marion Crane (Janet Leigh) meets with her lover, Sam Loomis (John Gavin), for an illicit sexual tryst in a seedy Phoenix hotel. The two, we are assured, are in love and would marry, were it not for the fact that Sam cannot afford a marriage because he is burdened by the assumption of his father's debts and by alimony payments to his ex-wife. Thus, a major theme of the film is established early on: the continuing oppression of the present by the past, a theme that will be played out thematically in the continuing psychic domination of Norman Bates by his dead mother and visually by the memorable image of the Victorian haunted Bates house looming darkly over the modern, if dilapidated, Bates Motel. As Spoto puts it "this film is really a meditation on the tyranny of past over present" (314). In *Psycho*, as in Marx's *Eighteenth Brumaire*, "the tradition of all the dead generations weighs like a nightmare on the brain of the living" (Marx and Engels 594). But, whereas for Marx human beings can awake from this nightmare by collective action to make their own history, Hitchcock's characters pursue only individual action and are doomed to failure. But that, of course, is part of the point of *Psycho*, a film in which all of the characters are far too alienated to be able to make genuine common cause with any of the others. As Brill puts it, "the central poverty of human life in *Psycho*, and the source of much of its miserable comedy and deep pessimism, derives from the inability of its characters to make contact" (229).

Marion's first action is to steal $40,000 deposited with her boss, a real estate agent, by Tom Cassidy (Frank Albertson), a blustering, obnoxious client who wants to purchase a house for his "baby" girl, who is being married. The film goes out of its way to emphasize that Cassidy can well afford to lose the $40,000 and that he even deserves to lose it, thus assuring that the audience will not condemn Marion for the theft. Indeed, the film works so deftly to establish audience identification with Marion that virtually no one seems to have noticed that the real victim of the theft is not the oily Cassidy but Marion's innocent boss, who would no doubt be legally responsible for the loss. Nor do we worry very much that Marion seems to take a certain thrill from the theft that has nothing to do with her love for Loomis, whose commitment to their relationship is already suspect given the easy resignation with which he accepts the economic impossibility of their union.

But, if we never really expect Marion to find domestic bliss with Loomis, we still *want* her to. In fact, almost all commentators on *Psycho* have noted the way in which the first 47 minutes of the film focus so centrally on Marion, making her the clear protagonist of the piece and making her sudden death not even halfway through the film all the more shocking. Hitchcock here again plays with the mechanics of audience identification, clearly encouraging viewers to identify with Marion during the first part of the film, then shifting the primary focus of identification to the problematic Norman Bates (Anthony Perkins), perhaps the best remembered character of Hitchcock's entire career. This shift in identification is surprisingly effective. Who has not watched the film and shared Norman's anxiety when, for a moment, it appears that the car bearing Marion's body and the $40,000 seems as if it will not sink out of sight after Norman pushes it into a swamp?

This sliding audience identification is a bit unnerving in that it requires audiences to undergo a shift in their own identities, much like the unstable postmodernist schizo-characters described by Jameson as having no "sense of the persistence of the 'I' and the 'me' over time" ("Postmodernism" 119). Indeed, Spoto notes the prominence of schizoid images of various kinds in *Psycho*, the attack on Marion being only one of many images of cutting and splitting that proliferate throughout the film. But this attack is nevertheless the central such image, precipitating a shift in audience identification that is made particularly jarring by the sudden and brutal way in which Marion is removed from the scene, leaving us with the haunting memory of the shower murder and of Marion's dead eye staring out of the screen at us as if in accusation of our voyeuristic complicity in her death. Our mixed feelings over viewing the shower scene reinforce the schizoid tendencies of the film, which, as Spoto notes, "becomes a series of our own schizoid feelings, our wanting to see and our wanting not to see" (320).

Of course, all the emphasis on voyeurism (and on Marion's sense of being under surveillance after her theft) evokes the prevalence of surveillance in the security state of Cold War America. This is particularly the case in the scenes involving the film's sinister-looking highway patrolman, whose mirrored sunglasses allow him to see without being seen, much in the mode of Foucault's panopticon. In this sense, the film would seem to be a perfect illustration of Corber's thesis about the centrality of the discourse of national security in Hitchcock's work. However, as Corber points out, *Psycho*'s refusal to suggest that anything good can come of all this surveillance actually tends to challenge and even subvert the rhetoric of the security state. For Corber, then, *Psycho* is a sort of anti–*North by Northwest* that "represents a kind of paranoid fantasy in which the discourses of national security not only fail to guarantee the individual's consent to the postwar settlement but actually encourage her/his resistance to them" (*Name* 217).

It is certainly the case that *Psycho* poses severe challenges to the official discourse of Cold War America. Indeed, the film systematically poses, then rejects most of the official strategies that are supposed, in the context of the 1950s, to bring individual happiness and contentment. For Spoto, *Psycho* is "a statement on the American dream turned nightmare … a ruthless exposition of American Puritanism and exaggerated Momism" (314). Indeed, the film contains a considerable amount of commentary on American society in the long 1950s. The rhetoric of consumerism and affluence interferes with the romance between Marion and Loomis, causing him, at least, to conclude that they cannot possibly be happy if they are not rich. Meanwhile, both Loomis and Norman realize the American dream of owning their own businesses, but Loomis's hardware store seems to pull him deeper into debt, while Norman's motel is a crucial source of his psychic breakdown.

From this point of view, Marion's theft becomes a parody of the American dream of sudden wealth, and the fact that this money only gets her into worse trouble can be taken as a commentary on the anxiety of affluence in Cold War America. Indeed, one gets the sense that, even if she had not encountered Norman Bates along the way, the $40,000 would not have led to happiness with Loomis, whose lack of true devotion to Marion becomes clear in his oddly affectless reaction to her murder. In *Psycho*, romance, so often problematic in Hitchcock, collapses altogether as a solution to the alienation and psychic fragmentation experienced by the characters. Here, families are traps, not havens, and the typical Hitchcockian theme of the sinister effect of excessive mothering reaches its most chilling conclusion, with Norman's identity finally, in the end, completely absorbed within that of his mother.

Of course, Norman's unstable identity is still another example of the schizoid tendencies of the film. But it is a postmodernist metafictional moment as well, providing a chilling instantiation of the experience of identification with the Other that is so central to the watching of films. *Psycho*, like so many Hitchcock films, is, of course, a film about watching films — and about *looking* in general, even if it shows that we cannot always believe our eyes. In this, it participates in a very postmodern skepticism about the stability of reality, while also commenting in a particular way on the cinema itself as a realm in which the visual faculty is crucial, but not necessarily reliable. As Spoto puts it, crucial here is *Psycho*'s "self-referential character, for it's a moviemaker's movie about moviemaking" (323). Of course, as R. Barton Palmer, among others, has noted, *Rear Window* and *Vertigo* are also highly metafictional, and Hitchcock's overall tendency to make movies that are, at least on some level, about making (and watching) movies is no doubt a crucial element in his auteurist reputation.

But the self-referentiality of *Psycho*, more than that in either *Rear Window* or *Vertigo*, is also postmodernist self-parody. Thus, we should not get too carried away with either descriptions of Hitchcock's tyrannical manipulation of audiences or admiration for Hitchcock's genius to realize how excessive and, in fact, downright campy *Psycho* really is. Hitchcock himself notoriously described it as a "fun" picture made essentially with tongue in cheek, and Sterritt rightly calls it one of Hitchcock's "most playful exercises," despite the serious implications of its depiction of the performativity of human identity (112). Among other things, this view of the film casts a different light on the psychiatrist's final explanation of Norman's mental illness, an explanation often criticized as superfluous and certainly overly lengthy but one that now becomes a send-up of psychiatric explanations in general. As Corber points out, the psychiatrist's diagnosis, which for many viewers of the film seems to tie up all the films loose ends all too neatly, really does not explain much and, in fact, does not make sense (*Name* 190). Meanwhile, Corber further points out the way in which the portrayal of the psychiatrist serves as a commentary on the growing authority of "experts" in America in the 1950s, and reading this scene as a send-up of psychiatry can then be taken as a parodic challenge to that authority.

Of course, the ultimate target of the parodic tendencies of *Psycho* would appear to be audiences, whose gullibility is played upon so mercilessly in the film. Still, audiences get to play along as well. According to Linda Williams, *Psycho* is Hitchcock's most popular film not because audiences are awed by its artistry but because they enjoy watching it, playing with their own performative identities as they do so. For her, *Psycho*

needs to be seen not as an exceptional and transgressive experience working against the classical norms of visual pleasure, but rather as an important turning point in the pleasurable destabilizing of sexual identity in American film history: it is the moment when the experience of going to the movies began to be constituted as providing a certain generally transgressive sexualized thrill of promiscuous abandonment to indeterminate, "other" identities. (103)

At the same time, Williams notes that *Psycho*, with its famous policy of not allowing anyone to enter the theater after the film had started, also marked an important turning point in the disciplining of once-unruly American film audiences. But this enforced routinization is also part of the fun. Indeed, Williams specifically compares this aspect of the film to theme parks such as Disneyland, suggesting that "the sort of discipline that Hitchcock was teaching was more like that of the crowds at these theme parks than any kind of simple audience taming" (107).

The experience of audiences who attended Hitchcock's next film, *The Birds* (1963), was even more analogous to visiting a theme park. Here, Hitchcock continues his relentless assault on conventional narrative logic, constructing a film that is driven not by plot but by a series of episodic thrills, very much like a sort of roller-coaster ride. The film begins in San Francisco in the mode of a romantic (perhaps screwball) comedy, as two young people, clearly coded as potential lovers, meet in a pet shop tellingly filled with caged birds. Then, the woman, Melanie Daniels (Tippi Hedren) buys a pair of lovebirds to give to the man, Mitch Brenner (Rod Taylor), largely as a sort of prank. When she discovers that he has gone north to the pastoral seaside town of Bodega Bay for the week-

end, she drives there to deliver the birds. However, by the time she successfully leaves them in the home of Mitch's mother, Lydia Brenner (Jes-
sica Tandy), as a birthday gift for Mitch's younger sister, Cathy (Veronica
Cartwright), the prank has been dropped and the gift of the birds has become a legitimate romantic gesture.

These early parts of the film clearly play on the traditional romantic
associations that are attached to birds, as seemingly symbolized in the
scene in which Melanie steers her small sports car along the coastal
highway, with the two lovebirds swaying back and forth in tandem as
she negotiates the curves. Such togetherness seems to imply romantic attachment (these are, after all, *lovebirds*), but such moments also contribute
to the growing suspense. Even the first theater audiences of the film
would have known full well that birds were going to be sinister and
dangerous in this film, as they had often been in Hitchcock, from the
early days of his evocation, in *Sabotage*, of the murderous bird in Disney's
*Who Killed Cock Robin?* (1935), to the more recent images of the ominous
stuffed birds in *Psycho*.

Audiences did not have to wait long for this threat to materialize.
Melanie, in fact, is attacked by a gull on her way back from delivering
the lovebirds, and from that moment the bird attacks gradually escalate
in intensity, the synchronized swaying of the lovebirds suddenly becoming an image of the strange ability of birds to work together to take collective action, even to the point of carrying out seemingly well planned
and coordinated military assaults. Meanwhile, in contrast, the humans of
the film have no such ability. All are frustrated and thwarted in their
personal relationships, which are hollow, superficial, and unsatisfactory.
Indeed, for Spoto, the bird attacks allegorize the alienation of the human
characters. He argues that the birds "have nothing to do with capricious
nature" but are instead "poetic representations of everything shallow
and undermining in human relationships" (335). Similarly, Zizek, drawing on the obvious psychoanalytic possibilities inherent in the bird imagery, sees the bird attacks as "the incarnation of a fundamental disorder
in family relationships" (132).

Indeed, much of Mitch's seeming lack of emotional development
seems to be attributable, in the standard Hitchcock mode, to his excessive
attachment to his widowed mother, whose fears of being "abandoned"
have already destroyed a promising romantic relationship between
Mitch and Annie Hayworth (Suzanne Pleshette), now the local spinster
school marm. Melanie's emotional growth, on the other hand, seems to
be attributable to her childhood abandonment by her mother, who flew
the coop when Melanie was 11, thus just approaching puberty. The
Daniels and Brenner families are presumably less pathological than the
Bates family, but we are nevertheless encouraged in the film—in direct
opposition to most of the official rhetoric of the long 1950s—to see families as a source of problems, not solutions. We are assured (by Annie)

that Lydia is not a clinging and possessive mother, that she is not afraid of losing Mitch, but merely of being abandoned. Most critics seem to take this explanation at face value, without noting that the distinction made by Annie makes no sense. Losing Mitch and being abandoned seem, in Lydia's mind, to be one and the same thing, and the psychic effect on Mitch, who is rendered incapable of maintaining a mature sexual relationship with a woman, is also the same in either case.

By the logic of conventional narrative, we expect the characters to experience various trials, over which they will triumph and then emerge with a new maturity that will help them to overcome their initial alienation and sterility. The bird attacks certainly offer trials, but they also short-circuit the narrative machinery. Once the attacks begin in earnest, the human relationships in the film become entirely secondary. As a sheer matter of survival, the characters begin to work together to some extent, but, caught up in the life-and-death struggle with the birds, they have no opportunity to develop profound emotional attachments to one another. Indeed, the various personal problems of the characters suddenly seem trivial in the light of the looming crisis, just as the narrative development of the film up to the time of the bird attacks is rendered irrelevant. By the end of the film, meanwhile, Melanie is so traumatized by a near-fatal bird attack (the staging of which obviously recalls the shower scene in *Psycho*) that she seems to have withdrawn altogether. Then, in the film's famous final scene, the Brenners slowly drive away from their house, attempting to get Melanie to a hospital. The birds, apparently resting from their rigors for the moment, remained massed around the house, and the film then suddenly ends with nothing resolved. We do not know whether Melanie will survive, or whether the car will make it safely out of Bodega Bay. We do not find out whether the birds will finally be defeated by human technology, or whether they will emerge triumphant, the new rulers of Bodega Bay, and perhaps elsewhere.

This sudden unresolved ending is the film's most radical assault on the logic of conventional narrative, suggesting an impossibility of closure that is profoundly pessimistic and anti-utopian. The film's conflicts are not resolved, because the film itself is based on the premise that nothing is ever resolved and that human problems are never solved. They simply go on, with each generation passing its pathologies onto the next in a never-ending cycle in which the present can never escape the past and can therefore never move forward into a new and better future. As Sterritt puts it, "the movie's lack of a conventionally resolved ending signals Hitchcock's ultimate gesture of despair over the power not only of words but of screenwriting and storytelling itself" (143).

Of course, the very ambiguity of the ending means that it can be read in numerous ways, but most of the content of the film supports this pessimistic reading. Robin Wood, for example, notes the "awareness of fragility and insecurity that is the basis of the whole film," and it is certainly the case that here, as so often in Hitchcock, we are reminded that our mundane everyday lives might be interrupted by tragedy at any moment (162). To an extent, what is particularly frightening about the bird attacks is that they make no real sense and cannot be explained. Thus, the film's "expert," an amateur ornithologist, is at a loss to explain what is going on, while the alternative metaphysical explanation ("it's the end of the world"), offered up, tellingly, by the town drunk, is not very helpful, either. Thus, Wood concludes that "the film derives its disturbing power from the absolute meaninglessness and unpredictability of the attacks" (162).

However, I would argue that this very meaninglessness has a clear meaning, especially within the Cold War context of the long 1950s, when so many Americans felt a vague sense of being threatened by forces that made no sense to them. Indeed, while critics such as Spoto are dismissive of the notion that the film is "a parable on the bomb, with all that destruction from the air," I would argue that the film functions quite specifically as an expression of Cold War anxieties (330). In this case, however, the fear comes not from the bomb per se but from the perception of all those teeming masses all over the world, living lives of quiet desperation and just waiting for their opportunity to take revenge on the United States for its relative wealth and power. It is surely not insignificant, for example, that the most sinister of the avian attackers are crows, which had been clearly coded in American popular culture as African American, at least since the Negroid crows of Disney's *Dumbo* (1941). In addition, the birds are described in the film as being particularly primitive creatures and as deriving their strength from numbers, there being so many of them all over the world that they cannot possibly be wiped out even by American military technology. In short, they are described in precisely the Orientalist terms that were consistently applied to both communists and the threatening denizens of the Third World throughout the Cold War.

If the seemingly mindless attacks of the birds offer obvious psychological interpretations as a sort of return of the repressed, they also offer political interpretations as a return of the oppressed masses of the Third World. The climactic scene in which Melanie and the Brenners are claustrophobically boarded up inside the Brenner home while huge numbers of birds batter away at the perimeter is a classic representation of the sense of embattlement felt by many Americans during the long 1950s: here, the affluent Brenner home becomes America, and the birds become all those (incredibly numerous) unwashed foreigners banging away at the nation's doors, trying to get in to share (or spitefully destroy) the wealth.

Perhaps less obvious, but possibly more important as a Cold War allegory is the attack of the crow army on the Bodega Bay school, made all the more frightening by the sinister blackness of the birds and the presumably pristine innocence of the assaulted children. The scene thus offers all sorts of metaphysical and psychoanalytic interpretations as a parable on the destruction of innocence by the prevalence of evil in the world or simply by the looming fact of puberty and sexuality. However, given that the children are attacked in school, one can also read the attack in a social way as an assault on the well-organized efforts of the American Ideological State Apparatus to construct children as ideologically orthodox subjects, able to function efficiently in the modern consumer capitalist world. In addition, the school functions as an emblem of knowledge and education, so that the crow attack becomes an allegory of the threat posed by the unenlightened Third World to the entire rationalist legacy of the Enlightenment.

This aspect of the attack can perhaps best be understood by a comparison to a companion scene that appears in Francis Ford Coppola's *Apocalypse Now* (1979). In this scene, which mirrors (thus both repeats and reverses) the attack on the school in *The Birds*, a squadron of American helicopters descends (with Wagner blaring from their loudspeakers) on a peaceful Vietnamese village, in which schoolchildren are seen going about their daily educational activities. The helicopters, like the crows, rain senseless and overwhelming destruction from the air, but here the forces of death are precisely the products of the Western Enlightenment that, in *The Birds*, is under attack. What has come between, of course, is the experience of Vietnam itself, which made it clear once and for all that the Third World had more to fear from us than we did from them, that it was the forces of global capitalism, backed up by American military might, that were assaulting the Third World, and not the reverse.

Of course, Vietnam and associated experiences of the 1960s changed a lot of things about American culture, among other things rendering untenable the version of American reality that had been conveyed by filmmakers such as Hitchcock, and especially Disney, throughout the long 1950s. It is thus not coincidental that the golden age of Disney animation, which began with the release of *Snow White* in 1937, ended roughly with the long 1950s and that the golden age of Hitchcock ended at about the same time. That the Disney company, seemingly so in tune with postwar America, was particularly out of step in the 1960s can be seen from the fact that the Disney studios began their postwar output with the 1946 release of the technically innovative *Song of the South*, which mixes live actors and animated figures in an adaptation of the Uncle Remus tales so racist that even the Disney folks have been embarrassed by it, especially after the rise of the civil rights movement in the 1960s. The film has thus never been released on video, though it was rereleased in theaters several times. Of course, this embarrassment did not prevent Disney from continuing to fill their films with racist stereotypes, though the stereotypes tended to be more subtle in later films, such as *Aladdin* (1992), an astonishingly Orientalist production that most American audiences embraced with enthusiasm, perhaps because they themselves had so recently been doused with Orientalist propaganda in the 1991 Gulf War.

Of course, the happy, singing, dancing African Americans of *Song of the South* contribute to a vision of the antebellum South as an idyllic paradise, thus resonating with a somewhat similar, if more subtle, strain in the thought of the New Critics and thus addressing one of the principal forms of bad utopianism in the culture of the long 1950s. Indeed, this utopianism is doubly bad: not only does it point to a past that can never be retrieved, but it also constructs its utopia on the backs of black slaves. Of course, as in most modernist efforts, the real utopian component of Disney's animated features of the long 1950s lies primarily in the their technical achievements. But these achievements were often empty, with little connection to practical reality. Thus, the technical advances of *Song of the South* mark a move, in the long 1950s, toward much more complex and elaborate productions, eschewing the relative simplicity of *Snow White* and the downright primitivism of *Steamboat Willie* (Mickey Mouse's 1928 debut and the first cartoon to have an integrated sound track) in favor of modernist sophistication that, in keeping with the glorification of modernism by the decade's critics, often seemed to emphasize technique for technique's sake. As Richard Schickel puts it,

The wonderful simplicity that Disney's graphic art naturally possessed in the beginning and that he may have distrusted as betraying its humble and primitive origins, disappeared. In the late films complexity of draftsmanship was used to demonstrate virtuosity and often became an end in itself, a way of demonstrating what was a kind of growth in technical resourcefulness but not, unfortunately, in artfulness. (178)

Several minor Disney films followed *Song of the South*, but the Disney Company got back on track in its inexorable production of children's classics with the release of *Cinderella* in 1950. This time race is no issue, but the search for an ideal life remains at the center of the text. The basic plot of the film stays relatively true to the original Perrault fairy tale, supplemented liberally with Disney's trademark musical embellishments and scenes of cavorting animals, especially mice. Indeed, the Disney Company makes the story very much its own, marking the company's "arrogant" tendency to claim any and all aspects of the Western cultural tradition as "grist for a mighty mill" (Schickel 296).[14] The mice of *Cinderella* are a particularly Disnified elaboration. It was, after all, a cavorting mouse that made Disney famous, and the Disney animators had discovered early on that humanized animals were actually far easier to animate convincingly than actual human figures. In this case, the household mice are the allies of the stately, but downtrodden, Cinderella, who responds in kind by feeding them and protecting them from the evil family cat, Lucifer. With her kindly father deceased, Cinderella is treated cruelly and made into a servant by her wicked stepmother and ugly stepsisters. Nevertheless, she retains her ability to dream. Thus, she endures her lot patiently, working obediently and diligently, while consoling herself with reminders that "they can't order you to stop dreaming."

If this motif sounds almost like Bloch's emphasis on the importance of hope, the rest of the film makes very clear its conservative insistence that there is no need to transform society. For Bloch, hope can lead to a transformation of the social order; for Disney, if one works hard, does what one is told, and doesn't rock the boat, then one's dreams can come true, with no systemic changes required. What's worse, in Cinderella's feminine case, the dreams are entirely passive. As Doris Day would later urge in *The Man Who Knew Too Much*, Cinderella simply takes life as it comes. Rather than fantasize about taking action to improve her lot, she simply hopes that something will happen to save her. As in *The Wrong Man*, something does happen, of course. Through the magical intervention of her fairy godmother, she gets a chance to impress the local Prince Charming, who falls madly in love with her. After the requisite complications, the prince and Cinderella are wed, to live happily ever after. Some scenes (such as the one in which Cinderella is locked away in her room as the Duke seeks the wearer of the glass slipper) involve almost Hitchcockian suspense, but with a lighter edge, though it is also the case that *Cinderella*, like most Disney films, involves considerably more actual violence than most Hitchcock films. A surprising percentage of the film's 74 minutes is spent on scenes in which the evil Lucifer attempts (unsuccessfully, of course) to murder and devour various cute and cuddly mice, while one of the film's most extended scenes shows the local king attempting to dismember the Duke, his most trusted advisor, with the royal sword.

The cartoon format and the idyllic ending presumably allay any anxieties introduced by these scenes of violence. In fact, this ending aims to leave no room for lingering doubt that all is well in the kingdom or in the life of Cinderella, even though she moves directly from the domination of her stepmother and stepsisters into the control of a powerful man whom she hardly knows. Meanwhile, Cinderella can achieve even this questionable utopia only by the sudden intervention of magic, which makes this utopia a bad sort indeed, especially as it encourages American children to be obedient and hardworking, while waiting for a similar intervention that will never come. It also helps that Cinderella is strikingly beautiful and has really small feet, but pointing out the astonishingly sexist implications of this situation (and of the tale as a whole) is almost too easy to be useful. What is more interesting (and telling) is that the film was very well received at the time and triggered very little in the way of complaints about its treatment of gender, indicating its basic consistency with the dominant gender codes of the time. Further, Cinderella's delicate feet are also a sign of her class superiority, and it is important that Cinderella is coded as a natural aristocrat throughout the film, so that her marriage to the prince is a conservative gesture that merely restores her to her rightful position, rather than posing a potentially disruptive threat to the stability of class boundaries.[15]

*Cinderella* was a major box-office smash, continuing the commercial success Disney had first achieved with *Snow White and the Seven Dwarfs*, then sustained with one hit after another, despite disruptions such as the notorious Disney cartoonists' strike of 1941.[16] This economic success, meanwhile, calls attention to the consumerist implications of the film. For example, the scene in which the fairy godmother produces Cinderella's carriage, gown, and servants is pure consumerist fantasy, as expensive goods are produced from thin air. On the other hand, the disappearance of all these goods at midnight is an inadvertent reminder of the tenuousness of capitalist wealth, as all that had been solid suddenly melts back into the air from which it came. All is well, however. Cinderella not only finds love, but love with someone who is very rich and can resume the flow of fancy commodities begun by the fairy godmother.

*Cinderella* was quickly followed by *Alice in Wonderland* (1951), as the Disney company continued its Shakespearean search for preexisting narrative frames on which to hang its animated magic. Disney's adaptation required considerable bowdlerization of the Lewis Carroll original, but in many ways Carroll's work was ideal for Disney, filled as it was with numerous absurd characters that were ripe for animation — though the ultra-conformist Walt Disney himself groused that the film was too "full of weird characters" (Schickel 295). Still, though lacking the life of the original Alice books, the film is one of the more colorful and unusual (though least successful) of the Disney productions of the long 1950s. *Alice in Wonderland* also well illustrates many of the crucial features of American culture in the 1950s. For one thing, its transplantation, without comment, of a nineteenth-century British classic into American culture of the 1950s potentially shows a postmodern obliviousness to historical context. This lack of historical sense is also reflected in the film's extremely weak narrative component. The film has only a rudimentary plot (Alice, in a dream, follows the white rabbit into Wonderland, meets some bizarre characters, has a few scrapes with danger, then returns safely home), and is really nothing more than a series of pageants, spectacles, and, of course, weird characters. Meanwhile, Alice is the only truly human character in Wonderland, which reinforces the text's individualism. However, it is a somewhat anxious individualism, as Alice herself admits that, in this absurdist environment, she no longer knows who she is, feeling that her identity is shifting from one strange experience to the next.

Alice's vertiginous shifts in identity reinforce the strongly anti-utopian orientation of the film. As the film begins, Alice daydreams of living in an alternative world of her own, where conditions would be determined not by the constraints of material reality but by the projections of her individual fantasies. In short, this world would be a classic case of what Freud described as delusion. In this, of course, she follows in the footsteps of both Nabokov's Humbert Humbert and Hitchcock's Scottie Ferguson. But, like Humbert and Ferguson, she finds that this projected fantasy world is far from utopian. *Alice in Wonderland* is ostensibly meant as whimsical, light entertainment for children, but one of the most striking things about the film is its basic darkness. Alice, while in Wonderland, is consistently troubled and disoriented, extremely fearful of the absurd and threatening situations in which she finds herself. In the end, she narrowly escapes death at the hands of the decapitation-crazy Queen of Hearts, and only then because she awakes from her dream, finding herself back in a real world that suddenly looks much better than her fantasy alternative.

The message of *Alice in Wonderland* seems abundantly clear: accept the status quo or risk serious consequences. In this sense, the Queen of Hearts is a particularly important character. Portrayed in the film as large, uncouth, and extremely masculine (as opposed to the small, effeminate King of Hearts, whom she clearly dominates), the Queen of Hearts here functions rather clearly as an image of the woman who refuses to accept her feminine, subservient domestic role. Indeed, her penchant for decapitation could not be more obvious as an emblem of her status as the castrating female. Asserting her authority despite her gender, she becomes a sinister and threatening figure, the polar opposite of Alice, who remains throughout the film passive, demure, and unequivocally feminine, returning in the end to her proper place, having learned a valuable lesson about the dangers of venturing out of the domestic sphere.

*Peter Pan* (1953) similarly associated utopianism with childishness, while equating maturity with adjustment to the status quo. In this well-known story, young Wendy Darling, on the verge of maturity (read puberty, with all the attendant complications) and thus exile from the world of childhood, follows the impish Peter Pan off to Neverland, taking her younger brothers along for the ride. Neverland is a fairy-tale world (complete with a real fairy, in Tinker Bell), precisely the opposite of the routinized environment of modern corporate capitalism. Here, presumably, nothing is routine, and everything is shot through with magic. Somewhat like Baum's Land of Oz, Neverland does present dangers, though they are relatively easily surmounted. The greatest of these dangers is presented by the swarthy, beak-nosed Captain Hook, whose basic vileness is (in classic Disney fashion) coded in his ethnicized appearance. (In Disney Anglo-Saxons are normal; all others are ethnic.) But, of course, Hook is no match for the talented Peter Pan, and one seldom gets much sense that the pirate and his crew (also heavily ethnicized) have much chance of success against their flying green opponent.

In addition, at one point, Wendy and her brothers are abducted by savage Indians who threaten to burn them at the stake. These burlesque Indians are again preposterously ethnicized, not even appearing fully human, but this threat is even less serious than that posed by Captain Hook. The Indians turn out to be Peter Pan's allies, and the children are quickly freed. In the meantime, this modern captivity narrative also gives the children a chance to learn all about Indian lore. They hear, for example, an Indian version of the story of the original sin, discovering that "red men" are red out of sexual shame, dating back to the primal scene when the first brave was kissed by the first squaw and then subsequently became embarrassed.

From the point of view of my examination of utopian thought, what is most important about Neverland (as the name indicates) is its timelessness. It is, then, a bad utopia, explicitly blocked off from the historical process. Moreover, Neverland's separation from the flow of history means that children who go there will never have to grow old or face the mature responsibilities of adulthood. Indeed, we are told in the film that *only* children can go there and that it is off-limits for adults, who lack sufficient imagination to travel there.[17] (Apparently the pirates and Indians who inhabit Neverland do not count as subjects, but are merely objects on the landscape of this amusement-park world.) Of course, by the end of the film, Wendy realizes it is time to go home and face the fall from childhood grace that constitutes adulthood, entering the sexual economy and producing children of her own, so that the cycle can continue.[18] Return home she does, delivering the same message as *Alice in Wonderland*: at some point it is time to put away childish things, where utopian imaginings are identified as the most childish things of all. Oddly enough, there is no sign of the brothers at the end of the film; being younger (and male, thereby inherently more immature), they appear to have stayed in Neverland, though neither Wendy nor their parents appear to notice their absence.

The implied sexualization of Wendy's maturation is one of the most striking things about *Peter Pan*. From this point of view, it is interesting that Wendy seems to be the first girl to have ever entered Neverland, previously the province only of boys, several of whom (the "lost boys") have come there to live permanently. Femininity is, in fact, a barrier in various ways in this film. Note, for example, the amazing early scene in which the rather well endowed Tinker Bell regards her own callipygian form with considerable alarm, then is unable to fit through a keyhole because her ass gets stuck.[19] In any case, Wendy's presence in Neverland is specifically presented as a feminine disturbance of the ongoing male fun, Tinker Bell and a few Indian squaws (who again do not appear to count as people) being the only female inhabitants of the land. The squaws are safely contained within an extremely patriarchal environment, but Tinker Bell is more of a problem. Thus, the only time Peter Pan ever seems in any real danger from Hook comes about because Peter's obvious sexual fascination with Wendy leads to a crisis when Tinker Bell (being a typical female) becomes madly jealous, causing a rift that Hook is nearly able to exploit to Peter Pan's fatal detriment.

Females do not really belong in the adventure world of Neverland, because they are associated, in the discourse of the 1950s, with domesticity and orderliness, one of their functions being to "tame" males, who will then overcome their natural rowdiness, put their gray-flanneled noses to the grindstone, and produce and support families. Indeed, as Alan Nadel has elaborated in considerable detail, the "containment" mentality of the peak Cold War years extended well beyond capitalist containment of socialist expansion to include the containment of masculine sexual energies by the taming influence of feminine domesticity. It is significant in this regard that Wendy, the female protagonist, must take responsibility in the film for her own maturation. Males, in the Disney universe, do not have to mature on their own: it is the responsibility of females to capture them and force them into maturity. Given that the necessity of maturation and acceptance of responsibility is the key message of all of Disney's films of the long 1950s, it is not surprising that Disney protagonists from the period are almost always female. After all, it is females, despite their seemingly weak and passive conditions, who must first mature, providing an anchor for wayward men. Thus, Cinderella at last convinces the prodigal Prince Charming to settle down and raise a family, while Sleeping Beauty later lures her own prince into marriage, so that he will stop his dalliances with peasant girls in the woods.

In the long 1950s, mothers, as well as wives, were crucial in this regard: Peter Pan and the lost boys do not grow up precisely because they have no mothers. (Wendy at one point insists to her brothers that they must return home with her from Neverland precisely because they need a mother.) The overt glorification of motherhood in *Peter Pan* participates in a much larger discourse of the period, of course. However, motherhood is double-edged, and the threat of momism is ever-present: whereas fathers must submit to the allure of mothers in order to become mature family men, sons must ultimately surmount the oedipal attraction of their mothers in order to be eligible for the same maturity.

The vague subtext of feminine threat that underlies the main plot of *Peter Pan* is also informed by a self-contradictory doubleness: the film suggests that sexual maturity for men is, however necessary, a form of entrapment (note how thoroughly tamed the Darling father appears to be), with feminine sexual allure serving as a snare that ends up spoiling boyhood fun. After all, Wendy with her budding breasts and hips just beginning to flare, nearly leads Peter Pan to his death, just as the seductive Eve Kendall nearly causes Roger Thornhill to be decapitated (read castrated) by a biplane. Indeed, in its treatment of such issues, *Peter Pan* resembles nothing more than *North by Northwest*, in which Thornhill must overcome his unnatural (immature) attachment to his mother, while giving up his boyish philandering, in order to achieve mature genital bliss with Eve, who will presumably now become the mother to little Thornhills.

In *Lady and the Tramp* (1955), the free-spirited Tramp also achieves domestic bliss (and, ultimately fatherhood) by submitting to the castrating sexual allures of the prissy Lady. Indeed, as Nadel notes, this film was a classic case of the attempt during the long 1950s to promote "the cult of domesticity as a form of political and social containment of the sexual energies of post–World War II teenagers and young adults, congruent to and commensurate with the American foreign and domestic policy of containing communism" (117). This film represents a rare case in Disney in which utopian imagery is actually associated with the real world, rather than with the childish imagination. However, it locates utopia not in a transformed social world but merely in the affluent, sheltered world of American suburbia. At that, the film, as Disney films tend to do, still locates its utopia in an idyllic past—in this case, America at the beginning of the twentieth century. The plot of the film is straightforward. Lady is a pampered cocker spaniel who lives with an affluent young couple in their posh suburban home. Her life is complicated when the couple (doing what couples are supposed to do) has a baby, but she still has it made until her owners go away for a brief vacation, leaving their Aunt Sarah in charge of the baby. Aunt Sarah, unfortunately, is a cat person, and in a Disney film that means bad news. Indeed, after a run-in with Aunt Sarah's twin Siamese cats, Lady is literally in the doghouse—so much so that she runs away, finding herself lost in a strange urban setting in which she does not know how to survive.

Luckily, she is rescued by the streetwise Tramp, a stray mutt that she had briefly met earlier. Tramp shows her the ropes of life on the dole, which he views as a utopian alternative to the routinized confines of Lady's suburbia, a land of fences, collars, and leashes. Indeed, Tramp does not have it bad at all, living high on the hog from handouts he gets from various families and restaurants. The film thus makes a mockery of poverty, depicting the underclasses as carefree beggars, happy to live off handouts, thus avoiding work and responsibility.[20] But the film clearly prefers Lady's more bourgeois ideology. After a series of adventures, she and Tramp settle down and start their own family, living in domestic wedded bliss with Lady's original bourgeois family.

In its focus on dogs, *Lady and the Tramp* relies on animated animals even more than most Disney films. In fact, the humans are entirely marginal and generally appear on-screen in fleeting shots that show only parts of their bodies. Their faces are seldom seen at all. Presumably, this device is intended to suggest that we are seeing the humans as they might appear to Lady and the other dogs, but it is also the case that this technique further marginalizes the humans and increases the film's focus on the dogs, which are easier to animate convincingly but which are also easier to portray sympathetically. The Disney company was quite well aware that one of the principal features of bourgeois ideology is an intense sentimentality that tends to focus on animals, kindness to animals thus serving as a utopian compensation for the cruelty and alienation to which humans are subjected in a capitalist environment. After all, even the German Nazis were notoriously fond of dogs.[21]

Of course, in the Disney universe, this same sentimentality is not extended to cats, who predictably appear as sinister, sneaky, and conniving creatures bent on working mischief at the expense of the innocent Lady. What is particularly significant here is the film's emphasis on the fact that these cats are Siamese, that is, Oriental, driven home at great length in their performance of an ostentatiously Oriental song ("we are Siamee-uz, if you plee-uz") and accompanying slinky Oriental dance. In fact, the sneakiness and treachery of the slanty-eyed cats are closely associated with their Oriental ethnicity, suggesting that such behavior is only to be expected of Orientals and producing some of the most strikingly Orientalist images in the entire Disney oeuvre. As Eleanor Byrne and Martin McQuillan put it, the cats are depicted as "wily, duplicitous, troublemaking, freeloading, Asian illegal immigrants" (97).

Of course, the United States had a long history of suspicion toward Asian immigrants, as can be seen in the Chinese Exclusion Act of 1882. The virulent racism of anti-Japanese propaganda (and the oppression of Japanese Americans) during World War II indicated that Orientalist racism was still alive and well. Indeed, Nadel notes that the depiction of the cats "draws heavily on the images of the Asian associated with World War II and Korean War propaganda" (122). Guilt feelings over the atomic bombings of Hiroshima and Nagasaki gave this racism a new nervous edge in the long 1950s, and this nervousness was quickly exacerbated by the successful communist revolution in China and the subsequent Korean War, by which time fear and loathing of Orientals were, in the American mind, inextricably intertwined with anticommunist hysteria. Indeed, the depiction of the Siamese cats in *Lady and the Tramp* as sly and insidious embodies not only a number of stock Orientalist stereotypes but communist stereotypes as well, and it is probably not an exaggeration to say that cats function quite generally in the Disney animated films of the long 1950s as figures of communism.[22]

The threat posed to Lady's domestic bliss by these felonious felines surely images the feeling of many Americans in the mid-1950s that their comfortable lives were endangered by sinister foreigners. The dangers experienced by Lady once she wanders out of the shelter of her posh suburb reinforce this same theme of a tranquil island surrounded by a threatening and stormy sea. But never fear: she returns safely home and takes the Tramp with her, taming his unruly masculine sexual energies. The message conveyed to American children was clear: your best bet for a good life is to stay home, follow the rules, and avoid all contaminating truck with foreigners and poor people. Meanwhile, little boys can be boys for a while, but little girls have the responsibility of domesticating them and putting them to useful work by the time they reach adulthood. As Nadel puts it, "the national agenda too has been served, with Tramp assimilated into the stable domestic setting, adding extra protection against the future subversion by cats, or invasion by rats, and forever divorced from the ethnically and socially marginal, who are left to be purged by the elements, both natural and social" (125).

If *Lady and the Tramp* relied almost entirely on animal characters, the Disney Company topped off the 1950s proper with the release of *Sleeping Beauty*, which involved significant advances in the sophistication of their animation of human figures—so much so that this film centers almost entirely on humans, with animals playing only backup roles. The backgrounds in this film are particularly impressive as well, having been developed and stylized by Disney's artists after extensive study of medieval art, allowing them to use the backgrounds to enhance the notion that the film is set in the fourteenth century, as the audience is repeatedly reminded in the course of the film. Of course, the film's primary audience of children could not have been expected to factor in the historical setting with any sophistication, but this placement of the action in the distant past is a crucial indicator of the film's problematic utopianism. Thus, in the end, we are assured that Princess Aurora and Prince Phillip will not only be married but live happily ever after. This seems promising, except that the film makes it clear that such things happen only in the distant past and cannot be expected to recur in the future. Further, such things happen only to royalty, so that ordinary citizens should in no way expect to achieve such happiness.

The treatment of gender in *Sleeping Beauty* is even more problematic than in most Disney films. For one thing, the heroine is once again staggeringly stereotypical, remarkable primarily for her beauty but also for other feminine accomplishments, such as singing and dancing. Betrothed at birth, she has spent her entire life (though she does not know it) in preparation for her wedding. But these preparations are interrupted when she is thrust into an even more feminine predicament, cast through evil magic into the passivity of a permanent sleep from which she can awaken only through the agency of a kiss from her beloved prince. Finally, this magic is wielded by the dark sorceress Maleficent, another in the string of evil females who together constitute the central villains in the Disney canon. Maleficent, aided by an army of evil black birds that are the forerunners of the winged attackers in *The Birds*, is, in fact, the bad woman who serves to highlight Aurora's goodness. A strong and independent woman, Maleficent is the epitome of the threatening female, the exact opposite of the beautiful, but submissive, Aurora, just as the evil witch-queen is paired off against the ostentatiously pure Snow

White, the wicked stepmother against the virtuous Cinderella, and the crazed Queen of Hearts against Alice.

The anthropocentric *Sleeping Beauty* was another great success for Disney, but the company returned to its tried-and-true focus on animated dogs in *One Hundred and One Dalmatians* (1961), which is literally swarming with cute cartoon canines. As in *Lady and the Tramp*, the human protagonists are dog owners who figure only marginally in the film. In fact, in this film, the only important human figures are the evil villains, led by Cruella De Ville, another of Disney's sinister female villains. Indeed, Cruella, who masterminds the kidnapping of 99 Dalmatian puppies that she horrifically plans to kill and skin for fur coats, may be the most despicable of Disney's bad girls, though she is presented as comically inept, presumably to avoid frightening small children. In this film, meanwhile, all animals are kind and good, even including a cat, so that the film is essentially structured around a polar opposition between good animals and bad humans, a motif that powerfully reinforces the sentimental bourgeois tendency to feel more sympathy for animals than for humans. However, as with so many polar oppositions in the long 1950s, this human-animal dichotomy is not a simple one. Thus, as Patrick Murphy points out, "the animals are most noble when most nearly 'human,' while the human is most ignoble when most nearly 'inhuman'" (128).

Otherwise, *One Hundred and One Dalmatians* is a relatively slight work, lacking the mythic resonances of many of the Disney animated classics of the long 1950s. In fact, the film can be taken as the marker of the beginning of a period of decline in Disney animation, in which the Disney company focused more and more on live action films. The Disney company attempted another (rather unsuccessful) animated story with mythic proportions in *The Sword in the Stone* (1963), based on the Arthurian legends, and it scored a major hit with the release of *The Jungle Book* (1967), perhaps the height (or depth) of Disnified racist Orientalism. Then the company would not produce another true animated classic until the release of *The Little Mermaid* (1989), which announced the beginning of a new string of successful animated films that ran through the 1990s, resurrecting numerous motifs (including sexist and racist ones) from the 1950s in a clear nostalgia play. At that, only *The Lion King* (1994), continuing the Disney project of scouring the Third World for material by depicting Africa primarily as the home of exotic jungle animals, rather than human beings, was a box-office hit on the order of the classics of the 1950s.

Of course, if the films of both Disney and Hitchcock are saturated with the ideology of the Cold War, then it should come as no surprise that the peak periods of both Hitchcock and Disney should both end roughly at the same time as the peak years of Cold War hysteria. Similarly, it is not by sheer accident that, at this same pivotal historical moment, Stanley Kubrick's *Dr. Strangelove* (1963) and Fuller's *Shock Corridor*

(1963), respectively, marked the ends of the science fiction and film noir cycles of the long 1950s. At this point, the Cold War consensus began to crack at the seams, providing at least a brief opportunity for alternative visions to shine through. The subsequent oppositional political movements of the 1960s, however weakened by their failure to challenge the class-based structural premises of capitalism, did at least show a momentary flowering of utopian thought, a sort of last-gasp protest against the approaching completion of the global hegemony of late capitalism. Thus, noting the widely acknowledged dearth of utopian thought, Jameson sees Herbert Marcuse's *One-Dimensional Man*, tellingly published in 1964 and thus at the very end of the long 1950s, as the beginning of a protest against this dearth. For Jameson, in the 1960s, "'Marcuse' virtually becomes the name for a whole explosive renewal of Utopian thinking and imagination, and for a rebirth of the older narrative form" (*Postmodernism* 160).

Jameson grants, however, that the newly emergent utopias of the 1960s (which really means 1964 to 1975 or so) tended to lack any genuine historical vision. Instead of this temporal orientation, they tended to be spatial, envisioning utopia not as a future goal for the transformation of the present society but as an alternative place (generally located in "nature") to which one might go to escape the present society. As a result, the energies released by this moment were comparatively weak and did not survive the mid-1970s intact, though Jameson sees in this phenomenon, however short-lived, a glimmer of hope. Utopian thought is not dead but in a coma. It thus maintains a heartbeat, however faint, and might someday be resurrected to full health. This resurrection, however, requires a proper diagnosis of the ailments that led to the coma in the first place. It is hoped that the interrogation, in this volume, of the weakness of utopian energy in American Cold War culture can serve as an early contribution to this diagnosis by at least pointing toward the complex involvement of anti-utopian thought in the ideology of the Cold War.

# Postscript

In his very useful survey of the historical evolution of the idea of the postmodern, Perry Anderson notes that the term was already being used in the United States in the late 1950s. However, 1950s intellectuals, such as C. Wright Mills and Irving Howe, generally used the term in a pejorative sense to indicate a decline in American culture (from the heights of modernism) brought about by creeping routinization, commodification, and conformity (Anderson 12–13). Anderson notes that the idea of postmodernism as we now know it began to take shape in the 1960s, with the work of figures such as Charles Jencks (on architecture) and Ihab Hassan (on literature). By the end of the 1960s, the term had come into full-blown currency with the theoretical work of thinkers such as Jean-François Lyotard.

As a result of this history, many observers have come to think of postmodernism itself as beginning sometime around the end of the 1960s. As Anderson notes, much of the recent theoretical interest in postmodernism has involved such issues of periodization, especially as this placement of postmodernism as beginning at the end of the 1960s seems to make Jameson's influential vision of postmodernism problematic (78–79). After all, Jameson's vision of postmodernism as the cultural logic of late capitalism would seem to place the beginnings of postmodernism in the late 1940s, while Jameson himself seems to locate the real rise of postmodernist culture in the early 1970s. Similarly, David Harvey, while employing a slightly different Marxist model that relates postmodernism to a crisis in post-Fordist capital accumulation, sees postmodernism as a cultural phenomenon that began in the early 1960s and "asserted itself as hegemonic in the early 1970s" (63). Harvey also sees the political unrest of 1968 as a "harbinger" of the coming of postmodernity (38). Meanwhile, Alex Callinicos, who doubts that postmodernism even exists, except as an artifact created by theorists, locates this invention of postmodernism in the flurry of postmodernist discourse that arose at the end of the 1960s in the wake of the collapse of the radical political movements of that decade. For Callinicos, the invention of postmodernity is intimately linked to a "rejection of socialist revolution as either feasible or desirable" (9). Finally, Terry Eagleton, while accepting the notion that postmodernism is a real phenomenon, also locates much of the impetus behind postmodernism to the experience of political defeat for the Left, a defeat that, by the end of the 1960s, left no "utopic space" beyond the "prevailing system" (*Illusions* 18).

In other words, both Callinicos and Eagleton, whatever their other differences, see the phenomenon of postmodernism (whether real or illusory) as arising from a loss of faith in the utopian alternatives provided by the possibility of socialist revolution. Anderson himself emphasizes the same point. Discussing the well-known suggestion by Lyotard that postmodernism is informed by a basic "incredulity toward metanarratives" (xxiv), he offers a convincing argument that by "metanarratives" Lyotard really means only one metanarrative, that of classical Marxism. Further, Anderson argues that Lyotard's rejection of Marxism is part of a thoroughgoing rejection of all utopian alternatives to the existing capitalist order. Indeed, Anderson concludes that the various versions of postmodernism, as they developed in the work of thinkers otherwise as various as Hassan, Jencks, Lyotard, and Jürgen Habermas, were united by a consistent antipathy toward the traditional utopian values of socialism and the Left: "Common to all was a subscription to the principles of what Lyotard — once the most radical — called liberal democracy, as the unsurpassable horizon of the time. There could be nothing but capitalism. The postmodern was a sentence on alternative illusions" (46).

For Anderson, as for Callinicos and Eagleton, the postmodern rejection of these utopian "illusions" is closely related to the disillusionment that arose after the failure of the radical movements of the 1960s to bring about sweeping systemic changes in capitalist society, which again seems to locate the rise of postmodernism at the end of the 1960s or beginning of the 1970s. In any case, this model again locates the rise of postmodernism in an experience of defeat for the Left. But Jameson's different spin on this phenomenon — which locates the rise of postmodernism in the experience of victory for capitalism, rather than defeat for socialism — is surely more to the point. It is discourse on postmodernism, including the Marxist work of Anderson, Harvey, Callinicos, Eagleton, and Jameson himself, as well as the postmodern theorization of former Marxists such as Lyotard, that arises out of disillusionment on the Left. Postmodernity itself (a real historical phenomenon, as opposed to discourse about that phenomenon) arises out of the post–World War II triumph of capitalism.

But this view should, again, locate the beginnings of postmodernism in the long 1950s, rather than the late 1960s or early 1970s. Indeed, even if

one chooses to see postmodernism as arising primarily from the experience of defeat for the Left, it is certainly the case that, in a Western context, this experience itself hardly began with the collapse of the May 1968
general strike in France. In many ways, it began with the compromises of
the Popular Front in the 1930s and was certainly well under way after the
1939 Ribbentrop-Molotov pact, with the events of 1956 (including the
Soviet intervention in Hungary and Khrushchev's "revelations" concerning Stalin) sounding a death knell that was all but final for "traditional"
Soviet-led world socialism. In America, the repressive climate of the Cold
War completely destroyed the Communist Party and all but completely
destroyed the trade union movement, well before the advent of the
1960s.

That so many observers would seem to locate the beginnings of postmodernism in or after the 1960s is largely a matter of terminology. It is at
the end of the 1960s that postmodernism becomes *hegemonic* in the West,
but it is well before that time that postmodernism becomes an emergent
phenomenon. The weakness of utopian vision in American culture in the
long 1950s is, I think, one of the clearest signs of this emergence. After all,
sweeping cultural and historical phenomena do not appear (or disap-
pear) overnight, as Raymond Williams has perhaps best reminded us
with his elegant formulation of the notion of emergent, dominant, and
residual historical phenomena (121–27). Thus, if postmodernism was a
cultural dominant at the beginning of the 1970s, then it surely must have
been an emergent cultural phenomenon for some time before that.

It is crucial to understand this emergence if we are to get a better grip
on the nature and implications of postmodernism as a cultural phenomenon. For example, Callinicos consistently argues that postmodernism must not be real because so many of the cultural motifs identified as
postmodern after the explosion of postmodern theory at the beginning of
the 1970s were already present in the 1950s. Thus, he concludes that
there is nothing postmodern about the use of Brechtian alienation effects
in the 1980s television series *Moonlighting*, because a similar phenomenon
had already occurred in the use of expressionist techniques in film noir
decades earlier (156). But, if one locates the beginnings of postmodernism in the long 1950s and thus sees that film noir was *already* postmodern
to an extent, then Callinicos's argument here collapses.

Locating the rise of postmodernism in the long 1950s may thus help to
make the point that postmodernism is not merely an illusion arising from
theoretical elaborations that began in the late 1960s. But thus identifying
postmodernism as a part of the historical matrix of the long 1950s also
does more. For one thing, it adds support to Jameson's vision of postmodernism as the cultural logic of late capitalism, because it makes the
rise of postmodernism historically congruent with the postwar rise of late
capitalism. For another, locating the emergence of postmodernism in the
long 1950s suggests an intimate relationship between postmodernism

and the Cold War. Indeed, a lack of attention to the importance of the Cold War is, to my mind, a crucial missing piece to the theoretical puzzle that Marxist theorists such as Jameson, Anderson, Callinicos, Harvey, and Eagleton have attempted to put together.

Modernism was informed, first and foremost, by a sense of cultural crisis brought about by the rapid social and technological changes that swept Europe and North America in the period roughly from 1890 to 1930. During the long 1950s, at the height of the Cold War, this sense of crisis became all the more pronounced, even as the project of modernity seemed, in many ways, to be fulfilling its promise. For one thing, the very texture of Western culture was changing even more rapidly than at the beginning of the century, with the rise of American television now leading the way. If nothing else, the widespread terror of nuclear holo-caust, especially in the United States (where this terror was particularly intense), ensured that the unprecedented economic prosperity of the postwar years brought about little in the way of comfort and content-ment. However, as I have argued in *Monsters, Mushroom Clouds, and the Cold War*, the particular vehemence of Cold War hysteria in the United States cannot be accounted for in any simple way but can only be seen as the product of a number of different, interacting phenomena. Certainly, the fear of nuclear holocaust was important, but that alone does not ex-plain why Cold War hysteria was so much more pronounced in the United States than anywhere else. Many other fears, both domestic and international, made contributions as well. Further, as Eric Hobsbawm notes, much of the particularly apocalyptic tone of American Cold War rhetoric can be attributed to the fact that numerous American politicians did all they could to encourage Cold War hysteria as a means of winning votes (*Age of Extremes* 235–37). It is certainly the case that anticommunist hysteria was actively encouraged by a corporate America bent on crip-pling the trade unions that had gained so much ground during the 1930s.

The success of such strategies for the demonization of socialism cer-tainly contributed to the triumph of capitalism during the long 1950s, but it also contributed to the decided ambivalence with which that success was greeted, even by an American population that reaped most of the benefits of this triumph. For example, the effective removal of socialism as a utopian alternative to capitalism made the routinization and homog-enization that capitalism was bringing about in American society seem all the more suffocating. Indeed, the very sense that capitalism (and, by extension, the Enlightenment) was at last achieving its historical goals turned out to be oppressive to an increasingly affluent American society the citizens of which began more and more to wonder if that was all there was. This environment helped to breed a cynicism that was surely one of the most important conditions of possibility of postmodernity.

In this sense, postmodernism might be seen as a reaction *against* capi-talism. Of course, Jameson's argument that postmodernism is best understood as the cultural logic of late capitalism in no way implies that postmodernism cannot contain certain anticapitalist impulses. After all, as Marx understood long ago, capitalism itself includes strong anticapitalist impulses, potentially containing the seeds of its own destruction. Thus, any properly dialectical Marxist analysis of the relationship between capitalism and postmodernism would surely have to consider the possibility that postmodernism has an anticapitalist side, somewhat along the lines of Hal Foster's suggestion some time ago that postmodernism involves competing impulses of resistance to, and celebration of, the capitalist status quo (xi–xii). Some of the antirationalist impulses of postmodernism can certainly be seen as protests against capitalist routinization, while the postmodernist depiction of fragmented subjectivity can be seen as complaint about the growing alienation of the individual in the long 1950s. In the climate of the Cold War, however, these seemingly anticapitalist inclinations were largely conscripted as anti*socialist* impulses, with socialism now being portrayed as the principal threat to individualism in the modern world, while the dehumanizing tendencies of Enlightenment rationality came to be associated with a coldly logical, inhumanly superscientific socialism.

Thus, the climate of the Cold War was crucial to the development of postmodernism as the cultural logic of late capitalism, helping to resolve the dialectical tension between anticapitalist and procapitalist postmodernism almost entirely in favor of the latter. Central to this resolution was the perceived absence of any utopian alternative to the capitalist order, a perception that, as I have demonstrated in this volume, permeated American culture in the long 1950s, paving the way for the evolution of postmodernism in directions that were primarily congruent with the growing global hegemony of capitalism. Thus, the opposition between postmodernisms of resistance and reaction indicated by Foster (or Teresa Ebert's somewhat similar distinction between a postmodernism of resistance and a "ludic" postmodernism) had essentially collapsed by the end of the Cold War, though a certain strain of postmodernist cultural production (which one might term "anxious" postmodernism, as opposed to the continuing ludic strain) remains less than celebratory with regard to the nature of life in the late capitalist world.

But this anxious strain of postmodernism poses no real challenge to the hegemony of late capitalism, partly because of the ongoing absence of any effective utopian alternative. Nevertheless, it is worth remembering that hegemony does not imply total control. Anticapitalist forces remain in the world, especially in the Third World, and many of these forces may, in fact, turn out to be emergent, rather than residual, in Williams's sense. Meanwhile, a few utopian, anticapitalist impulses remain even within postmodernism itself. Critics of postmodernist culture would do well to seek out these impulses through careful analysis, rather than merely to decry the feebleness of postmodernist resistance to capitalism.

After all, it remains to be seen, as we enter a new millennium, whether these impulses, however weak and residual, might evolve in new and productive directions, perhaps joining forces with the emerging anticapitalist forces of the Third World to produce new constellations of utopian ideas unforeseen in the thought of the twentieth century. With history, as with baseball, it ain't over till it's over. And it ain't over.

# Notes

## INTRODUCTION

1. For a discussion of the role of the SDS in the radical politics of the 1960s, see James Miller. The entire Port Huron statement can be found on-line at http://lists.village.virginia.edu/sixties/HTML_docs/Resources/Primary/Mani festos/SDS_Port_Huron.html.

2. In *Monsters, Mushroom Clouds, and the Cold War*, I argue that it makes sense, in terms of periodization, to treat the peak Cold War years of 1946–1964 as a unit (which I call the long 1950s), rather than arbitrarily limiting oneself to the 1950s proper. I will typically use the term "1950s" to indicate this longer period in this work.

3. Compare Blanche DuBois, the "heroine" of Tennessee Williams's *A Streetcar Named Desire* (1947), whose taste for teenage boys, fueled by the loss of her young husband years earlier, drives her to madness and incarceration in an asylum.

4. Jameson here draws crucially upon Ernest Mandel's important elaboration of the notion of late capitalism.

5. Jameson himself, I should note, appears to locate the beginnings of postmodernist literature in the early 1970s, as does David Harvey.

6. See also Firdous Azim for an extended study of the interrelationship between the novel and the ideology of colonialism.

7. For a recent extended study of *Moby-Dick* within the context of the work of Pease and other "New Americanists," see Spanos's *The Errant Art of* Moby-Dick.

8. See Slotkin's magisterial three-volume study of the role of racial frontier violence in the formation of the American national identity, comprising *Regeneration through Violence, The Fatal Environment*, and *Gunfighter Nation*.

9. For a reading of Baum's book as a populist parable critical of capitalism, see Littlefield.

10. Tarzan's centrality as an icon of American culture was solidified by the MGM films, featuring Johnny Weismuller as Tarzan, which began with *Tarzan the Ape Man* in 1932, and ran all the way to *Tarzan and the Mermaids* in 1948,

when an aging and fattening Weismuller (44 years old in 1948) finally gave way to Lex Barker in the title role.

11. Bloch here is speaking primarily of the cinema of the 1940s. He grants that there was sometimes a vague social criticism in earlier American films but concludes that this criticism "was, as regards capitalism, little more than the refinement of a critical apology" (410).

12. For an excellent study of the American proletarian literature of the 1930s, see Barbara Foley's *Radical Representations*.

## CHAPTER 1

1. In his next novel, *Barbary Shore* (1951), Mailer would suggest that the United States was not all that different from its former ally and new Cold War enemy, the Soviet Union. Here, Mailer envisions a coming American–Soviet war as a "conflict between two virtually identical forms of exploitation," both sides having succumbed to the same bureaucratic routinization (278).

2. Tony Tanner notes that *Catch-22* conducts a number of interesting dialogues with both *The Naked and the Dead* and *From Here to Eternity* (23–25).

3. See Raeburn for a reading of *Catch-22* within the context of the 1950s.

4. In this same interview, published in the *Detroit News* on September 13, 1970, Heller also specifically claimed that the "elements that inspired the ideas" in his book were derived from "the civilian situation in this country in the 1950s." Reprinted in *A* Catch-22 *Casebook* (64).

5. See Tanner (59–70)

6. For a succinct discussion of the carnivalesque aspects of *Henderson the Rain King* (based on his doctoral dissertation on the same topic), see Renaux.

7. The term "ugly American," of course, comes from the 1958 Lederer and Burdick novel of the same title. Note, however, that the real point of the novel is not that Americans abroad do not sufficiently understand indigenous cultures but that America does not sufficiently understand the cleverness and ruthlessness of our Soviet rivals in the Cold War, thus virtually assuring a Soviet victory. The opposite, of course, was the case, with the Soviets being no match for America's greater economic resources or for an American propaganda machine driven by sophisticated Madison Avenue strategies of mind control.

8. For a different, Third World, view of this scene, see Anita Desai's admiring description of the power of this "terrible image of water gone to waste in the desert" (64).

9. In addition to the spoof of Wilhelm Reich in the description of the personality therapy practiced by Dahfu on Henderson, *Henderson the Rain King* also lampoons Freudian psychoanalysis and Freudian personality theory. See Moss for a discussion of the some of the book's Freudian themes. On Bellow and Reich, see Rodrigues.

10. But see my argument elsewhere that many of Radek's complaints about Joyce are perfectly reasonable and probably justified (Ulysses 20–25).

11. See Robert Penn Warren's summary of the pre–World War II critical reputation of Faulkner as "a combination of Thomas Nelson Page, a fascist and a psychopath" (328).

12. See Grimwood for a discussion of Faullkner's animosity toward uppity poor whites (163–64).

13. On this and other aspects of Faulkner's dialogue with consumer culture in the Snopes Trilogy, see Ownby.

14. Nadel notes that Holden's vigilant search for phonies echoes the paranoid political climate of the Cold War (71–89). However, the phonies of the book are not communists but conformist, mainstream Americans.

15. On the crucial role played by anticommunist politics in *Invisible Man*, see Foley's "The Rhetoric of Anticommunism in *Invisible Man*." Ellison's rejection of communism, given his earlier flirtation with radical politics, is a typical sign of the turn from utopian thought in the long 1950s. On the leftist inclination of Ellison's early fiction, see Foley's "Reading Redness."

16. See my discussion of *Lolita* in *Literature and Domination* (70–89).

17. This is the scenario as the book presents it, but the complexities of the book's mixtures are such that it is not entirely clear how we are to regard the authorship of the poem and the commentary. Within the world of the text, it is possible that Shade may have written both the poem and the commentary (see Field) or that Kinbote may have written both (see Stegner). Boyd, showing the complexity of the text, agrees with Field that Shade wrote both (and thus created Kinbote) but also suggests that Kinbote is "the demented fantasy of Vveslav Botkin, a refugee scholar in the Russian department" at Wordsmith College, where Shade also teaches (433).

18. Interestingly, Doctorow performs a similar combination of modernist technique, leftist ideology, and popular genre in his second novel, *Big as Life* (1966), which might be described as revisionary science fiction.

19. Andreas Huyssen's *Beyond the Great Divide* is perhaps the most influential statement of this position, though, in Huyssen's case, this statement is only one part of a more complicated argument.

## CHAPTER 2

1. For a discussion of the actual strike on which the film was based, see Cargill. For an extensive discussion of the film and the opposition it faced, with Michael Wilson's screenplay included, see Rosenfelt. For a firsthand account of the film and its tribulations, see Biberman. On official attempts to suppress the film, see Lorence.

2. Even in Britain, traditionally far more class-conscious than America, some on the Left, such as Anthony Crosland, argued for the development of new modes of leftist critique that transcended the old emphasis on class, while also (tellingly) singing the virtues of American-style liberalism. On the other hand, such important British New Leftists as E. P. Thompson, Eric Hobsbawm, and Raymond Williams maintained a strong focus on class, assuring that class would

not be obliterated from British leftist discourse to the extent that it was in America. For a discussion of some of these debates, see Dworkin.

3. Of course, this tendency to focus on style, rather than substance, has often been the result of specific readings of literary texts more than the texts themselves. Thus, the important (especially anticolonial) political content in the work of Joyce was long ignored by critics more concerned with placing him in the mainstream of Western culture by emphasizing the formal sophistication of his work.

4. Probably the best description of the absorption of the avant-garde by mainstream bourgeois culture is Peter Bürger's.

5. See James F. Murphy for a detailed and well-documented argument that the *Partisan Review* narrative of the cultural history of the 1930s "remains one of the most glaring misinterpretations in the writing of recent American history" (195).

6. Schaub further associates this erosion of class with the rise of postmodernism.

7. Here, Killens follows in the footsteps of William Attaway's *Blood on the Forge* (1941), with its central treatment of employer-engineered antagonisms between Slavic and African American steelworkers, a theme that is also central to Phillip Bonosky's *Burning Valley* (1953) , reissued in 1997 with an extensive introduction by Wald.

8. Much of this "betrayal," of course, consisted merely of a moderation in the Party's antiracist rhetoric during the Popular Front period and especially during World War II as part of a general cessation in radical critique of American society that grew out of a desire not to undermine the battle against fascism. The party also moderated its criticisms in terms of class and gender during the same period.

9. For more on Du Bois, see the recent two-volume biography by David Levering Lewis.

10. For a study of Du Bois's "literary legacy," see Aptheker.

11. Watson was a real historical personage; he also figures in Carl Marzani's leftist novel, *The Survivor.*

12. For a discussion of the Gallup Strike, see Rubenstein.

13. In the early 1930s, Stevenson himself lived in Taos, the later home of Nichols. It was presumably there that Stevenson became interested in the Gallup Strike and in the tribulations of New Mexican miners in general. On the background of Stevenson's sequence in New Mexico history, see Thorson and Thorson. For a moving elegy to Stevenson, see Maltz.

14. See Pizer for a description of the ways in which Mailer's first book "is a 1930s novel" (90).

15. Mailer's principal political statement during this period is *The White Negro* (1957), an individualist, beat-influenced work the title of which also suggests the replacement of class by race in American leftist discourse of the long 1950s.

16. In his introduction to the 1997 republication of *The Great Midland*, Saxton acknowledges that he remains "bitterly ashamed of the compromise" but notes that he still sees no other way he could have gotten the novel published at all at the time (xxii).

17. The full history of the impact of the anticommunism purges on American academic and intellectual life—and of the complicity of academe in these purges—has yet to be written. But works such as Ellen Schrecker's *No Ivory Tower* and Sigmund Diamond's *Compromised Campus* do at least begin to indicate the scope of the problem. For some of the most recent thoughts on this topic, see the collection edited by André Schiffrin.

18. Lest my discomfort with McCarthy's book be construed as verification of the rumor that leftists have no sense of humor, I might note that Ring Lardner, Jr. also treats the anticommunist purges in a comic mode in *The Ecstasy of Owen Muir* (1954). Lardner, who wrote the book while in prison for his political beliefs, makes clear in it that he understands the seriousness of the repression that was sweeping America at the time in a way that Mary McCarthy apparently did not.

19. McCarthy's novel thus suggests that the recent right-wing assault on political correctness may, in fact, be rooted in the anticommunist purges of the 1950s. For an extended study of the counterfeit basis of this right-wing project, see Wilson.

20. Dodd provides similar links in *The Searching Light*. She had observed German Nazism first-hand while in Berlin during the 1930s with her father, the American ambassador to Germany. On Dodd's experiences during in Germany, see *Through Embassy Eyes*.

21. For a much more positive reading of Swados's treatment of union activity in the book, see Wald (*New York Intellectuals* 336–38).

22. Swados's book has other problems as well, not the least of which is its treatment of gender. Most of his workers (who are all men) seem more oppressed by their demanding wives than by the unequal class structure of capitalism.

23. Indeed, trends in Britain paralleled those in America in numerous ways. On the other hand, Alan Sillitoe, a writer often associated with Barstow, Braine, and Waterhouse, maintains a better sense of connection to the long British tradition of working-class culture. Meanwhile, writers such as Sid Chaplin, Jack Common, and Len Doherty were still, in the 1950s, producing novels with a strong working-class orientation, even if they tended to shy away from a rhetoric of revolutionary class struggle. Writers such as Sillitoe, Barry Hines, David Storey, Pat Barker, and James Kelman continued this trend into subsequent decades. See the summaries of the work of these writers in my *The Modern British Novel of the Left*.

24. Incidentally, Swados and other members of the New York Intellectuals were not necessarily as independent in their own minds as they have later been portrayed. Many of them, at least at times, thought of themselves as followers of Leon Trotsky, though, in fact, their citations of Trotsky appear often to have been instances of convenient (anti-Stalinist) name-dropping more than literal ideological influence.

25. As Eric Hobsbawm points out, racism itself evolved in the nineteenth century as a technique for the rationalization of the mismatch between capitalist practice and bourgeois rhetoric. Arguments, often based on "scientific" data, that some groups of people were by nature inferior to others helped to justify the

contradictory status of the new capitalist system as "a fundamentally inegalitarian society based upon a fundamentally egalitarian ideology" (296).

26. From this point of view it is interesting to note that genuinely leftist literature virtually disappears from American culture not in the 1950s, when dozens of leftist novels were published, but in the 1960s, when there were very few.

## CHAPTER 3

1. One character, given Thompson's party name, Robert Dillon, is a figure of the author himself in his childhood, though his date of birth has been shifted to 1900, rather than 1906.

2. He also provides an exposition on the glories of marriage that is, to say the least, radically inconsistent with the skepticism toward marriage shown in Thompson's novel.

3. Both film versions of *The Getaway* roughly replicate the scene in the manure pile by having the stars dumped into landfills from garbage trucks, but neither film version is able to capture the Menippean energies of the scene in the book.

4. With little else going for it, this lackluster film was also issued on videotape in a special unrated version that featured even steamier sex scenes.

5. Overt or not, the commentary can still be read in different ways: as an offensively sexist locker room joke or as a parodic criticism of such jokes.

6. See Brian McHale's extended argument that such mixtures of ontological levels are crucial to the strategies of much postmodernist fiction.

7. Note, however, Michael André Bernstein's argument that Bakhtin's vision of the carnivalesque, generally seen by critics as celebratory, itself has an extremely dark side.

8. This "castration" theme is, in fact, a common one in modern fiction. See my discussion of this motif elsewhere (*Techniques* 132–61).

9. Such passing mentions of the McCarthyite anticommunist crusades also appear in *Now and on Earth*, where Jim Dillon is investigated by the FBI because of his former membership in the Communist Party and in *Recoil*, where the right-wing demagogue Fanning Arnholt (a neo-Nazi who functions, after the fact, as a forerunner of religious Right leaders such as Pat Robertson and Jerry Falwell) crusades against "Un-Americanism" as part of his own scheme to gain wealth and power.

10. Polito notes that the character was, in fact, originally called Lou Ford but that Thompson apparently changed the name to avoid complications in the sale of future film rights to *The Killer Inside Me* or *Wild Town* (442).

11. Perhaps the closest literary parallel to Thompson's almost recurring characters involves the the appearance of Quentin Compson as the protagonist of both William Faulkner's *The Sound and the Fury* (1929) and its apparent prequel, *Absalom, Absalom!* (1936). Subtle inconsistencies between the two texts suggest that the Quentin of the latter book is not quite the same person as the Quentin of the former book. In Faulkner's case these inconsistencies reinforce the theme of the unreliability of historical memory that informs *Absalom, Absalom!* On the

other hand, Faulkner's repeated use of settings from his fictional Yoknapataw-pha County generally enhances the sense of that county as a real place. Polito cites Thompson's wife, Alberta, to the effect that Faulkner was Thompson's favorite novelist (226).

## CHAPTER 4

1. See, for example, the collection *Inside the Mouse*, edited by Susan Willis and the "Project on Disney."

2. The entire AFI list can be found on-line at http://www.afionline.org /100movies/.

3. Hitchcock's rage for order has been widely discussed. Regarding routinization, see Ferrara for a useful discussion of Hitchcock's "consistent oblique criticism of the restraints which bourgeois society places on individuals" (84).

4. As Robert Sklar notes, *The Stranger*, in this sense, resembles Hitchcock's earlier *Shadow of a Doubt* (1943), which locates "its intense anxiety, and claustrophobic fear in a benign, sunny small-town setting" (253).

5. That important Nazis had fled to South America in the wake of their defeat in the war was, of course, an established fact. Thus, the Nazis of *Cornered* also operate in South America.

6. Spoto notes that Hitchcock, in the film, "drew on the tradition of the fairground as the place where the demented aspects of life are concentrated and expressed, where the Dionysian riots and the repressions of the year are set free" (193).

7. On Stewart as a paragon of the postwar crisis in American masculinity, see Amy Lawrence. Note that, in Stanley Kubrick's film version of *Lolita* (1962), the role of Humbert was played by James Mason, that paragon of suave, continental corruption. In the world of Hitchcock, of course, Mason would appear not as a protagonist but as a decadent communist agent in *North by Northwest*.

8. Numerous critics have commented on the postmodernist tendencies of *Vertigo*. Marantz Cohen, for example, feels that the film challenges, in a postmodernist way, conventional notions of stable subjectivity and narrative coherence (166–70). Similarly, Katie Trumpener feels that the film is postmodernist in its self-referential tendency to deconstruct the ontological boundary between fiction and reality (183).

9. For more on the issue of class in the film, see Corber ("'Thumbprints'" 303–5).

10. See West for a discussion of the postmodernist metafictional aspects of *Vertigo*.

11. Alternatively, this shift in background suggests the extent to which Ferguson's projected fantasies are beginning to overwhelm reality.

12. Corber points particularly to the discussion of the negative impact of "momism" in Philip Wylie's rightist *Generation of Vipers* (1942) (*Name* 197).

13. Jameson thus notes that Grant's schematic acting style is virtually Brechtian in the way it calls attention to itself as signification ("Spatial" 49).

14. See Zipes for an extended discussion of Disney's appropriation of fairy tales in a way that "capitalized on American innocence and utopianism to reinforce the social and political status quo" (21–22).

15. Elizabeth Bell suggests that Cinderella is reminiscent of Hitchcock favorite Grace Kelly, thus providing another link between Hitchcock and Disney (109–10).

16. For an excellent discussion of this strike and of the Disney Company's determined efforts to break the union that instituted it, see Denning (403–22).

17. In this, *Peter Pan* differs from Baum's much more utopian depiction of the Land of Oz, which is accessible even to adults—and which appears to be real, not just imaginary.

18. Cyclicity is, in fact, a key trope in *Peter Pan*. Note that the film begins with a narrator's announcement that "all this has happened before, and it will happen again."

19. Note Schickel's description of Disney's version of Tinker Bell as a "midget ... nymphet, though she is considerable more voluptuous than Nabokov's young Lolita" (234). Indeed, Tinker Bell here directly parallels the difficulties experienced by Marilyn Monroe in attempting to climb through a ship's porthole in Howard Hawks's *Gentlemen Prefer Blondes* (1953).

20. These underclasses are also vaguely associated with suspect ethnics. When Lady is briefly imprisoned in the dog pound, the denizens of the pound include a Mexican Chihuahua, a German (read Nazi) dachsund, and a Cockney (read working-class) bulldog. There is also a suspect Gorky-quoting Russian wolfhound, whose portrayal associates the underclasses with Russians and communists. Byrne and McQuillan also argue that this wolfhound is portrayed as Jewish, but then Jews and communists were often linked in the Cold War discourse of the long 1950s (99).

21. See my extensive discussion of bourgeois sentimentality in Ulysses, *Capitalism, and Colonialism* (147-68).

22. See Pietz for a discussion of the use, during the Cold War, of Orientalist stereotypes to characterize Soviets and other communists.

# Works Cited

**BOOKS AND ARTICLES**

Alter, Robert. "*Invitation to a Beheading*: Nabokov and the Art of Politics." *Triquarterly* 17 (1970): 41-59.

Althusser, Louis. *Lenin and Philosophy and Other Essays*. Trans. Ben Brewster. London: Monthly Review Press, 1971, 170-83.

Anderson, Perry. *The Origins of Postmodernity*. London: Verso, 1998.

Aptheker, Herbert. *The Literary Legacy of W.E.B. Du Bois*. White Plains, NY: Kraus International, 1989.

Arnow, Harriette. *The Dollmaker*. New York: Macmillan, 1954.

Attaway, William. *Blood on the Forge*. 1941. New York: Monthly Review P, 1987.

Azim, Firdous. *The Colonial Rise of the Novel*. London: Routledge, 1993.

Baer, Barbara. "Harriette Arnow's Chronicles of Destruction." *Harriette Simpson Arnow: Critical Essays on Her Work*. Ed. Haeja K. Chung. East Lansing: Michigan State UP, 1995. 53-62.

Balzac, Honoré de. *Lost Illusions*. 1837-1843. Trans. Herbert J. Hunt. New York: Penguin, 1971.

Baudrillard, Jean. *Selected Writings*. Ed. Mark Poster. Stanford, CA: Stanford UP, 1988.

Barzman, Ben. *Twinkle, Twinkle Little Star*. New York: G. P. Putnam's Sons, 1960.

Baum, L. Frank. *The Wonderful Wizard of Oz*. 1900. New York: Oxford UP, 2000.

Behn, Aphra. *Oroonoko*. 1688. New York: Norton, 1997.

Bell, Daniel. *The End of Ideology: On the Exhaustion of Political Ideas in the Fifties*. 1960. Cambridge, MA: Harvard UP, 1988.

Bell, Elizabeth. "Somatexts at the Disney Shop: Constructing the Pentimentos of Women's Animated Bodies." *From Mouse to Mermaid: The Politics of Film, Gender, and Culture*. Ed. Elizabeth Bell, Lynda Haas, and Laura Sells. Bloomington: Indiana UP, 1995. 107-24.

Bellamy, Edward. *Looking Backward: 2000-1887*. 1888. Boston: Houghton-Mifflin, 1926.

Bellow, Saul. *Henderson the Rain King*. New York: Viking, 1959.

Benjamin, Walter. *Illuminations*. Trans. Harry Zohn. Ed. Hannah Arendt. New
    York: Harcourt, Brace and World, 1955.
Bercovitch, Sacvan. "The Problem of Ideology in American Literary History."
    *Critical Inquiry* 12.1 (1986):
Bernstein, Michael André. *Bitter Carnival:* Ressentiment *and the Abject Hero*.
    Princeton, NJ: Princeton UP, 1992.
Bessie, Alvah. *The Un-Americans*. New York: Cameron, 1957.
Biberman, Herbert. Salt of the Earth: *The Story of a Film*. Boston: Beacon, 1965.
Bloch, Ernst. *The Principle of Hope*. 1954–1959. 3 vols. Trans. Neville Plaice,
    Stephen Plaice, and Paul Knight. 1986. Cambridge, MA: MIT P, 1996.
Bloom, James D. *Left Letters: The Culture Wars of Mike Gold and Joseph Freeman*.
    New York: Columbia UP, 1992.
Bluestone, George. *Novels into Film*. Berkeley: U of California P, 1957.
Blumberg, Paul. *Inequality in an Age of Decline*. New York: Oxford UP, 1980.
Bonosky, Phillip. *Burning Valley*. New York: Masses and Mainstream, 1953.
Booker, M. Keith. *Literature and Domination: Sex, Knowledge, and Power in Modern
    Fiction*. Gainesville: UP of Florida, 1993.
———. *The Modern British Novel of the Left: A Research Guide*. Westport, CT:
    Greenwood, 1998.
———. *Monsters, Mushroom Clouds, and the Cold War: American Science Fiction and
    the Birth of Postmodernism, 1946–1964*. Westport, CT: Greenwood, 2001.
———. *Ulysses, Capitalism, and Colonialism: Reading Joyce after the Cold War*.
    Westport, CT: Greenwood, 2001.
Boyd, Brian. *Vladimir Nabokov: The American Years*. Princeton, NJ: Princeton UP,
    1991.
———. *Vladimir Nabokov: The Russian Years*. Princeton, NJ: Princeton UP, 1990.
Bradbury, Malcolm. *The Modern American Novel*. New York: Viking, 1993.
Brill, Lesley. *The Hitchcock Romance: Love and Irony in Hitchcock's Films*. Princeton,
    NJ: Princeton UP, 1988.
Brinkmeyer, Robert H., Jr. "Faulkner and the Democratic Crisis." *Faulkner and
    Ideology*. Ed. Donald M. Kartiganer and Ann J. Abadie. Jackson: UP of Missis-
    sippi, 1995. 70–94.
Brecht, Bertolt. *The Threepenny Opera*. Trans. Desmond Vesey and Eric Bentley.
    New York: Grove Weidenfeld, 1960.
Brewer, Gay. *Laughing Like Hell: The Harrowing Satires of Jim Thompson*. San Ber-
    nardino, CA: Brownstone Books, 1996.
Brooks, Cleanth. *William Faulkner: The Yoknapatawpha Country*. New Haven, CT:
    Yale UP, 1963.
Brown, Lloyd. "'The Deep Pit': A Review of Ralph Ellison's *Invisible Man*."
    *Masses & Mainstream* 5.6 (June 1952).
———. *Iron City*. 1951. Boston: Northeastern UP, 1994.
Bruce-Novoa, Juan. "There's Many a Slip between Good Intentions and Script:
    *The Milagro Beanfield War*." *Post Script* 16.1 (1996): 53–63.
Bürger, Peter. *Theory of the Avant-garde*. Trans. Michael Shaw. Minneapolis: U of
    Minnesota P, 1984.
Burke, Fielding. *Call Home the Heart*. 1932. Old Westbury: Feminist P, 1983.
———. *A Stone Came Rolling*. New York: International, 1935.
Burroughs, Edgar Rice. *A Princess of Mars*. 1911. New York: Ballantine, 1999.

————. *Tarzan of the Apes*. 1914. New York: Penguin, 1990.

Burroughs, William S. *Naked Lunch*. 1959. New York: Grove, 1966.

Bus, Heiner. "John Nichols' *The Milagro Beanfield War* (1974): The View from Within and/or the View from Without?" *Missions in Conflict: Essays on U.S.-Mexican Relations and Chicano Culture*. Ed. Renate von Bardeleben, Dietrich Briesemeister, and Juan Bruce-Novoa. Tübingen: Narr, 1986. 215–25.

Byerman, Keith E. *Seizing the Word: History, Art, and Self in the Work of W.E.B. Du Bois*. Athens: U of Georgia P, 1994.

Byrne, Eleanor, and Martin McQuillan. *Deconstructing Disney*. London: Pluto P, 1999.

Calinescu, Matei. *Five Faces of Modernity*. Durham, NC: Duke UP, 1987.

Callinicos, Alex. *Against Postmodernism: A Marxist Critique*. New York: St. Martin's, 1989.

Cameron, Ardis. "Open Secrets: Rereading *Peyton Place*." Introduction to *Peyton Place* by Grace Metalious. Boston: Northeastern UP, 1999. vii–xxx.

Cargill, Jack. "Empire and Opposition: The 'Salt of the Earth' Strike." *Labor in New Mexico*. Ed. Robert Kern. Albuquerque: U of New Mexico P, 1983. 182–267.

Chase, Richard. *The American Novel and Its Tradition*. New York: Anchor, 1957.

————. *Herman Melville: A Critical Study*. 1949. New York: Hafner, 1971.

Coiner, Constance. *Better Red: The Writing and Resistance of Tillie Olsen and Meridel Le Sueur*. New York: Oxford UP, 1995.

————. "The Old Left and Cross-Gendered Writing." Critical introduction to *The Great Midland* by Alexander Saxton. Urbana: U of Illinois P, 1997. xi–xiv.

Conrad, Joseph. *Heart of Darkness*. 1899. New York: Penguin, 1999.

Conroy, Jack. *The Disinherited*. 1933. Cambridge: Robert Bentley, 1979.

Corber, Robert J. *In the Name of National Security: Hitchcock, Homophobia, and the Political Construction of Gender in Postwar America*. Durham, NC: Duke UP, 1993.

————. "Resisting History: *Rear Window* and the Limits of the Postwar Settlement." *National Identities and Post-Americanist Narratives*. Ed. Donald E. Pease. Durham, NC: Duke UP, 1994. 121–48.

————. "'You wanna check my thumbprints?': *Vertigo*, the Trope of Invisibility and Cold War Nationalism." *Alfred Hitchcock: Centenary Essays*. Ed. Richard Allen and S. Ishii Gonzalès. London: British Film Institute, 1999. 307–14.

Cronin, Gloria L. "*Henderson the Rain King*: A Parodic Exposé of the Modern Novel." *Arizona Quarterly* 39.3 (1983): 266–76.

Crossman, R.H.S., ed. *The God That Failed*. New York: Harper, 1949.

Dayton, Timothy Arthur. "Recontextualizing U.S. Literary Modernism: Randolph Bourne, F. Scott Fitzgerald, Tillie Olsen, Jim Thompson." Diss. Duke University, 1990.

Defoe, Daniel. *The Fortunes and Misfortunes of the Famous Moll Flanders*. 1722. New York: Oxford UP, 1981.

————. *The Life and Strange and Surprising Adventures of Robinson Crusoe*. 1719. New York: Penguin, 1994.

Denning, Michael. *The Cultural Front: The Laboring of American Culture in the Twentieth Century*. London: Verso, 1996.

Desai, Anita. "Bellow, the Rain King." *Salmagundi* 106/107 (1995): 63–65.

Diamond, Sigmund. *Compromised Campus: The Collaboration of Universities with the Intelligence Community, 1945-1955.* New York: Oxford UP, 1992.

Dirlik, Arif. *The Postcolonial Aura: Third World Criticism in the Age of Global Capitalism.* Boulder, CO: Westview P, 1997.

Doctorow, E. L. *The Book of Daniel.* New York: Random House, 1971.

———. *Welcome to Hard Times.* New York: Random House, 1960.

Dodd, Martha. *The Searching Light.* New York: Citadel, 1955.

———. *Through Embassy Eyes.* New York: Harcourt, Brace, 1939.

Dos Passos, John. *Adventures of a Young Man.* Boston: Houghton Mifflin, 1939.

———. *U.S.A. (The 42nd Parallel, 1919, and The Big Money).* 1930–1936. New York: Library of America, 1996.

Dreiser, Theodore. *An American Tragedy.* 1925. New York: Thomas Crowell, 1974.

———. *The Financier.* 1912. New York: Meridian-Penguin, 1995.

———. *Sister Carrie.* 1900. *Dreiser: Sister Carrie, Jennie Gerhardt, Twelve Men.* New York: Library of America, 1996. 1–455.

Du Bois, W.E.B. *Mansart Builds a School.* New York: Mainstream, 1959.

———. *The Ordeal of Mansart.* New York: Mainstream, 1957.

———. *Worlds of Color.* New York: Mainstream, 1961.

Dworkin, Dennis. *Cultural Marxism in Postwar Britain: History, the New Left, and the Origins of Cultural Studies.* Durham, NC: Duke UP, 1997.

Eagleton, Terry. *The Illusions of Postmodernism.* Oxford: Blackwell, 1996.

———. "Nationalism: Irony and Commitment." *National, Colonialism, and Literature.* Comp. Seamus Deane. Minneapolis: U of Minnesota P, 1990. 23-39.

Ebert, Teresa. *Ludic Feminism and After.* Ann Arbor: U of Michigan P, 1996.

Ellison, Ralph. *Invisible Man.* New York: Random House, 1952.

Engelhardt, Tom. *The End of Victory Culture: Cold War America and the Disillusioning of a Generation.* New York: Basic Books, 1995.

Fanon, Frantz. *The Wretched of the Earth.* Trans. Constance Farrington. New York: Grove P, 1968.

Fast, Howard. *Clarkton.* New York: Duell, Sloan, and Pearce, 1947.

———. *Silas Timberman.* New York: Blue Heron, 1954.

———. *Spartacus.* 1951. Armonk, NY: North Castle, 1996.

Faulkner, William. *Absalom, Absalom!* 1936. New York: Vintage-Random House, 1990.

———. *As I Lay Dying.* 1930. New York: Vintage-Random House, 1987.

———. *A Fable.* New York: Random House, 1954.

———. *The Hamlet.* 1931. New York: Vintage-Random House, 1991.

———. *Light in August.* 1932. New York: Vintage-Random House, 1990.

———. *The Mansion.* New York: Random House, 1959.

———. *The Reivers: A Reminiscence.* New York: Vintage-Random House, 1962.

———. *Requiem for a Nun.* New York: Random House, 1950.

———. *The Sound and the Fury.* 1929. New York: Vintage-Random House, 1990.

———. *The Town.* New York: Random House, 1957.

Fearing, Kenneth. *The Big Clock.* New York: Harcourt, Brace, 1946.

Ferrara, Patricia. "The Discontented Bourgeois: Bourgeois Morality and the Interplay of Light and Dark Strains in Hitchcock's Films." *New Orleans Review* 14.4 (1987): 79-87.

Field, Andrew. *Nabokov: His Life in Art.* Boston: Little, Brown, 1967.

Finkelstein, Sidney. "W.E.B. Du Bois' Trilogy: A Literary Triumph." *Critical Essays on W.E.B. Du Bois*. Ed. William L. Andrews. Boston: G. K. Hall, 1985. 194–201.

Fitzgerald, F. Scott. *The Great Gatsby*. 1925. New York: Scribner's, 1995.

———. *The Last Tycoon*. New York: Scribner's, 1941.

Foley, Barbara. *Radical Representations: Politics and Form in U.S. Proletarian Fiction, 1929-1941*. Durham, NC: Duke UP, 1993.

———. "Reading Redness: Politics and Audience in Ralph Ellison's Early Short Fiction." *Journal of Narrative Technique* 29.3 (1999): 323–39.

———. "The Rhetoric of Anticommunism in *Invisible Man*." *College English* 59.5 (1997): 530–47.

Folsom, Michael Brewster. "The Book of Poverty." Review of *Jews Without Money* by Michael Gold. *Nation* (February 28, 1966): 242–45.

———. "The Education of Mike Gold." *Proletarian Writers of the Thirties*. Ed. David Madden. Carbondale: Southern Illinois UP, 1968. 222–51.

Foster, Hal. "Postmodernism: A Preface." *The Anti-Aesthetic: Essays on Postmodern Culture*. Ed. Hal Foster. Port Townsend, WA, 1983. ix–xvi.

Foucault, Michel. *Discipline and Punish: The Birth of the Prison*. Trans. Alan Sheridan. New York: Vintage-Random House, 1979.

———. *The History of Sexuality, Volume I: An Introduction*. Trans. Robert Hurley. New York: Vintage-Random House, 1980.

———. *Madness and Civilization*. Trans. Richard Howard. New York: Vintage, 1973.

Fussell, Paul. *Class*. New York: Ballantine, 1984.

Gaddis, William. *The Recognitions*. 1955. New York: Penguin, 1985.

Gibson, Donald B. "Richard Wright." *The Oxford Companion to African American Literature*. Ed. William L. Andrews, Frances Smith Foster, and Trudier Harris. New York: Oxford UP, 1997. 793–95.

Giroux, Henry A. *The Mouse That Roared: Disney and the End of Innocence*. Lanham, MD: Rowman and Littlefield, 1999.

Goffman, Erving. *Asylums: Essays on the Social Situation of Mental Patients and Other Inmates*. New York: Anchor-Doubleday, 1961.

Gold, Mike. "Dick Wright Gives America a Significant Picture in *Native Son*." *Sunday Worker* (March 31, 1940): 2.7.

———. *Jews Without Money*. 1930. New York: Carroll and Graf, 1984.

Greenblatt, Stephen. *Marvelous Possessions: The Wonder of the New World*. Chicago: U of Chicago P, 1991.

Grimwood, Michael. *Heart in Conflict: Faulkner's Struggles with Vocation*. Athens: U of Georgia P, 1987.

Guilbaut, Serge. *How New York Stole the Idea of Modern Art: Abstract Expressionism, Freedom, and the Cold War*. Trans. Arthur Goldhammer. Chicago: U of Chicago P, 1983.

Hackett, Alice Payne, and James Henry Burke. *80 Years of Best Sellers, 1895–1975*. New York: Bowker, 1977.

Hapke, Laura. *Labor's Text: The Worker in American Fiction*. New Brunswick, NJ: Rutgers UP, 2001.

Harvey, David. *The Condition of Postmodernity: An Enquiry into the Origins of Cultural Change*. Cambridge, MA: Blackwell, 1990.

Heller, Joseph. *Catch-22*. 1961. New York: Scribner's-Simon and Schuster, 1996.

Hemingway, Ernest. *A Farewell to Arms*. New York: Scribner's, 1929.

Hemingway, Ernest. *For Whom the Bell Tolls*. New York: Scribner's, 1940.

Hemingway, Ernest. *To Have and Have Not*. New York: Scribner's, 1937.

Heym, Stefan. *Goldsborough*. 1953. London: Cassell, 1961.

Hilfer, Tony. *American Fiction since 1940*. London: Longman, 1992.

Himes, Chester. *If He Hollers Let Him Go*. 1945. Chatham, NJ: Chatham Bookseller, 1973.

Himes, Chester. *Lonely Crusade*. New York: Knopf, 1947.

Hitchens, Christopher. *Blood, Class, and Nostalgia: Anglo-American Ironies*. New York: Farrar, Straus, Giroux, 1990.

Hobbs, Glenda. "A Portrait of the Artist as Mother: Harriette Arnow and *The Dollmaker*." *Harriette Simpson Arnow: Critical Essays on Her Work*. Ed. Haeja K. Chung. East Lansing: Michigan State UP, 1995. 169-83.

Hobsbawm, Eric. *The Age of Capital, 1848-1875*. New York: Scribner's, 1975.

———. *The Age of Empire, 1875-1914*. New York: Pantheon, 1987.

———. *The Age of Extremes: A History of the World, 1914-1991*. New York: Pantheon, 1994.

Hoover, J, Edgar. *Masters of Deceit: What the Communist Bosses Are Doing Now to Bring America to Its Knees*. New York: Henry Holt, 1958.

Horne, Gerald. *Black and Red: W.E.B. Du Bois and the Afro-American Response to the Cold War, 1944-63*. Albany: State U of New York P, 1986.

Howe, Irving and Louis Coser. *The American Communist Party: A Critical History (1919-1957)*. Boston: Beacon, 1957.

Howells, William Dean. *The Rise of Silas Lapham*. 1885. New York: Penguin, 1986.

———. *A Traveler from Altruria*. 1894. New York: Bedford-St. Martin's, 1996.

Hutcheon, Linda. *A Poetics of Postmodernism: History, Theory, Fiction*. New York: Routledge, 1988.

Hyman, Stanley Edgar. "The Handle: *Invitation to a Beheading* and *Bend Sinister*." *Triquarterly* 17 (1970): 60-71.

Jameson, Fredric. *Marxism and Form: Twentieth-Century Dialectical Theories of Literature*. Princeton, NJ: Princeton UP, 1971.

———. *The Political Unconscious: Narrative as a Socially Symbolic Act*. Ithaca, New York: Cornell UP, 1981.

———. "Postmodernism and Consumer Society." *The Anti-Aesthetic: Essays on Postmodern Culture*. Ed. Hal Foster. Port Townsend, WA, 1983. 111-25.

———. *Postmodernism, or, The Cultural Logic of Late Capitalism*. Durham, NC: Duke UP, 1991.

———. *Signatures of the Visible*. New York: Routledge, 1992.

———. "Spatial Systems in *North by Northwest*." *Everything You Always Wanted to Know about Lacan (But Were Afraid to Ask Hitchcock)*. Ed. Slavoj Zizek. London: Verso, 1992. 47-72.

Jones, James. *From Here to Eternity*. New York: Scribner's, 1951.

Joyce, James. *Ulysses: The Corrected Text*. Ed. Hans Walter Gabler with Wolfhard Steppe and Claus Melchior. New York: Random House, 1986.

Kalaidjian, Walter. *American Culture Between the Wars: Revisionary Modernism and Postmodern Critique*. New York: Columbia UP, 1993.

Karl, Frederick R. *American Fictions 1940–1980: A Comprehensive History and Critical Evaluation.* New York: Harper and Row, 1983.

Kazin, Alfred. *On Native Grounds: An Interpretation of Modern American Prose Literature.* 1942. San Diego: Harcourt, Brace, 1995.

Kesey, Ken. *One Flew over the Cuckoo's Nest.* 1962. New York: Penguin, 1976.

Kiley, Frederick, and Walter McDonald, eds. *A* Catch-22 *Casebook.* New York: Crowell, 1973.

Killens, John O. *Youngblood.* New York: Dial, 1954.

Kinnamon, Keneth. *The Emergence of Richard Wright: A Study in Literature and Society.* Urbana: U of Illinois P, 1972.

Klugman, Karen, Jane Kuenz, Shelton Waldrep, and Susan Willis. *Inside the Mouse: Work and Play at Disney World.* Durham, NC: Duke UP, 1995.

Kostelanetz, Richard. "Fictions for a Negro Politics: The Neglected Novels of W.E.B. Du Bois." *Critical Essays on W.E.B. Du Bois.* Ed. William L. Andrews. Boston: G. K. Hall, 1985. 173–94.

Laclau, Ernesto, and Chantal Mouffe. *Hegemony and Socialist Strategy: Towards a Radical Democratic Politics.* London: Verso, 1985.

Lacy, Ed. *Room to Swing.* New York: Harper, 1957.

Lardner, Ring, Jr. *The Ecstasy of Owen Muir.* 1954. Amherst, NY: Prometheus, 1997.

Larmour, David H. J. "The Classical Allusions in *Bend Sinister.*" *Russian Literary Triquarterly* 24 (1990): 163–72.

Lawrence, Amy. "American Shame: *Rope,* James Stewart, and the Postwar Crisis in American Masculinity." *Hitchcock's America.* Ed. Jonathan Freedman and Richard Millington. New York: Oxford UP, 1999. 55–76.

Leach, William. *Land of Desire: Merchants, Power, and the Rise of a New American Culture.* New York: Vintage-Random House, 1994.

Lederer, William J., and Eugene Burdick. 1958. *The Ugly American.* New York: Fawcett, 1983.

Le Sueur, Meridel. *The Girl.* Rev. ed. Albuquerque: West End P, 1990.

Leitch, Thomas M. "It's the Cold War, Stupid: An Obvious History of Political Hitchcock." *Literature/Film Quarterly* 27.1 (1999): 3–15.

Lewis, David Levering. *W.E.B. Du Bois: Biography of a Race, 1868–1919.* New York: Henry Holt, 1993.

———. *W.E.B. Du Bois: The Fight for Equality, 1919–1963.* New York: Henry Holt, 2000.

Littlefield, Henry. "The Wizard of Oz: Parable of Populism." *American Quarterly* (Spring 1964): 47–58.

Lorence, James J. *The Suppression of* Salt of the Earth: *How Hollywood, Big Labor, and Politicians Blacklisted a Movie in Cold War America.* Albuquerque: U of New Mexico P, 1999.

Lukács, Georg. *The Destruction of Reason.* Trans. Peter Palmer. Atlantic Highlands, NJ: Humanities P, 1981.

———. *The Historical Novel.* Trans. Hannah Mitchell and Stanley Mitchell. Lincoln: U of Nebraska P, 1983.

———. *The Meaning of Contemporary Realism.* Trans. John Mander and Necke Mander. London: Merlin P, 1963.

————. *Studies in European Realism*. Trans. anon. New York: Grosset and Dunlap, 1964.

Lynch, Kevin. *The Image of the City*. Cambridge, MA: MIT P, 1960.

Lyotard, Jean-François. *The Postmodern Condition: A Report on Knowledge*. Trans. Geoff Bennington and Brian Massumi. Minneapolis: U of Minnesota P, 1984.

Mailer, Norman. *Barbary Shore*. 1951. New York: Vintage-Random House, 1997.

————. *The Naked and the Dead*. 1948. New York: Henry Holt, 1981.

————. *The White Negro*. San Francisco: City Lights Books, 1957.

Maltz, Albert. "In Memoriam Philip Stevenson (Lars Lawrence)." *Zeitschrift für Anglistik und Amerikanistik* 14 (1966): 377–80.

Mandel, Ernest. *Late Capitalism*. Trans. Joris De Bres. London: NLB, 1975.

Marantz Cohen, Paula. "Hitchcock's Revised American Vision: *The Wrong Man* and *Vertigo*." *Hitchcock's America*. Ed. Jonathan Freedman and Richard Millington. New York: Oxford UP, 1999. 155–72.

Marcuse, Herbert. *One-Dimensional Man: Studies in the Ideology of Advanced Industrial Society*. Boston: Beacon P, 1964.

Marx, Karl, and Friedrich Engels. *The Marx-Engels Reader*. Ed. Robert C. Tucker. New York: W. W. Norton, 1978.

Marzani, Carl. *The Survivor*. New York: Cameron, 1958.

————. *We Can Be Friends*. New York: Topical Books, 1952.

Matthiessen, F. O. *American Renaissance: Art and Expression in the Age of Emerson and Whitman*. New York: Oxford UP, 1941.

May, Elaine Tyler. *Homeward Bound: American Families in the Cold War Era*. New York: Basic Books, 1988.

McCarthy, Mary. *The Groves of Academe*. New York: Harcourt, Brace, 1952.

McCauley, Michael J. *Jim Thompson: Sleep with the Devil*. New York: Mysterious P, 1991.

McHale, Brian. *Postmodernist Fiction*. New York: Methuen, 1987.

Melville, Herman. *Moby-Dick, or, The Whale*. 1851. New York: Modern Library, 2000.

Metalious, Grace. *Peyton Place*. 1956. Boston: Northeastern UP, 1999.

Michaels, Walter Benn. *The Gold Standard and the Logic of Capitalism: American Literature at the Turn of the Century*. Berkeley: U of California P, 1987.

Miller, James. *"Democracy Is in the Streets": From Port Huron to the Siege of Chicago*. New York: Simon and Schuster, 1987.

Miller, Warren. *The Cool World*. Boston: Little, Brown, 1959.

Mills, C. Wright. *The Power Elite*. London: Oxford UP, 1956.

Moss, Judith. "The Body as Symbol in Saul Bellow's *Henderson the Rain King*." *Literature and Psychology* 20 (1970): 51–61.

Motley, Willard. *Knock on Any Door*. New York: Appleton-Century, 1947.

Murphy, James F. *The Proletarian Moment: The Controversy over Leftism in Literature*. Urbana: U of Illinois P, 1991.

Murphy, Patrick D. "'The Whole Wide World Was Scrubbed Clean': The Androcentric Animation of Denatured Disney." *From Mouse to Mermaid: The Politics of Film, Gender, and Culture*. Ed. Elizabeth Bell, Lynda Haas, and Laura Sells. Bloomington: Indiana UP, 1995. 125–36.

Nabokov, Vladimir. *The Annotated Lolita*. Ed. Alfred Appel, Jr. New York: McGraw-Hill, 1970.

————. *Bend Sinister*. New York: Henry Holt, 1947.

————. *Conclusive Evidence*. New York: Harper, 1951.

————. *The Gift*. Trans. Michael Scammel with the collaboration of the author. New York: Wideview/Perigee Books, 1963.

————. *Invitation to a Beheading*. 1938. Trans. Dmitri Nabokov and Vladimir Nabokov. New York: Putnam, 1959.

————. *Pale Fire*. 1962. New York: Perigee-Putnam's, 1980.

————. *Strong Opinions*. New York: McGraw-Hill, 1981.

Nadel, Alan. *Containment Culture: American Narratives, Postmodernism, and the Atomic Age*. Durham, NC: Duke UP, 1995.

Naremore, James. "Hitchcock at the Margins of Noir." *Alfred Hitchcock: Centenary Essays*. Ed. Richard Allen and S. Ishii Gonzalès. London: British Film Institute, 1999. 263–77.

Nelson, Cary. *Repression and Recovery: Modern American Poetry and the Politics of Cultural Memory, 1914–1945*. Madison, U of Wisconsin P, 1989.

Nichols, John. *The Magic Journey*. 1978. New York: Ballantine, 1983.

————. *The Milagro Beanfield War*. 1974. New York: Ballantine, 1976.

————. *The Nirvana Blues*. 1981. New York: Ballantine, 1983.

O'Brien, Geoffrey. *Hardboiled America: Lurid Paperbacks and the Masters of Noir*. 1981. Expanded ed. New York: Da Capo, 1997.

O'Connor, Flannery. *Wise Blood*. 1952. New York: Farrar, Straus, and Giroux, 1999.

Olsen, Tillie. *Yonnondio: From the Thirties*. New York: Delta-Dell, 1974.

Ornitz, Samuel. *Bride of the Sabbath*. New York: Rinehart and Company, 1951.

"Our Country and Our Culture." *Partisan Review* 19 (May-June 1952): 283–326.

Ownby, Ted. "The Snopes Trilogy and the Emergence of Consumer Culture." *Faulkner and Ideology*. Ed. Donald M. Kartiganer and Ann J. Abadie. Jackson: UP of Mississippi, 1995. 95–128.

Page, Dorothy Myra. *Gathering Storm: A Story of the Black Belt*. New York: International Publishers, 1932.

Page, Myra. *Moscow Yankee*. 1935. Urbana: U of Illinois P, 1995.

————. *With Sun in Our Blood*. New York: Citadel, 1950.

Palmer, R. Barton. "The Metafictional Hitchcock: The Experience of Viewing and the Viewing of Experience in *Rear Window* and *Psycho*." *Perspectives on Alfred Hitchcock*. New York: G. K. Hall, 1995.

Pease, Donald. *Visionary Compacts: American Renaissance Writings in Cultural Context*. Madison: U of Wisconsin P, 1987.

Pells, Richard H. *The Liberal Mind in a Conservative Age: American Intellectuals in the 1940s and 1950s*. New York: Harper and Row, 1985.

Petrey, Sandy. "The Language of Realism, The Language of False Consciousness: A Reading of *Sister Carrie*." *Novel* 10.2 (1977): 101–13.

Phillips, Lily Wiatrowski. "W.E.B. Du Bois and Soviet Communism: *The Black Flame* as Socialist Realism." *South Atlantic Quarterly* 94.3 (1995): 837–64.

Pietz, William. "The 'Post-Colonialism' of Cold War Discourse." *Social Text* 19–20 (Fall 1988): 55–75.

Pizer, Donald. *Twentieth-Century American Literary Naturalism: An Interpretation*. Carbondale: Southern Illinois UP, 1982.

Pohl, Frederik, and C. M. Kornbluth. *The Space Merchants.* 1952. New York: St. Martin's, 1987.

Poirier, Richard. *The Performing Self: Compositions and Decompositions in the Languages of Contemporary Life.* New York: Oxford UP, 1971.

Polito, Robert. *Savage Art: A Biography of Jim Thompson.* New York: Vintage-Random House, 1995.

Polonsky, Abraham. *A Season of Fear.* New York: Cameron Associates, 1956.

Potter, David M. *People of Plenty: Economic Abundance and the American Character.* Chicago: U of Chicago P, 1954.

Pynchon, Thomas. *Vineland.* Boston: Little, Brown, 1990.

Quin, Mike. *The Big Strike.* Olema, CA: Olema, 1949.

Rabinowitz, Paula. *Labor and Desire: Women's Revolutionary Fiction in Depression America.* Chapel Hill: U of North Carolina P, 1991.

Radek, Karl. "Contemporary World Literature and the Tasks of Proletarian Art." *Problems of Soviet Literature: Reports and Speeches at the First Soviet Writers' Congress.* Ed. H. G. Scott. Westport, CT: Greenwood, 1979. 73–182.

Raeburn, John. "*Catch-22* and the Culture of the 1950s." *American Studies in Scandinavia* 25 (1993): 119–28.

Rahv, Philip. Review of *Absalom, Absalom!* 1936. *William Faulkner: The Critical Heritage.* Ed. John Bassett. London: Routledge and Kegan Paul, 1975.

Railton, Stephen. "Pilgrims' Politics: Steinbeck's Art of Conversion." *New Essays on* The Grapes of Wrath. Ed. David Wyatt. Cambridge: Cambridge UP, 1990. 27–46.

Rampersad, Arnold. *The Art and Imagination of W.E.B. Du Bois.* Cambridge, MA: Harvard UP, 1976.

Rampton, David. *Vladimir Nabokov: A Critical Study of the Novels.* Cambridge: Cambridge University Press, 1984.

Ray, Robert B. *A Certain Tendency of the Hollywood Cinema, 1930–1980.* Princeton, NJ: Princeton UP, 1985.

Renaux, Sigrid. "The Hero's Last Ordeal." *American Studies International* 35 (February 1997): 44–49.

Rideout, Walter. *The Radical Novel in the United States, 1900-1954.* 1956. New York: Columbia UP, 1992.

Riesman, David, with Reuel Denney and Nathan Glazer. *The Lonely Crowd: A Study of the Changing American Character.* New Haven, CT: Yale UP, 1950.

Rodrigues, Eusebio L. "Reichianism in *Henderson the Rain King.*" *Criticism* 15 (1973): 212–33.

Rosenfelt, Deborah Silverton. "Commentary." *Salt of the Earth.* New York: Feminist P, 1978. 93–168.

Rubenstein, Harry R. "Political Repression in New Mexico: The Destruction of the National Miner's Union in Gallup." *Labor in New Mexico.* Ed. Robert Kern. Albuquerque: U of New Mexico P, 1983. 91–142.

Said, Edward. *Culture and Imperialism.* New York: Knopf, 1993.

Salinger, J. D. *The Catcher in the Rye.* Boston: Little, Brown, 1951.

Saunders, Frances Stonor. *The Cultural Cold War: The CIA and the World of Arts and Letters.* New York: New P, 1999.

Saxton, Alexander. *Bright Web in the Darkness.* New York: St. Martin's, 1959.

———. *The Great Midland.* 1948. Urbana: U of Illinois P, 1997.

Schatz, Thomas. *The Genius of the System: Hollywood Filmmaking in the Studio Era.* New York: Henry Holt, 1996.

Schaub, Thomas. *American Fiction in the Cold War.* Madison: U of Wisconsin P, 1991.

Schickel, Richard. *The Disney Version: The Life, Times, Art and Commerce of Walt Disney.* 3rd edition. Chicago: Ivan R. Dee, 1997.

Schiffrin, André, ed. *The Cold War and the University: Toward an Intellectual History of the Postwar Years.* New York: New P, 1997.

Schrecker, Ellen W. *No Ivory Tower: McCarthyism and the Universities.* New York: Oxford UP, 1986.

Schulberg, Budd. *Waterfront.* New York: Random House, 1955.

Schwartz, Lawrence. *Creating Faulkner's Reputation: The Politics of Modern Literary Criticism.* Knoxville: U of Tennessee P, 1988.

Seelye, John. Introduction to *Tarzan of the Apes* by Edgar Rice Burroughs. New York: Penguin, 1990. vii–xxviii.

Sigal, Clancy. *Going Away.* 1961. New York: Carroll and Graf, 1984.

———. *Weekend in Dinlock.* London: Secker and Warburg, 1960.

Sinclair, Upton. *The Return of Lanny Budd.* New York: Viking, 1953.

Sklar, Robert. *Movie-Made America: A Cultural History of American Movies.* New York: Vintage-Random House, 1994.

Slotkin, Richard. *The Fatal Environment: The Myth of the Frontier in the Age of Industrialization, 1800–1890.* 1985, Norman: U of Oklahoma P, 1998.

———. *Gunfighter Nation: The Myth of the Frontier in Twentieth-Century America.* 1992. Norman: U of Oklahoma P, 1998.

———. *Regeneration through Violence: The Mythology of the American Frontier, 1600–1860.* 1973. Norman: U of Oklahoma P, 2000.

Smedley, Agnes. *Daughter of Earth.* 1929. Old Westbury, NY: Feminist P, 1973.

Smith, William Gardner. *Anger at Innocence.* 1950. Chatham, NJ: Chatham Bookseller, 1973.

Spanos, William V. *The Errant Art of* Moby-Dick: *The Canon, the Cold War, and the Struggle for American Studies.* Durham, NC: Duke UP, 1995.

Spoto, Donald. *The Art of Alfred Hitchcock: Fifty Years of His Motion Pictures.* 2nd ed. New York: Anchor-Doubleday, 1992.

Stannard, David E. *American Holocaust: Columbus and the Conquest of the New World.* New York: Oxford UP, 1992.

Stansberry, Domenic. *Manifesto for the Dead.* Sag Harbor, NY: Permanent P, 2000.

Stegner, Page. *Escape into Aesthetics: The Art of Vladimir Nabokov.* New York: Dial, 1966.

Steinbeck, John. *The Grapes of Wrath.* 1939. *John Steinbeck:* The Grapes of Wrath *and Other Writings, 1936-1941.* New York: Library of America, 1996. 207-692.

Sterritt, David. *The Films of Alfred Hitchcock.* Cambridge: Cambridge UP, 1993.

Stevenson, Philip. (Lars Lawrence). *The Hoax.* New York: International, 1961.

———. *Morning, Noon, and Night.* New York: Putnam, 1954.

———. *Old Father Antic.* New York: International,1961.

———. *Out of the Dust.* New York: Putnam, 1956.

Stimpson, Catharine R. "Literature as Radical Statement." *Columbia Literary History of the United States.* Ed. Emory Elliott. New York: Columbia UP, 1988. 1060-76.

Stuart, Dabney. *Nabokov: The Dimensions of Parody*. Baton Rouge: Louisiana State UP, 1978.

Swados, Harvey. *On the Line*. Boston: Little, Brown, 1957.

Tanner, Tony. *The Fiction of Joseph Heller: Against the Grain*. New York: St. Martin's, 1989.

Thompson, Jim. *After Dark, My Sweet*. 1955. New York: Vintage Crime/Black Lizard, 1990.

————. *Bad Boy*. 1953. New York: Vintage Crime/Black Lizard, 1997.

————. *The Criminal*. 1953. New York: Vintage Crime/Black Lizard, 1993.

————. *Cropper's Cabin*. 1952. New York: Vintage Crime/Black Lizard, 1992.

————. *The Getaway*. 1958. New York: Vintage Crime/Black Lizard, 1994.

————. *The Grifters*. 1963. New York: Vintage Crime/Black Lizard, 1990.

————. *Heed the Thunder*. 1947. New York: Vintage Crime/Black Lizard, 1994.

————. *A Hell of a Woman*. 1954. New York: Vintage Crime/Black Lizard, 1990.

————. *The Killer Inside Me*. 1952. *Crime Novels : American Noir of the 1950s*. Ed. Robert Polito. New York: Library of America, 1997. 1–160.

————. *The Kill-Off*. 1957. New York: Vintage Crime/Black Lizard, 1999.

————. *The Nothing Man*. 1954. New York: Vintage Crime/Black Lizard, 1997.

————. *Nothing More Than Murder*. 1949. New York: Vintage Crime/Black Lizard, 1991.

————. *Now and on Earth*. 1942. New York: Vintage Crime/Black Lizard, 1994.

————. *Pop. 1280*. 1964. New York: Vintage Crime/Black Lizard, 1990.

————. *Recoil*. 1953. New York: Vintage Crime/Black Lizard, 1992.

————. *Roughneck*. 1954. New York: Vintage Crime/Black Lizard, 1998.

————. *Savage Night*. 1953. New York: Vintage Crime/Black Lizard, 1991.

————. *South of Heaven*. 1967. New York: Vintage Crime/Black Lizard, 1994.

————. *A Swell-Looking Babe*. 1954. New York: Vintage Crime/Black Lizard, 1991.

————. *Texas by the Tail*. 1965. New York: Vintage Crime/Black Lizard, 1994.

————. *The Transgressors*. 1961. New York: Vintage Crime/Black Lizard, 1994.

————. *Wild Town*. 1957. New York: Vintage Crime/Black Lizard, 1993.

Thorson, Connie Capers, and James L. Thorson. "Gomorrah on the Puerco: A Critical Study of Philip Stevenson's Proletarian Epic *The Seed*." *Labor in New Mexico: Unions, Strikes, and Social History since 1881*. Ed. Robert Kern. Albuquerque: U of New Mexico P, 1983. 183–270.

Tichi, Cecelia. "American Literary Studies to the Civil War." *Redrawing the Boundaries: The Transformation of English and American Literary Studies*. Ed. Stephen Greenblatt and Giles Gunn. New York: Modern Language Association, 1992. 209–31.

Timmerman, John H. *John Steinbeck's Fiction: The Aesthetics of the Road Taken*. Norman: U of Oklahoma P, 1986.

Todd, Ruthven. *Over the Mountain*. New York: Knopf, 1939.

Trumpener, Katie. "Fragments of the Mirror: Self-Reference, Mise-en-Abyme, *Vertigo*. *Hitchcock's Rereleased Films: From* Rope *to* Vertigo. Ed. Walter Raubicheck and Walter Srebnick. Detroit: Wayne State UP, 1991. 175–88.

Vonnegut, Kurt, Jr. *Cat's Cradle*. New York: Delacorte, 1963.

Wald, Alan. *The New York Intellectuals: The Rise and Decline of the Anti-Stalinist Left from the 1930s to the 1960s*. Chapel Hill: U of North Carolina P, 1987.

———. *Writing from the Left: New Essays on Radical Culture and Politics*. London: Verso, 1994.

Warner, Rex. *The Wild Goose Chase*. London: John Lane the Bodley Head, 1937.

Warren, Robert Penn. "Cowley's Faulkner." *William Faulkner: The Critical Heritage*. Ed. John Bassett. London: Routledge and Kegan Paul, 1975.

Way, Brian. "Formal Experiment and Social Discontent: Joseph Heller's *Catch-22*." *American Studies* 2.2 (1968): 253–70.

Weber, Max. *The Protestant Ethic and the Spirit of Capitalism.* 1904–1905. Trans. Talcott Parsons. 1930. London: Routledge, 1995.

Wellmer, Albrecht. "Reason, Utopia, and the *Dialectic of Enlightenment*." In *Habermas and Modernity*. Ed. Richard J. Bernstein. Cambridge, Massachusetts: MIT Press, 1985, 35-66.

West, Ann. "The Concept of the Fantastic in *Vertigo*." *Hitchcock's Rereleased Films: From* Rope *to* Vertigo. Ed. Walter Raubicheck and Walter Srebnick. Detroit: Wayne State UP, 1991. 163–74.

Whyte, William. *The Organization Man*. New York: Simon and Schuster, 1956.

Williams, Linda. "Discipline and Distraction: *Psycho*, Visual Culture, and Postmodern Cinema." *"Culture" and the Problem of the Disciplines*. Ed. John Carlos Rowe. New York: Columbia UP, 1998. 87-120.

Williams, Raymond. *Marxism and Literature*. New York: Oxford UP, 1977.

Willis, Susan, et al., eds. *Inside the Mouse: Work and Play at Disney World*. Durham, NC: Duke UP, 1995.

Wilson, John K. *The Myth of Political Correctness: The Conservative Attack on Higher Education*. Durham, NC: Duke UP, 1995.

Wilson, Sloan. *The Man in the Gray Flannel Suit*. New York: Simon and Schuster, 1955.

Wixson, Douglas. *Worker-Writer in America: Jack Conroy and the Tradition of Midwestern Literary Radicalism, 1898–1990*. Urbana: U of Illinois P, 1994.

Wood, Robin. *Hitchcock's Films Revisited*. New York: Columbia UP, 1989.

Wood, Ruth Pirsig. *Lolita in* Peyton Place: *Highbrow, Middlebrow, and Lowbrow Novels of the 1950s*. New York: Garland, 1995.

Woolf, Michael. "The Haunted House: Jewish-American Autobiography." *First Person Singular: Studies in American Autobiography*. Ed. A. Robert Lee. New York: St. Martin's, 1988. 198-216.

Wright, Richard. *Native Son*. 1940. *Richard Wright: Early Works*. New York: Library of America, 1991. 443-850.

Wylie, Philip. *Generation of Vipers*. New York: Rinehart, 1942.

Zamyatin, Yevgeny. *We*. Trans. Mirra Ginsberg. New York: Avon, 1983.

Zinberg, Len. *Hold with the Hares*. Garden City, NY: Doubleday, 1948.

Zipes, Jack. "Breaking the Disney Spell." *From Mouse to Mermaid: The Politics of Film, Gender, and Culture*. Ed. Elizabeth Bell, Lynda Haas, and Laura Sells. Bloomington: Indiana UP, 1995. 21–42.

Zizek, Slavoj. "The Hitchcockian Blot." *Alfred Hitchcock: Centenary Essays*. Ed. Richard Allen and S. Ishii Gonzalès. London: British Film Institute, 1999. 123-39.

Zola, Émile. *Germinal*. 1885. Trans. Havelock Ellis. New York: Vintage-Random House, 1994.

## FILMS

*Aladdin*. Dir. Ron Clements and John Mukser. Disney, 1992.

*Alice in Wonderland*. Dir. Clyde Geronimi, Hamilton Luske, and Wilfred Jackson. Disney, 1951.

*Apocalypse Now*. Dir. Francis Ford Coppola. Zoetrope, 1979.

*Around the World in Eighty Days*. Dir. Michael Anderson and Kevin McClory. United Artists, 1956.

*The Asphalt Jungle*. Dir. John Huston. MGM, 1950.

*The Birds*. Dir. Alfred Hitchcock. Universal, 1963.

*Body and Soul*. Dir. Robert Rossen. Enterprise, 1947.

*Cinderella*. Dir. Wilfred Jackson, Hamilton Luske, and Clyde Geronimi. Disney, 1950.

*Citizen Kane*. Dir. Orson Welles. RKO, 1941.

*Cornered*. Dir. Edward Dmytryk. RKO, 1945.

*Dead End*. Dir. William Wyler. Samuel Goldwyn, 1937.

*Dial M for Murder*. Dir. Alfred Hitchcock. Warner, 1954.

*D.O.A.* Dir. Rudolph Maté. United Artists, 1950.

*Dr. Strangelove; or, How I Learn to Stop Worrying and Love the Bomb*. Dir. Stanley Kubrick. Columbia, 1963.

*Double Indemnity*. Dir. Billy Wilder. Paramount, 1944.

*Duck Soup*. Dir. Leo McCarey. Paramount, 1933.

*Dumbo*. Dir. Ben Sharpsteen. Disney, 1941.

*Fantasia*. Dir. Ben Sharpsteen. Disney, 1940.

*Force of Evil*. Dir. Abraham Polonsky. MGM/Enterprise, 1948

*From Here to Eternity*. Dir. Fred Zinnemann. Columbia, 1953.

*Fury*. Dir. Fritz Lang. MGM, 1936.

*Gentlemen Prefer Blondes*. Dir. Howard Hawks. Twentieth Century Fox, 1953.

*The Getaway*. Dir. Sam Peckinpah. Solar, 1972.

*The Getaway*. Dir. Roger Donaldson. Universal, 1993.

*Gold Diggers of 1933*. Dir. Mervyn LeRoy. Warner, 1933.

*Gone with the Wind*. Dir. Victor Fleming. MGM, 1939.

*The Harder They Fall*. Dir. Mark Robson. Columbia, 1956.

*Heart of Spain*. Dir. Herbert Kline. CBC Canada, 1937.

*Heroes for Sale*. Dir. William Wellman. Warner, 1933.

*High Noon*. Dir. Fred Zinnemann. Stanley Kramer, 1952.

*I Am a Fugitive from a Chain Gang*. Dir. Mervyn LeRoy. Warner, 1932.

*It's a Wonderful Life*. Dir. Frank Capra. RKO, 1946.

*The Jungle Book*. Dir. Wolfgang Reitherman. Disney, 1967.

*Lady and the Tramp*. Dir. Hamilton Luske, Clyde Geronimi, and Wilfred Jackson. Disney, 1955.

*The Lady from Shanghai*. Dir. Orson Welles. Columbia, 1948.

*Laura*. Dir. Otto Preminger. 20th Century Fox, 1944.

*The Lion King*. Dir. Roger Allers and Rob Minkoff. Disney, 1994.

*The Little Mermaid*. Dir. Ron Clements and John Musker. Disney, 1989.

*Lolita*. Dir. Stanley Kubrick. MGM, 1962.

*Lost Weekend*. Dir. Billy Wilder. Paramount, 1945.

*Madame Bovary*. Dir. Vincente Minelli. MGM, 1949.

*The Maltese Falcon.* Dir. John Huston. Warner, 1941.

*The Man Who Knew Too Much.* Dir. Alfred Hitchcock. Gaumont, 1934.

*The Man Who Knew Too Much.* Dir. Alfred Hitchcock. Paramount, 1956.

*The Milagro Beanfield War.* Dir. Robert Redford. Universal, 1988.

*Mr. and Mrs. Smith.* Dir. Alfred Hitchcock. RKO, 1941.

*Modern Times.* Dir. Charles Chaplin. Charles Chaplin, 1936.

*Murder, My Sweet.* Dir. Edward Dmytryk. RKO, 1944.

*North by Northwest.* Dir. Alfred Hitchcock. MGM, 1959.

*Notorious.* Dir. Alfred Hitchcock. RKO, 1946.

*On the Waterfront.* Dir. Elia Kazan. Columbia, 1954.

*One Hundred and One Dalmatians.* Dir. Wolfgang Reitherman, Hamilton S. Luske, and Clyde Geronimi. Disney, 1961.

*Our Daily Bread.* Dir. King Vidor. United Artists, 1934.

*People of the Cumberland.* Dir. Sidney Myers, Jay Leyda, and Elia Kazan. Frontier, 1938.

*Peter Pan.* Dir. Wilfred Jackson, Clyde Geronimi, and Hamilton Luske. Disney, 1953.

*Peyton Place.* Dir. Mark Robson. 20th Century Fox, 1957.

*Pie in the Sky.* Dir. Ralph Steiner, 1934.

"Plutopia." Dir. Charles A. Nichols. Disney, 1951.

*Psycho.* Dir. Alfred Hitchcock. Paramount, 1960.

*Rear Window.* Dir. Alfred Hitchcock. Paramount, 1954.

*The Robe.* Dir. Henry Koster. 20th Century Fox, 1953.

*Rope.* Dir. Alfred Hitchcock. Transatlantic, 1948.

*Sabotage.* Dir. Alfred Hitchcock. Gaumont British, 1936.

*Salt of the Earth.* Dir. Herbert Biberman. Independent Productions, 1954.

*The Searchers.* Dir. John Ford. Warner, 1956.

*Shadow of a Doubt.* Dir. Alfred Hitchcock. Universal, 1943.

*Shane.* Dir. George Stevens. Paramount, 1953.

*Shock Corridor.* Dir. Samuel Fuller. Leon Fromkiss/Sam Firks, 1963.

*Sleeping Beauty.* Dir. Clyde Geronimi. Disney, 1959.

*Snow White and the Seven Dwarfs.* Dir. David Hand. Disney, 1937.

*Song of the South.* Dir. Harve Foster. Disney, 1946.

*South Pacific.* Dir. Joshua Logan. Magna, 1958.

*The Spanish Earth.* Dir. Joris Ivens. Prometheus, 1937.

*Stage Fright.* Dir. Alfred Hitchcock. Warner, 1950.

"Steamboat Willie." Dir. Walt Disney and Ub Iwerks. Disney, 1928.

*The Stranger.* Dir. Orson Welles. International, 1946.

*Strangers on a Train.* Dir. Alfred Hitchcock. Warner, 1951.

*Sunset Boulevard.* Dir. Billy Wilder. Paramount, 1950.

*Sweet Smell of Success.* Dir. Alexander Mackendrick. United Artists, 1957.

*The Sword in the Stone.* Dir. Wolfgang Reitherman. Disney, 1963.

*Tarzan the Ape Man.* Dir. W. S. Van Dyke. MGM, 1932.

*Tarzan and the Mermaids.* Dir. Robert Florey. RKO, 1948.

*The Ten Commandments.* Dir. Cecil B. de Mille. Paramount, 1956.

*To Catch a Thief.* Dir. Albert Hitchock. Paramount, 1955.

*Touch of Evil.* Dir. Orson Welles. United International, 1958.

*The Trouble with Harry.* Dir. Alfred Hitchcock. Paramount, 1955.

*Vertigo*. Dir. Alfred Hitchcock. Paramount, 1958.

"Who Killed Cock Robin?" Dir. David Hand. Disney, 1935.

*Wild Boys of the Road*. Dir. William Wellman. Warner, 1933.

*Will Success Spoil Rock Hunter?* Dir. Frank Tashlin. 20th Century Fox, 1957.

*The Wizard of Oz*. Dir. Mervyn LeRoy. MGM, 1939.

*The Wrong Man*. Dir. Alfred Hitchcock. Warner, 1957.

*Young and Innocent*. Dir. Alfred Hitchcock. GFD/Gainsborough, 1937.

# Index

**About the Author**

M. KEITH BOOKER is Professor of English at the University of Arkansas. He is the author of numerous articles and books on modern literature and theory, including *Dystopian Literature: A Theory and Research Guide* (Greenwood, 1994), *Joyce, Bakhtin, and the Literary Tradition* (1996), *A Practical Introduction to Literary Theory and Criticism* (1996), *Colonial Power, Colonial Texts: India in the Modern British Novel* (1997), *The African Novel in English* (Heinemann, 1998), *The Modern British Novel of the Left* (Greenwood, 1998), *The Modern American Novel of the Left* (Greenwood, 1999), *Film and the American Left* (Greenwood, 1999), *Ulysses, Capitalism, and Colonialism* (Greenwood, 2000), and *Monsters, Mushroom Clouds, and the Cold War* (Greenwood, 2001).